MW01610997

Around and Around

Recollections of a NASA Bioengineer from the Bronx

Laurence R. Young
with Leslie A. Young

Cambridge, Massachusetts

AROUND AND AROUND: RECOLLECTIONS OF A BIOENGINEER FROM THE BRONX © 2022 by Laurence R. Young and Leslie A. Young. All rights reserved. No part of this book may be used or reproduced in any manner whatsoever without written permission except in the case of brief quotations embodied in critical articles and reviews.

Cover and interior design by Larry Yudelson

ISBN-13: 978-1-953829-93-1 pb, 978-1-953829-92-4 electronic

22 23 24 / 10 9 8 7 6 5 4 3 2 1   20220921

*This work is dedicated to everyone in Dad's final year
who let him end each day knowing he was loved.*

Contents

Preface

I write this preface as Larry Young, our Dad, is in home hospice with cancer. Larry revised his memoirs extensively in 2020 and showed an early version to friends, family, and colleagues in January 2021. We took that version and attempted a compilation of the unique sections of that work, imposing consistent formatting, making some judgements as to structure, and doing very light copy editing. That first edition was surely full of typos and shows arbitrary organization. Our hope is that this first edition will be a pleasure to read, and will be more amenable to further editing. Most importantly, our hope it that it will bring Larry joy. [*It has done so!* —*LRY*]

Leslie Young
February 21, 2021

These reflections began when I had my first of two knee replacements, in my seventies, and are being fully assembled in my eighty-fifth year and at home hospice. I was diagnosed with kidney cancer in the summer of 2020 and was being treated with chemotherapy and later with immunotherapy by a team of experts from Massachusetts General Hospital. This has been a terrible year for all of us. From COVID-19 to the economic downturn to the threat to our country by its forty-fifth president—it stinks! But rather than curse the darkness, I use these recollections to highlight the many bright spots in my life. My symptoms at this point are merely fatigue and memory loss, so let's blame them for any omissions or errors in these memoirs! My co-author, Leslie Young, an esteemed planetary scientist in her own right, has worked with me on assembling the final version of this memoir, with the able assistance of my granddaughter, Viv.

Larry Young
Cambridge, Massachusetts
April 2, 2021

We were given a gift of six unexpected months with Larry, due in no small part to the courageous and wise actions of his wife, Vicki Goldberg. Larry enjoyed working on his memoirs nearly every day, and he and I spent many rewarding hours together before his passing on August 4, 2021, editing line-by-line, or talking about themes. After his passing, we have taken the remaining steps of sorting the work into the chapters you see here, chosen by Larry in the spring with the help of his granddaughter, Viv. I have made light corrections and added brief clarifications. For the remaining errors, they are being included as Larry remembered them, or his perception of the time or event. After all, it's his story.

Leslie Young
Raymond, Colorado
March 7, 2022

Introduction

Around and Around is a compilation of recollections, anecdotes and stories that have enlivened my life—and might amuse and inform my family and some others. They are arranged in no particular order but, then again, neither was my life.

Just when I was thinking that it was presumptive to write about my life, I read a *New York Times* Op-Ed ("What's So Great About Young Writers," April 24, 2015), which provided my justification. Robin Black wrote, "I have reached a point at which I care less about what people think. Partly, that is one of the true joys of middle age, and partly the Internet has taught us, if nothing beyond the infinite appeal of cats, that someone will always think you're becoming a jerk, so you may as well say what's on your mind."

Why do I call my memoirs *Around and Around*? Somehow, everything in my life and what it touches seems to repeat an earlier event or stage. My love life delightfully included a number of fortunate revisits of earlier loves. Much of my professional work on protecting astronauts against the debilitating effects of long-duration weightlessness has involved putting them on a rotating centrifuge, going around and around, and letting centrifugal force substitute for gravity. I started experimenting with people and animals on centrifuges in the 1950s.

For my Sc.D. dissertation, I measured the eye movements of volunteers as they looked at spots moving around on a screen. (See what I mean?) Later I began to move the subject, rather than the target, thereby stimulating the inner ear (the vestibular system) and generating another class of eye movements. I spun my subjects on a centrifuge at the Massachusetts Institute of Technology (MIT) Instrumentation Lab, normally used for testing gyroscopes. This was long before the requirements to have our experimental program approved by an Institutional Review Board (IRB). Nobody was injured and, in the best scientific tradition, I served as my own first subject. My early centrifuge forays were not limited to human subjects. During a wonderful stay in Puerto Rico, I spun crabs around and measured their eye movement, the vestibular-ocular reflexes (VOR). For the next thirty years or so, I continued to spin people and monkeys. Sometimes we would accelerate them down a track to determine how gravity and body motion influence spatial orientation. When we ran an International Symposium on Artificial Gravity in Galveston, Texas, in 1997, and again in Palo Alto, California, I was still at it. I've been widely quoted as saying that "Artificial Gravity is a concept whose time has come around—and around—and around."

And so, in a way, have my life, my occupations and preoccupations spun around. I have been trying my whole career to make sense of the way the brain deals with gravity, and how spatial orientation adapts to different envi-

Here is what I looked like at age eighty. That is the face I expect to see in the mirror, once I splash some cold water on it.

ronments. Perception of gravity and the need to maintain balance come into play during travel to distant planets. It can produce vertigo when flying in the clouds. And it can add to the challenge of skiing in a "white out." So around and around I go, and I keep coming back to that same paradox: that gravity and linear acceleration are indistinguishable, as Einstein famously pointed out in his Equivalence Principle. The theme of these memoirs is simply that I have spent a life visiting and revisiting a series of challenges and opportunities—each time from a different perspective.

    It is clear that my grandchildren, Josh, Viv, David, Xander and Rachel, could tell when I was boasting—or just plain lying. So I might as well tell the truth to begin with. And that is pretty much what I intend to do here—except that sometimes, I must admit, the story gets modified to put me in a better light. The great physicist, Niels Bohr, reportedly dismissed Heisenberg's version of their Copenhagen atom bomb discussions by remarking, "Isn't memory marvelous? As you get older you start to remember things that never happened." As for me, I more often simply forget the story as it really unfolded. So I apologize for the errors and for the occasional boasting, but here are some of the tales of my life. I hope you are amused, or at least understand a bit about how amazed I am to have come from where I started—with lots of love and encouragement and a whole lot of luck—to have experienced all these adventures.

Family

Cast of Characters—Names and Dates

Family mattered a lot to us and was the trunk around which the garden—or perhaps more accurately, the tangle—of my childhood grew. Both sets of grandparents were immigrants from Russia during that great wave around the turn of the 20th century. I don't have the genealogy documents, but my cousin, Evan Rotner (Minna's eldest son) has been working on it for the Retman (Mother's) family and Tina Kraskow has been doing that for the Youngs.

My father, Ben (no middle name—they were too poor, he joked) was born in Russia, August 15, 1903, and arrived in New York with his mother when he was five, I think. A bright boy, he briefly went to Townsend Harris High School (the Stuyvesant/Science of its day) but left to go to De Witt Clinton High School in the Bronx and then went to work in his uncle's haberdashery shop. The uncle thought Dad was too smart to stay in that business and convinced him to become a lawyer, so off he went to a preparatory school and New York Law School. He shortened his name from Youngelman to Young to escape the anticipated antisemitism in starting his practice.

My mom, Bess, was born to Louis and Molly Retman in New York on October 9, 1908. Her family moved to Mt. Vernon, New York, in Westchester County, to improve their social status and their daughters' marriage prospects.

From left to right: Minna, Anne, Jonnie (Ethel's daughter), Ethel. This photo was taken after our mother, Bess, died.

After high school, she worked for her father, Louis, until she married Dad, in the late 1920s. Their romance was interrupted by Louis, who didn't want to lose his last assistant because she wanted to marry a poor lawyer.

I was born on December 19, 1935, at New York Hospital, and Ellen was born five years later, on September 28, 1940. Jody Fisher and I were married on June 12, 1960, in Spring Valley, New York. Eliot Fisher Young was born in Boston, Massachusetts, on August 25, 1962. Leslie Ann Young was born on March 4, 1965. By that time, we had moved from a rented apartment near Harvard Square, in Cambridge, Massachusetts, to a thirteen-room Victorian house in Newton Centre. Robert Retman Young followed on September 2, 1968, on Labor Day. We named him to honor Robert Kennedy, who had been assassinated earlier that summer. Ellen married Jerry Rosenberg September 11, 1960, and they had two daughters: Lauren Monica Rosenberg, born November 30, 1963, and Elizabeth Rosenberg, born August 14, 1966. I was divorced in 2000 and married Vicki Goldberg on May 8, 2008.

The Retmans

Louis Retman, my maternal grandfather, was the first of our family to immigrate, as a very young man, in about the 1870s. He trained in architecture and attended the competitive Cooper-Union public university in New York City. I believe the professional and creative accomplishments of our cousins stemmed from him—by genetics if not by environment. He was the grandparent who spoke English without any accent. He and Molly had six children, two of whom died as infants, including their only son. That may be why each firstborn son of each of the daughters (Evan, Harold and myself) was given the middle name of Retman—to keep the name from dying out. The surviving four sisters, Anne, Ethel, Minna and my mother, Bess, were very close all their lives, and their ten children formed a wonderful, tight, extended family. All of us lived in New York.

Louis invented a fireproof steel door, which he never patented, and established the Mott Haven Fireproof Door Company in a three-story building on Park Avenue. Not the ritzy part of Park Avenue on the Upper East Side, but the less desirable part uptown, where the trains emerge from the tunnel and rattle along on their way north. Evan reports that a friend told Grandpa that he would never marry off four daughters while living above the shop, and so they moved to Westchester County, to a house in Mt. Vernon—and indeed all four successfully married. All but Mom went to college (Normal School to get a teaching degree).

I loved Grandpa Retman and keep a picture of him taken by my cousin, Susan Wood, in our living room in New Hampshire. He was cagey, smart, and (according to Jonnie) overly devoted to women, especially after Molly's death in the early 1940s. Mom, as the youngest, was forced to keep working for Grandpa after high school, as bookkeeper, office manager, and truck driver. She was proud of being the first woman to drive through the Holland Tunnel, for which Grandpa had designed the big steel doors. Her romance with Dad, a beginning lawyer from the Bronx, was filled with drama and the triumph of love. Grandpa opposed it as a bad financial deal, and the sisters connived to have their engagement reinstated, according to Evan, based on Minna's (yet) unpublished memoirs.

The four Retman Girls stayed close after marriage. Anne, the oldest, was a talented pianist, and married Herman Judelson, a real estate agent, golfer and bridge player. They moved to Riverside Drive in Manhattan and had three children: Harold, Janet and Alan. Harold and Alan rooted for the Detroit Tigers because they had a famous Jewish first baseman, Hank Greenberg, playing for them. Harold was trained as a Navy officer in the V-12 Program

Partial Retman family tree, drawn on hotel stationary in Tokyo, Japan, 1990.

at Dartmouth, whereby he attended Dartmouth for three years and graduated
with both a bachelor's degree and a commission as an officer in the US Navy.
He was a big, cheerful guy, about twelve years older than me, and sent me
a red navy sailor cap to wear. Harold was bothered by antisemitic taunts at
Dartmouth until he entered the undergraduate boxing tournament and won
the heavyweight championship. Only then did the taunting stop.

Harold, the eldest of us, was the only family member to serve in World
War II. I was only ten years old in 1945, but I knew there was a war going on
because we needed a ration card for butter and sugar. In school, we contributed
to the war effort by collecting newspapers and silver foil from chewing gum
wrappers. Years later, I read that these were supplies of no strategic value.
They were collected by the school to convince the "home front" that we, too,
were part of the fight for the life of our nation. We sang patriotic war songs
in school, and not just from World War II. "From the Halls of Montezuma"
was sung along with "Anchors A-Weigh," and "Over There," which carried
over from World War I. For most of us the war was no closer to home than
the newspaper with its diagrams of the battle lines in Iwo Jima or Okinawa.
But Harold was in command of a Landing Ship, Tank (LST) in the Pacific.

Then, on August 6, 1945, the first atomic bomb was dropped on Hiroshima
and then a second one a week later on Nagasaki. Over the fierce objections of
their military, Japan's Emperor accepted President Truman's demand for an
unconditional surrender and the war ended. By September 2, Douglas McArthur and the Japanese military leaders signed the cease fire on the *USS Missouri*,
signaling V-J Day. At the Japanese military history museum I learned, many
years later, how deeply the Japanese hated us, and how they blamed Truman
for what they claimed to be unneeded deaths from the two atomic explosions.

But in our household, we were ready to celebrate, and to look forward to
Harold's safe return. On a bright Sunday, a large part of the US Navy's Pacific
Fleet steamed up the Hudson River from New York harbor, made a big turn
and returned to sea. Horns were tooted, drums were banged, girls were fa-
mously kissed, and the bloody war that began as the "Day of Infamy" at Pearl
Harbor was behind us. Our family, on my mother's side, gathered to see the
fleet pass upstream, from an ideal viewing spot. Aunt Anne's apartment was on
Riverside Drive at 92nd Street, and looked right at the Hudson. We celebrated.
The kids had cake and sang songs while the adults fought back their tears.

After the war, Harold moved his family to Mexico for work as a sales rep,
and briefly spent time near us in Newton when he worked for Gillette. A
lovely, thoughtful man. Then they moved to Chicago, where Harold played
competitive bridge, I heard. I lost contact and he died a couple of years ago.

Janet was a piece of work. Funny, talented, warm, and smart. Her first
husband, Lucien Felden, was a handsome gold-digging SOB. They lived in
Jamaica while married, and then were divorced. Janet remarried Irving Kissen,
a lawyer and real estate agent in New York who was as sane as anyone who

lived with Janet could be. Their children were Amanda (who became the ABC News Anchor in New York City) and Carl, who carried on his mom's humorous and imaginative influence as the successful producer of the Improv theatre in New York. (Janet and her husband lived in an apartment in a building he owned in Manhattan. One morning, at 2AM, Irving was running the electric floor sander over their hardwood living room floor. Janet answered the door to the police, responding to a complaint about the noise. She explained how hard it was to get any handyman, and that Irving was doing the work on his own against the wishes of his boss. So please let him finish. And they did!)

Alan was a good athlete, especially in roller hockey, with a willingness to let his younger cousins (Howie and me) tag along anywhere. His mother believed (or at least claimed) that I was a genius and Alan passed the story on down. I helped him with his math and reading some years later. Alan drew cartoons and caricatures delightfully, and attended Cooper Union. He married several times, each time saying after the divorce "never again," and had two children. His son, Howard was tragically killed in an auto accident when he was a young man. Alan was a drummer and worked as a commercial artist. He lived in Connecticut, where he complains that all of his tennis partners are now too old! The three Judelson cousins were the first of the ten of us to pass away. I credit Alan with saving my life when he pulled me out of the surf in Long Beach. I was not yet able to swim, but that hadn't stopped me from following the older cousins into the ocean—and suddenly was over my head. Thanks, Alan.

The Greenburgs were the richest of the extended Retman family. After leaving the West Side, they lived on Gracie Square and Ethel was a friend and advisor to Mayor Wagner. Her husband, Bill, a successful real estate agent and building owner, was a small man with a big heart and a strong ego, as well as a strong golf game. When he hit an occasional bad shot he blamed it on the ball, which went into a box to give to me. He was an early appreciator of modern art. Ethel was beautiful and gracious. Ellen and I would sometimes be parked at the Greenburg's apartment on West End Avenue while our parents went off on a Florida vacation. I slept in the maid's room, with its view out over the Hudson River at the electric sign over the Palisades that flashed S-P-R-Y, an ad for Lever Bros.' vegetable shortening.

My older cousins were wonderful. Jonnie, who is six years older than I am, took me to see my first Broadway show, a matinee, *Showboat* or maybe *Annie Get your Gun*. Jonnie was, and still is, glamorous and delightfully outrageous. She became a blonde, ran for Miss New York, became a talented dance critic, and declared that the first rule of her family was to not bore anyone. Susan found her outlet in photography and became highly recognized. She anticipated my liaison with Vicki before I did.

All of the New York cousins, Janet, Alan, Jonnie and Susan, Ellen and I, were fortunate enough to be admitted to one of the specialized high schools, the first four to Music and Art (now LaGuardia High School of Music & Art and Performing Arts), and Ellen and me to Bronx Science.

The Rotners

I didn't have a brother. And my sister, although funny, smart and a good sport, was five years younger and hardly a ball-playing brother. But I did have three very special cousins—the Rotner brothers. The Rotners were more like brothers than cousins. They lived nearby in Yonkers, where Uncle Phil was a dentist. He died of a tragic mistake at the local hospital when Howie and I were about nine, Bob was twelve and Evan was fourteen. Their mother, Minna, was very close to Mom, and hosted the big family celebrations. They had a country house in Monsey, New York and lived in Yonkers, a middle-class suburb next to the Bronx, but still in the tonier Westchester County. We lived over the border, only a few miles away in New York City, so that Dad could qualify for the judgeship he pursued in vain.

Bob, three years older than me, was the most creative—in drawing and music, and in cooking, too. When he attended Amherst and I went up north for a visit, I decided I wanted that too. (Others followed at Amherst, not just Howie and me, but his children, Pam and Phil, and my son, Eliot and two of his children, Josh and Viv. Eliot's wife, Diane, was a classmate of his at Amherst.) Following graduation from Amherst, Bob went on to get his architecture degree at Columbia and established a practice in the Hamptons.

Evan was my mentor and idol. I listened to all of his advice and tried to follow it. It never occurred to me that he might be anything but perfect. He convinced me that I could run fast enough to be on the track team. He told me I could never have enough math, so I studied as much math as I could until I reached my analytical wall in graduate school. I, too, worked on a ski patrol and, like Evan, I fell in love with sailing. And when he went off to study at the London School of Economics, I, too, studied abroad at the Sorbonne, and happily trekked to London to see Evan over the years.

Evan wasn't the top student in his class, and went to New York University rather than Amherst or any other "fancy pants" college. He had a good practical sense, which served him well in chemistry at NYU. He worked as the all-around assistant to an inventor and I thought it was the most glamorous job imaginable. He could fix cars. Once he drove back to basic training at Fort Dix, New Jersey, with brakes that were barely "good enough," he assured me, and I worried about him all night. In the army he got assigned to the motor pool, which was safe, and located at Fort Montauk on Long Island, which wasn't too bad. He studied abroad, at the London School of Economics (LSE), which had a reputation for educating the new left in the 1950s. He didn't baby me, but treated me as a junior partner in his adventures. And I gladly followed—one step after another.

One summer when the rest of the family swam in the ocean and biked on the boardwalk in Long Beach, Evan hitchhiked "out west" to make his way and some money, too. He worked logging in California and as deckhand on salmon boats in Alaska. It was right out of Jack Kerouac and the beat generation, and I loved to read his letters and hear his stories. His politics were always leftist and well supported by facts and figures. He remains overwhelming in his criticism of the establishment. The fact that he is right makes it informative to hear him out, even when he verges on the preachy political left fringe. Evan's wife, Sheila, an English woman and a trained architect, is an innovative artist with an imaginative use of materials. Evan retired from the World Bank and they live in Sag Harbor, New York, with their dogs. He enjoys the irony of identifying himself as a retired banker. We love visiting them.

My cousin Howie ("Cuz") was born a week after me in the same hospital—as I often reminded my little cousin. Except for school, Howie and I did everything together, from the time we were little kids right up until we were married.

We were both quite good students and enjoyed learning. I moved a year ahead of Howie in school since New York practiced the skipping of grades to accelerate gifted students but Westchester did not. However, we often took the same "Regents Exams," the statewide subject tests in physics, history and so forth. We studied from the old exam books while lounging on the deck of Howie's lovely home in Yonkers, and competed to match the published exam answers in the back of the book. We were both good, and enjoyed the competition as well as the learning and the lemonade.

We were not equals when it came to sports, however. Cuz had a natural grace and coordination that was a thing of beauty. On the basketball court, even the dirt field at first, he could dribble and fake and shoot like nobody else. When I see NBA star point guards of today, like Isaiah Thomas, or like Bob Cousy of our youth, I think of those moves—of looking one way, then starting the other way, and finally going back to the first direction to drive toward the basket. He was great and a high school star, but he had the good sense to turn down a basketball scholarship to Princeton in favor of an academic scholarship to Amherst, just in case he wasn't really up to that level of play. And he wasn't!

In baseball he was our pitcher and best hitter. We picked up tennis and golf together but his ability in both were evident, along with his natural athletic movements.

We both learned to ski in Van Cortland Park and followed Evan to bigger hills. At Amherst we were teammates on the alpine ski team and spent a lot of time going to and from training in the Berkshires. One memorable day, when we were in the back seat of the van driven by our slightly manic Hungarian coach, Steve Rostas, the speed as we approached the famous hairpin turn on Route 2 was way above a safe level. Howie put his head in his hands and moaned. That was all Steve, the driver, needed. He turned fully around and said, "Don't worry, Harvey," (he always had trouble saying "Howie") and proceeded to do a controlled race-style turn and drive on without further comment.

If I was a nerd at Amherst, Howie was a "hot rock" of the class of 1957. He was popular, a good athlete, a top student and an open and friendly guy. I lived in Theta Xi, a fraternity for oddballs and outsiders, although we considered ourselves the intellectual elite, along with the non-fraternity open admission Jeff Club. Howie, on the other hand, was rushed by everybody and joined Alpha Delta Phi, the most selective fraternity on campus. As its rush chairman, he combined his ability and charm throughout. Meanwhile, Cuz got top grades, majored in biology, and was admitted to Harvard Medical School.

Howie always worked when he could. We were both caddies in Oceanside, Long Island. We enjoyed being in the same Lido Beach cabana resort as some of our golfers. He had a summer job at the Chevrolet assembly plant in Tarrytown, New York—and best of all, he got to go to sea. At first it was just crossing the Hudson River as a deck hand on the Yonkers ferry. Then it was on a research vessel out of Woods Hole. And also, a summer or more as a seaman on a merchant marine ship. Meanwhile, I was working at low level technical jobs doing technical writing about building Dew Line facilities from an office in Manhattan.

Cuz and I spent our early summers at "Uncle Sam's" cottages in the Catskills, along with most of the Retman family. I was skinny and subject to bullying at my school, so Dad asked the bodyguard of Congressman Charlie Buckley to pass on some self-defense tricks. I learned about unbalancing an opponent by pushing up on his shoulder while sneaking one foot behind him—but it didn't work too well. One weekend, Dad came up from New York with boxing gloves for Howie and me. We set up a little ring and danced around, jabbing, the way we had seen Joe Louis and Billy Cahn do in the newsreels (way before TV). Within a few minutes, Cuz landed a solid jab to my nose, which began to bleed—and that was the end of our boxing.

Howie and I shared a bedroom at our summer cottage in Long Beach, New York. Each day we would get on our bikes, with a sandwich and a stick and our gloves, and head out to play one-on-one stickball. Or try to sink newspapers with stones in the slowly moving bay waters. Or run and play on the beach. Great freedom and true friendship.

Howie and his brothers got a sixteen-foot Cape Cod Dory, a small sloop, when Cuz was about thirteen, and we learned to sail it in Long Island Sound. It was moored in New Rochelle and the grand adventure always remained sailing across Long Island Sound to Long Island—but I never made it. We picked up our sailing together many years later. By this time, Cuz was a successful physician and head of the North Shore Hospital, with a house in Swampscott, Massachusetts, and a sailboat at the Eastern Yacht Club in Marblehead. I would race as his crew once a year, during Marblehead's Race Week. It was wonderful. I felt that we were kids again, taking off on our bikes again. But it wasn't the same. In the meantime, we had grown apart. No arguments or breaks—just separate lives.

We shared apartments in Boston when he was at Harvard Medical School and I was in graduate school at MIT. After we both married and graduated, we grew apart. Howie went off to serve our country as an army doctor in Georgia. I stayed in Massachusetts, and when Cuz and his wife, Sandy, moved back north, and lived in the same town that we did, Newton, I thought we would resume our close relationship. But it never happened. Who knows why? Perhaps it was just the result of growing children and competing interests. Howie was gracious enough to invite me as "Man of the Year," or some such honor tendered by the North Shore Medical Society, so that I could talk about how a professor plays astronaut, and we attended the big family events (Bar Mitzvahs and weddings) but otherwise we never saw each other.

Then Howie and Sandy settled into spending half the year in Sarasota and I moved to New Hampshire, and now we hardly ever see each other anymore. But the memories and the pleasure of growing up with Cuz are with me forever.

The Rothbergs

Mom's mother, or Grandma Retman, was born Molly Bernstein, and on her side of the family we had Tante Tilly, Tante Faiga and Tante Hahah. (Tante, of course, is the German and Yiddish word for Aunt, and used respectfully for contemporaries of my grandparents.) Sam and Tilly Rothberg had four sons in the service during World War II, and a large banner with four stars hung over the entrance drive. All four boys survived the war. Duffy and his brother Harry opened a garage in the Bronx, and years later, selected my first used car for me. Another brother, Richard Rollins, who we knew as "Diz," became a lawyer after having his novel, *I Find Treason*, favorably reviewed in the *New York Times* (March 1, 1941). Duffy, the pipe-smoking handsome brother, took me hunting for rabbits in his father's meadows and showed me how to shoot safely, but we never hit anything.

The Youngs

My cousin, Tina Kraskow (Molly's youngest daughter), is doing the genealogy for my father's side. I was never as close to them as to the Retmans. Suffice it to say that they all were forced out of Southern Russia (Tina says

Ruzhin and Pavolich, in or near current Ukraine) by antisemitic Russian society and its pogroms. Grandpa came to New York first, alone, and Molly followed later, with Dad. The story is that she pointed at the crowd on the dock in New York and said, "See that handsome man there? That's your father!" Maybe true and maybe not.

I had always thought of my background on my mother's side as Russian, but when I went to the Soviet Union in 1977, I was shocked to learn that the Russians don't consider the Jews to be Russian. The passports of Jews are not marked Russian, but Jewish. I have a wooden plaque with Grandpa Young's naturalization certificate, issued in 1916, on display in my MIT office—something I recovered from Dad's apartment after his death. [*It is now in Ellen's home in Amherst, Massachusetts.—LAY*] The spelling is variously "Youngleman" and "Youngelman."

Those ancestors lived tough lives and had meaningful stories of courage and grit that need to be told, but not by me. I cried when I recently read Malamud's *The Fixer* and imagined the lives of my ancestors and where I might be today if they had not had the gumption to leave Russia. On my frequent visits to Russia recently, trying without much success to work out a joint MIT-Russian Space Research Center, I was struck by the courage and determination of our forebears who made it to America. That generation all came to New York poor and they all reached, more or less, the American

Cousins in Kerhonkson, New York, in the Catskills, at Uncle Sam and Tante Tilly Rothberg's bungalow colony in 1938. Who are these little people? Presumably we are all the Retman cousins. I am in the front row at the extreme right at age 3-and-a-half. (Wish I still had some of that hair!) The others are Rotners and Judelsons. Front row: Bob, Howie and Larry. Second row: Alan. Back row: Harold.

dream of freedom and prosperity. We owe them so much!

On one such trip, I was attending a banquet with my Russian hosts, when I asked my tablemates how it was possible for everyone the room to drink a shot of vodka with every single toast.

"Ah," they said. "If you're a real man you can handle your vodka."

To which I proudly replied, "Don't give me that! All four of my grandparents are from the Ukraine."

This elicited an immediate change in their perception of me, and one of my hosts leaned over and whispered, "The secret is to drink water every other toast."

My father, Ben Young, was a personal hero of mine. He started out at Townsend Harris Hall, a highly selective public high school, sort of a predecessor to Bronx Science and Stuyvesant, in the 1920s. He later worked his way through law school, without attending college, and established a successful practice. Growing up, I faulted him only for worrying so much about his clients. "Larry," he told me, "that's what they pay me to do." That only drove me further into a science career, where the only enemy to worry about was nature herself, and, of course, the funding agencies. He told me that success

Photo from Grandpa Young's Certificate of Naturalization, stating "Be it known that Samuel Youngleman residing at 1960 Davidson Avenue, Bronx, New York, New York ... was naturalized by the Supreme Court of New York County at New York on June 22, 1916."

depends on luck—and the harder you work, the luckier you get. Both he and my mother, Bess Young, were presidents of the Science Parents Association and started the college scholarship fund. Her picture might still hang in the school as a member of the School Board when the new building was dedicated.

His encouragement to me and my sister, Ellen, and to Ellen's two daughters, all of whom later also attended Science, was to make the most of the education we were lucky enough to receive. It was certainly not wasted on us. And he hated waste. As Cousin Howie said at Ben's funeral, "He was the straightest arrow." All my life, I would judge my decisions according to what I could imagine my father saying about my choices. And those principles have served me well.

Dad was the oldest of four, followed by Molly, Willie and Celia. My grandma on my father's side, Yetta, was a traditional, devoted Jewish grandmother. She would take the bus and hike through the snow to bring us her special cookie if I was home with a cold. Grandpa was tall, and proud. He left Russia (Ukraine) under terrible circumstances and returned only to arrange for his wife and Dad (maybe Molly, too) to join him in New York. To get some idea of the cruelty imposed on Jews in their region of the Ukraine, and the city of Ruzhin, read http://kehilalinks.jewishgen.org/Ruzhin/ruzhin_files/Ruzhin_History.htm (from Gennady Makhorin's *Ruzhin's History: Tales & Documents*, published in Ukrainian, by Volin Publishing, Zhitomir, 2000).

Molly was such a dedicated leftie—on all issues—that she always made me feel reactionary, despite my Cambridge bona fides. I have lost touch with her three Kraskow daughters, except for Tina, with whom I occasionally exchange family reminiscences. Willie, who had a career in the Post Office, got me started on stamp collecting and arranged for me to be assigned to a nearby post office for my Christmas mailman job. Willie and Ruth's son, Arthur, stays in touch from California, and reminds me that he, too, went to Science and followed in my footsteps. Celia and her husband, Harry, lived on Long Island and had a charming daughter, Barbara, with whom we kept in touch for several years. All nice people, and I am proud to call them family.

Girls

Girls were always an attraction as far back as I can remember. In high school, I was drawn to the sexy ones in my class, and dated some of them, but I was such a complete geek, I had little romantic success. I wasn't so much disliked as ignored. I had plenty of friends who were girls, but no "girlfriends."

Over the course of my adult life I was in love four times. All four women (how can I say "girls"?) had some of the same characteristics. And for all four, I fell in love between the ages of sixteen and twenty—at least for the first time. All four were Jewish, were dark-haired, and three of them were tall. All four were smarter than me, funny, and academic high-achievers. Two went to Radcliffe and two went to Wellesley. And all four were adept at putting me in my place!

I was really lucky in love, as things turned out—though it didn't seem so at the time. Of the four, I had two great loves in my life. Both of them turned me down when I was really young. And both of them married me later! I met Jody Fisher when I was sixteen and worked for her father, Sam Fisher, and Uncle Leon at the Town and Country Day Camp, in Tibbets Brook Park in Yonkers, New York. She was smart and beautiful and I was in love. In the fall of 1952, I went off to start at Amherst and she went off to begin Radcliffe. I attempted to woo her, and she came to Amherst for one or two weekends, but she thought (she later told me) that we were rather silly (playing Frisbee on the lawn) in comparison to the serious guys at "Hahvahd."

That relationship went no further, until I saw her name on the list of people taking a Fortran programming course at MIT in 1959. I went to see if she remembered me. Second chance. She looked the same and she was surrounded by a phalanx of guys from the Joint Center for Urban Studies, who were about to shoo me away, until she recognized me. And then, as the story goes, love blossomed, we got together, and we talked, read, skied, laughed, and married in June 1960.

Jody and I were married for forty years—from 1960 to 2000—and that included amazing children, a growing academic career, lots of travel and, toward the end, too much stubbornness and hubris—on both sides. She once explained to a restaurant hostess in Halsee, Austria, that I should be shown to the table when I came in. How would the hostess know me? "That's easy," said Jody, "we look as though we should be together." And that was largely true, in interests and in background.

Jody has said that we had thirty really good years together, and I fully agree. The Zurich sabbatical was probably the best year of my married life with Jody! I am incredibly happy that she and John, her second husband, found happiness together. She deserves it after putting up with me!

I met Vicki Liebson in 1954 when I was fixed up on a blind date at Wellesley. My date was a tall, very attractive, very smart and funny freshman girl from St. Louis, dressed in a plaid kilt and radiant in that otherwise dreary Wellesley common room. I was smitten. We exchanged letters and the next year she came to visit at Amherst for a weekend or two. I eagerly looked forward to being in Boston, starting in 1955, and dated Vicki Liebson once or twice, including a ski weekend in New Hampshire, and lots of folk songs. She was fantastic. Then, by 1956 she informed me that she could no longer see me. She was engaged to an "older man" who was about to graduate from Harvard Law School. And off she went. I was heartbroken—so much so that my friends worried about me.

Jody and me in Newton, 1967.   Leonard McCombe/Life/Shutterstock.

I saw her on *The Today Show* several years later, discussing her Bourke-White biography, so I knew she was alive and a famous photo critic. I wrote her a fan letter from Houston when I read a terrific piece she had in the *Times*. We renewed our acquaintance, but that was all. Until, several years later, another second chance occurred. We married almost exactly fifty years after that first date. Lucky us.

I met Liz Keen, the younger sister of Eric Radin's old flame, Linda, in Huntington, Long Island, New York during the endless summer of 1955. She was cute, played tennis well, was ruthlessly amusing, and was already a serious modern dancer. She headed off to Radcliffe in the fall and I tried to woo her since I was down Mass Ave. at MIT, but I failed miserably. Liz was "taken" by a Filipino student at Harvard, and all of her spare time was spent on dance. A year or two later, she moved to New York and transferred to Barnard to pursue her very successful dance career. We met up again in 1958 and remained close friends for many years.

Yet another liaison was also through Eric. I dated his cousin, Pat Adel, beginning when she was a freshman at Wellesley in 1957. She was a poet and a pianist, and was full of romance and vigor. I pursued her for the rest of the year, and when I took the fellowship in France, she let me know that she would come over for a visit at the end of the next year. And so she did, along with her friend Ellen and my old roommate, Arnie. We travelled together to Spain and beyond. By the end of the summer of 1958 we were engaged, and I chose a job at MIT rather than Bell Labs and Columbia to be near her. But somehow, in the reality of Cambridge, the romance fell apart and so did our engagement. I am still not sure what turned it sour, nor were there any real misgivings on either side.

This picture, taken by Chehalis Hegner, was used in press handouts for Vicki Goldberg.

And that is all I am going to tell you about girls. After all, these recollections are intended for my grandchildren!

Pets

I never really had any pets. Oh, I used to like to pet my cousins' Irish setter, with its long golden-red hair, especially while I sat on the porch of their summer house in Monsey, New York. But no pets of my own—I really didn't want one. I was turned off by the slobber they left on my hand. And when a larger dog would jump up to greet me or hump my leg, I would be slightly scared. When I finally did have a pet, it was part of a package deal, and came with my wife, Jody.

Smutnik was the name of Jody's all-black cat. It was 1960, Jody and I were just married, and the cat's dark black fur at the time following the dawn of the Space Age led to the name that was given to one of the litters from David Feingold. (David had been the roommate or housemate of Robert, Jody's previous man, who was tragically killed in an auto accident from which Jody escaped—physically at least, but never mentally.)

Jody and I would leave our Cambridge apartment in the morning—Jody to the Harvard-MIT Joint Center for Urban Studies, working under Bob Wood, its director and her undergraduate advisor at Radcliffe. Jody was deservedly proud of her Radcliffe affiliation. (Years later, Leslie would answer the standard school question by saying, "I go to Harvard but my mother thinks I go to Radcliffe!") And I would go off to my research assistantship at Doc Draper's MIT Instrumentation Lab, in the old Whitemore shoe polish factory at 68 Albany St., seated along with the other grad students near the wall that separated us from the facility where radioactive beryllium was machined for gyros.

Then Smutnik would go about her daily task. We had left cat food and water for her, and she would proceed from one window seat to another, to gather her quota of warmth from the sun. Smutnik was convinced she was a person, and at night she would get into our bed before we did. We would find her lying on her back half under the covers, with her head out, checking out her domain. She was ushered out before we went to bed.

Sometimes we would take Smutnik for a walk. We bought Smutnik a collar and a leash and tried to take her for a stroll down Oxford Street, a very visible stretch near Harvard's Peabody Museum. But Smutnik had her own ideas, and the walk turned into an exercise in dragging this black fur ball, mostly on its back, and hoping not to see anyone we knew. The exercise was abandoned shortly afterward.

Nefertiti was the next cat I remember—a Tonkinese (cross between a Siamese and a Burmese), as Leslie reminds me. By this time, we were living in Newton Centre, Massachusetts. Nefertiti was a good mouser and the rodent population was reduced, if not eliminated. When she proudly brought in her catch one day, Leslie, who must have been around twelve, I guess, decided it was an opportunity to learn and practice taxidermy. I don't recall who taught her, but she gutted, stuffed and preserved the mouse, mounted it on a board, and labeled it, "Nefertiti's First Kill," along with the date. I kept it on display in our basement workshop until we sold the house in the late 1990s.

Sherman was the name of our first dog, acquired in the 1970s and loved by all five of us. A black Scottish terrier, with a squared-off snout that made him look somewhat like a Sherman tank, he was playful but stupid. Jody and Sherman went to school—but they both flunked out of obedience class. Sherman would harass the squirrels in our back yard and the squirrels in turn would bombard him with cherries or with acorns, according to the season. He stood about a foot high, and when he cavorted through the meadows or through the snow in Rumney, all we could see was the tail, sticking up. In the back seat of the car, Sherman was a highly desired prize. Stretched out, he could be petted by all three kids, "One for the waggy, one for the licky and one for the tummy," they said. Sherman loved roaming. He wasn't supposed to leave our enclosed yard in Newton, but managed to do so to visit his girlfriend some distance away. And boy, did Sherman love to roam in New Hampshire. But he always came back, until one day when he didn't.

Was he kidnapped? Attacked by a bear or a coyote? Who knows—but we missed him.

We had some big snowstorms even back in the 1970s. Here is Leslie, with Sherman, a few days after the 1978 blizzard that closed down Boston for a week or so. She didn't really need the snow shoes, she admits, but couldn't resist the chance to use them in Newton. Ah—Leslie! (Leslie and her husband, Paul, now live above 7,000 feet on the road from Boulder to Estes Park, Colorado, and get lots of snow).

Pluto was the next dog in our family, and he was really Jody's. Like her, he was very smart, inquisitive, and impossible to control. He would steal food from the table and jump on visitors. (Jody never did that.) We reached

Leslie walking Sherman in Newton Centre in the blizzard of 1978.

Young Pluto and I enjoy the sun in Rumney

common ground in playing Frisbee. I could sit on the back deck in Rumney, listen to music and toss the disc to him until he got exhausted and stopped returning it to me. It was fun and exercise for both of us. I still don't know the relation between the name of the dog and the name of the planet that played such a big part in the professional lives of Leslie and Eliot.

Where Are The Children?

I look at some "helicopter parents" and marvel at their apparent unending concern for the welfare and whereabouts of their children. I have good friends who are constantly in touch and who track their adult kids' airplane arrivals and the currency exchanges if they are abroad. And when their kids were of school age, my friends drove them wherever they were going and would never think of letting them take the bus home or walk alone.

NOT ME.

Maybe I was an uncaring father, and maybe I was trying to instill a sense of independence and self-confidence in them. Or maybe I just didn't know any better. But I love them and, at least so far, they turned out just fine.

That's not to say that there were no slip-ups.

When we lived in Zurich, Eliot was eleven, and already quite a good skier. He was one of the many who followed the legendary Wayne Wong, the first great free-style skier, at Waterville Valley, New Hampshire, and I was so pleased to have him ski with me in the Swiss Alps. I took one week by myself in the Engadine, staying in Pontresina and skiing everywhere from St. Moritz to Corvatch, looking for any field of powder to offer Eliot when he came down by train to join me for a couple of days. Of course he took the train alone—why the hell not?

Well, it was not a very good year for snow, and the only untracked powder snow I could find was a long steep gulley, between ugly rock outcroppings, at Piz LaGalp, a tough mountain near the Italian border. Not only was this gulley long and untracked—there were also no ski tracks or boot marks anywhere near it. It had to be a great find. So we took the cable car to the top and headed over, "off piste," toward the powder gulley. There were "closed to skiers" signs of course. This was Switzerland, after all. We took off our skis when the climbing got steep and then, as we reached the rocks, we had to climb very gingerly over the icy surfaces. This was not so easy, wearing ski boots! Holding on to rocks didn't help that much. We still had another fifty yards to get to the gulley, and easily that much behind us. I thought about turning back, and even mentioned it to Eliot, but that was out of the question. The way back over the icy rock was too precarious. So on we went, and all I could think about was getting across the rocks without sliding down the mountain. And what would I do if Eliot was injured—or even worse? And how would I ever be able to explain my bad judgment to Jody?

In the end we made it over to the untracked snow and made our way down in a series of well controlled, if not beautiful, linked turns, and never went back. Nor did we tell Jody about it.

A few years later, Eliot was working as a Hut Boy for the Appalachian Mountain Club, at the Lakes of the Clouds Hut on Mt. Washington. Part of their inter-hut games involved stealing things from another hut and sneaking back. One night in August, he hiked across the ridge of the northern Presidentials to the Madison Hut and was headed back, quite late, when the wind came up and got stronger and stronger—a full gale. He was nearly blown off the mountain and had to crawl on his hands and knees to make his way home, all alone in the storm. When he told me about it, some time later, I thought, "Oh my, what could have happened! What terrible judgment!" and then I remembered Piz LaGalp, and I said nothing.

Later, when he was a Boy Scout trip leader, guiding his group of young campers on their week in the mountains, he told me that he brought them down the "slippery when wet" South Peak of Tripyramid, a mountain not far from Waterville. Nobody was injured. But Eliot understood a bit more about my trepidation in the Alps.

Of our three children, Leslie was by far the champion at getting lost—even if she didn't think she was lost. We returned to Puerto Rico a few years after I had been a graduate student there, and stayed at a beach hotel. The kids loved the beach just outside San Juan, and built sand castles. Leslie may have been about six years old. And then she wasn't there anymore. Could she have drowned? Or been kidnapped? Or had she just wandered away? Some time passed and we finally reported her loss to the police.

No problem! One policeman, on horseback, came riding up to where we had our sand castles, and there was Leslie, on the horse, being held in place by the trooper, and having the time of her life!

And then there was the winter vacation in Zermatt, Switzerland. We were wandering around that wonderful town in the late afternoon after skiing, and noticed that Leslie was missing. We looked and called, but no Leslie. She was already eight and spoke enough German to be able to find her way, but we were staying in a rented chalet up the mountain road and didn't know what could have happened to her. Again, we checked with the police and found that there was a little American girl who was in a café partway up the mountain road. She was being fed hot chocolate and cookies, and the police or the innkeeper knew that we would come looking for her. And so we did.

Rob didn't exactly get lost. He knew where he was. But I didn't. And that seemed to not make any difference. Take the tree clearing for example. We have a grove of white pines not far from our house in Rumney, New Hampshire, and I decided to clear one out of the way of our driveway. It was big—probably thirty to forty feet high—with a trunk around two feet thick. I had a chain saw, of course, and was pleased that Rob, who was around nine years old at the time, wanted to help out. The trick is not in cutting the tree down. It is in making sure that it lands where you want it. And especially not either blocking the driveway (even temporarily) or hitting the house. I waited for a windless day. Then, first of all, I cut a wedge facing in the desired direction of fall. Since I was not very experienced, I also tied a rope around the tree and looped the other end around another tree in the direction of fall. Finally, before calling "TIMBER!" I cut through once more, just above the wedge, from the other side, to watch as the tree majestically fell, slowly at first, in exactly the right direction.

"Look!" I called out to Rob. Rob? I thought, *Where is he? Oh my God—right in the path of the falling tree!*

He saw it start to fall and got out of the way. He never talked about it and probably doesn't even remember how I nearly felled him too. But I remember.

Then, many years later, when Rob was in his twenties, he was once more "lost"—at least to me. Jody and I spent the night in Spring Valley, New York, to attend the opening of a Rockland County Park Trail named for her father, Samuel G. Fisher, who had been Park Commissioner. My mother-in-law, Ruth, as well as their friends and neighbors, were there for the occasion. Rob had his own car and was supposed to have driven down from Newton and joined us in the motel the previous night. But he didn't arrive. Well, I figured that it had been late and he would make the four-hour trip in the morning—but still no Rob and no call to the motel. (This was well before the days of cell phones.) I got worried and began calling the state police in both Massachusetts and New York. No accidents, no hospital emergency admissions, but still no Rob. He showed up some time later, after the ceremony, I think. I don't think I ever knew what or who kept him, and I didn't want to know. He wasn't lost—I just didn't know where he was.

The winter after his graduation, Rob worked for a Cable TV station in Winter Park, Colorado. I was with NASA in Houston at the time, and even though as an astronaut I was under strict instructions not to ski or risk injury in any way, I would fly off to Denver some weekends and visit with my youngest son at his workplace on the mountain. At the end of the season, when Rob tired of his next job as a DJ playing country music, he quit and drove back to Massachusetts. He noticed that his route would take him through Texas, and so he called and arranged to visit me in Houston for a few days. He evidently didn't look at the map carefully enough to see how big Texas is, or that Houston is very, very far from where his route would cut through Texas up near Oklahoma. He wasn't lost, I just didn't know where he was, once again. But he did arrive, a day or two later, and we did all sort of things I had wanted to do with him: renting jet skis on Clear Lake and eating crawfish etoufée in a Cajun restaurant. A great visit!

And now Eliot and Rob appear to be very careful dads, who carefully keep track of their children and their whereabouts. They'd better!

Grandchildren

Nothing makes one prouder than the grandchildren. Of course, they all are special—but what else could you imagine?

Vicki maintains closer ties to her children and grandchildren than I do—both geographically and familial. She is very good at it!

At Snow Mt. Ranch of the "Y" near Winter Park, Colorado, we rented a couple of cabins for a family reunion in June 2005. The extended Young family, sitting on the log are, from L-R, Larry, Xander, Viv, Eliot, David, Josh, Leslie, Liz, Rob, Rachel and Vicki. Diane and Paul are missing from the picture.

Vicki paddles with me and her granddaughter Tara, in the pond near our condo in Waterville Valley, New Hampshire in 2014.

Places

1935-1940: Infancy in the Bronx, New York

I read that I was born on Knox Place (or Street) in the North Bronx, but my earliest memories are from our airy apartment at 2450 Gates Place, across the street from the Mosholu Park Golf Course. We moved when I was five, so there was not much to recall. At that time, Mom kept a kosher kitchen out of respect for Grandma Retman. But otherwise we were not observant. I knew that we ate non-kosher when we went out, and one time I created a shocked hush over the large dining room in the Concord Hotel in the kosher Borscht Belt (for which Dad was doing legal work) by telling the waiter I wanted *bacon* with my eggs!

1940-1950: 3981 Saxon Avenue, Bronx, New York

We lived at 3981 Saxon Ave. in the Bronx, on the rented second floor of a private house, from about 1940 to 1950. When I was ready to enter school (probably the first grade—if there was any kindergarten, I don't remember it), we moved to the second floor of the three-family house owned by Mr. and Mrs. Karoli (I have no idea how it was spelled). Mr. Karoli had a metal lathe in the basement and he let me help him turn chess pieces of his own design, and allowed me to keep the curly metal shavings. We were on a quiet, tree-lined street across from one of the many buildings of the "Amalgam-ated," the cooperative apartments developed by the Amalgamated Clothing Workers. Ellen and I shared one room. I kept all of my "treasures" in a single tall cupboard whose door would swing open to reveal my belongings. Favorites included: a printing press in which I composed line-by-line articles by sliding rubber letters into a guide; a map game, in which the light would go on if you matched the state with the name of its capital; and a separate shelf for the sport of the season: baseball mitt, shoulder pads, skates. I would spy on the boxes after "lights out." We shopped in the Food Co-op in the Amalgamated building. The area was probably left leaning, but I only knew of one communist family.

As far back as I can remember I liked to play games, but hey—doesn't everyone? When Grandpa Retman came over to the house we would play cards, especially casino, with Mom. He was formal, yet fun.

1930s and 1940s: The Catskills

Mom's Uncle Sam and Tante Tilly had a summer bungalow colony in Kerhonkson, a sleepy farm region town in the Catskills in New York, now better known as the Borscht Belt. That was long before it became a vacation spot for New Yorkers. Mostly relatives stayed there. There was a swimming pool, but it was cracked and couldn't hold water, so we swam in the "black hole" in the creek, a short drive away. It was a pretty small swimming hole—but it seemed huge to a little kid.

Dad would come up on weekends. He would take the train up the Hudson to Beacon and ferry across the river to Newburgh. We would meet him there on Friday night and go to a movie together before heading home. On hot nights the "air cooled" theater was a welcome relief. The big stars were Ingrid Bergman and Humphrey Bogart—and there was no such thing as PG-13. I was overwhelmed by the sight of Jane Russell's audacious bosom in *The Outlaw*.

We cooked and ate together in a common kitchen. The men played pinochle in the evenings. Sometimes Dad would toss a baseball to me, though golf was more his game. The farm itself had frogs to catch and hay in the barn to jump on. I was very proud that Mom got to drive the hay wagon and to operate the cable-pulley system that lifted hay into the loft. Bathing was in an outdoor tub. On occasional outings into the town I would get to ride in the open "rumble seat" on the back of Uncle Sam's roadster. No seat belt. Just some instructions to stay in the seat. A miracle that I didn't bounce out onto the road!

1940s: Long Beach, New York

Our summers in Long Beach, on Long Island, New York, started somewhere in the 1940s, or perhaps even earlier. I have only the dimmest recollection of the summer in which we were staying in a hotel there, near a classic beach hotel. It had a large porch, and white rocking chairs, perfect for summer reading in those days way before TV. Right out of Norman Rockwell—or that is how I recall it. Ellen was born on Sept. 28, 1940, so I guess everything worked out.

Then, early in the war years, my parents bought our "bungalow" at 89 Oregon in Long Beach, New York, a block and a half from the ocean and half a block from the bay, in the less classy but affordable West End. (It cost $1,900. Everything was depressed because of rumors—later verified—that German U-Boats were patrolling just off the beach.) Cars all had their headlights half-covered and there were "lights out" drills to protect against enemy air attacks. Early on we shared the house with Grandpa and Grandma Retman, and later with the Rotners. Grandma died in 1943 and Uncle Phil Rotner in 1944.

Ours was like all the other bungalows, with a big front porch, bedrooms, a living room, a dining room, and out the back door, a shower. If you were the first one home from the beach you got to shower in warm water, heated by the mid-day sun. We had a long pine "saw-buck" dining table that Mom had a carpenter make to her drawings, and it was amply filled with people and food at dinner time. A memorable dinner was when Uncle Bill was arranging something in the attic and put his foot through the ceiling. Plaster and dust came tumbling down on Grandpa's plate. Dad thought it was deliberate, and that Bill might have used his X-Ray vision to locate the perfect spot to step.

I used to share a bedroom with my cousin and closest friend, Howie. Our serious disagreements were over baseball—he would listen only to the Giants' game and I would listen only to the Yankees. We had our separate radios tucked under our pillows. During most days we would hop on our bikes, with a tennis ball and broomstick, and head off for a day of one-on-one stickball. Or we would head over to the bay with its slow-moving current. There we would each throw some newspaper into the water and see who could sink his float first with a bombardment of rocks—or go out on the boardwalk with Mom and Dad at night to play Skee-Ball or arcade horse racing. It all seems so simple in these days of e-games. If we collected enough green winning tickets we might put them toward a stuffed animal or a flip-book. As we got into our teens our lives were squeaky-clean. We knew nobody who drank alcohol or took any drugs. We lived for sports and reading.

The bungalows were only separated by about ten to twenty feet, and you could clearly hear the conversation on the neighbors' porch. In this case our neighbors were a warm and intimate extended family, the Serinos. They would do their marketing together and then come home to do the arithmetic for the bill on the porch. They took a long time with it, saying, "Adding 26 and 13. Let's see—26 and 13?" So Mom would whisper, "39" and without a break the Serinos would continue, "That's a-right, 39," without noting where the answer had come from.

There was one recollection from Long Beach, involving a fatal accident, ending the life of a neighbor's little child on our street, which remains so painful that I cannot go into it, even sixty-five years later.

During summers in Long Beach, when I was still in high school, I practiced for the cross-country season by running from jetty to jetty. I can still feel the wet sand on my bare feet and the exhilaration. I loved the sensation and the sea air. To this day I adore walking on a beach.

Oh! What times they were, those endless summers! And how the three months of summer seemed timeless—at least a year long. Summers full of sports and swimming and reading and family. No worries about getting into college, or falling into or out of love, or money. If Mom and Dad intended to provide a happy and supportive surround for us, they certainly did that!

1950s: Riverdale, New York

Riverdale was a big step upward. At the end of the 1940s, after the war ended and Dad left his government job as the Chief Enforcement Attorney for the Office of Price Administration (OPA) (or perhaps it was the Office of Price Stabilization (OPS) by then), life changed quickly for my family. For the first time, Dad was making money in private practice—not an obscene amount, but more than the few thousand dollars per year paid by the government. We began spending the weekends looking for a house to buy. In Riverdale, no less, which had been a strictly non-Jewish, rather snooty, countryside part of the Bronx. Why Riverdale? I believe it was simply because Dad had invested so much of his ambition and volunteer work with the Bronx Democratic Party in hopes and expectation of eventually being nominated for a judgeship, and that would require residence in the Bronx, as well as a substantial party donation.

Well, that never happened, and it was a sad story and a miscarriage of justice. It hurt Dad. But we had a good life. New, bigger cars. Buick convertibles, because Dad thought it wouldn't look good to his clients to be driving a Cadillac. He later changed his mind. It was a lovely three-bedroom house at 6036 Spencer Avenue, at the top of a dead-end hill only two blocks from the Westchester line, but still in the Bronx. It had nice little yard, big trees, and a small lawn. (We still use the iron outdoor dining set that served us for many years. [*Liz Rosenberg, Larry's niece, has the dining set now.—LAY.*])

Dad's big invention was a string that allowed him to pull open the screen door separating the kitchen from the deck, while still seated at the table! Clearly Mom was the engineer. The only negatives I recall were the broad whitewalls on the Buick's tires, which I would have to scrub clean when I washed the car.

Mom and Dad had a membership in a Westchester Jewish country club (Briar Hall) and an active social life involving, mostly, the Riverdale Temple and Briar Hall members. I was partway through high school and not terribly influenced by Riverdale. I would socialize on Friday nights at the Fieldston School where Ethical Culture put on a teen evening—first basketball or automobile repair, and then a dance. (What did we smell like?) But I was too far from my friends at Bronx Science and too old for a new group of buddies in Riverdale.

I tried to earn money while still in high school, but utterly failed. I would scan the want ads in the newspaper Dad brought home (the *New York Post* or the *New York Times*), but never saw anything worth pursuing. The job I really wanted was to be in Yankee Stadium, selling hot dogs and Nedicks orange drink, but that never came about. In fact, I never applied.

One spring, in the week before Easter, my folks convinced our neighbor in Riverdale to hire me as a clerk in their flower shop. I was about fifteen at the time and their shop was near the subway station at Dyckman St., at the very north of Manhattan. I was shy. Very shy. And only with great hesitation did I approach strangers exiting the subway to ask if they wanted to buy flowers. One of the people who noticed my feeble efforts was a policeman. He asked to see my Working Papers, and then asked the shop owner. There were none, of course, and a summons ensued. Somehow, the neighbor got Dad to work things out politically and neither I nor the shop owner was fined or jailed. But I learned my first lesson about obeying the law!

By the time I was a "rising senior" in high school (Bronx Science), and sports editor of the school paper, the *Science Survey*, I thought I could be a sports writer. I had consistently opted for the journalism class instead of regular English in school. I read Jimmy Cannon's column in the *Post* and tried to copy his style, including his wise-cracking, "Nobody asked me but" column. I listed my pithy peeves in my column, "It Seems to Me That..." The one-liners are all collected in the red plastic scrapbook in which Mom kept all of my publications and awards—from my Arista (Honor Society) pin to the number I pinned to my shirt from my first 440-yard race at the Armory (I finished last). My writing was better than my running, but didn't compare to my hero, Red Smith of the *Herald Tribune*. Nevertheless, it was enough to get me a job as part-time sports writer for the *Riverdale Press*, a local weekly paper.

The publisher, Dave Stein, and the editor, Joe Fitzpatrick, were patient with me. I learned more from Joe than from my high school class, including how to write to a deadline. I was delighted for Dave Stein when the weekly won a Pulitzer many years later.

My "beat" was the evening softball league, played at the Riverdale Neighborhood House. The teams were each sponsored by a local tavern. Somebody from each team would maintain the official scorecard, with its universal language letting me know if a batter struck out, grounded to short, or hit a fly ball to right field. I would come by for the Thursday game, write it up with all of the color I could invent, assemble the highlights from the scorecards for the earlier games that week, and then go to the press office to type my story and hand it in. I learned from Joe to begin with a catchy sentence and to end with a series of "optional cuts" to allow the editors to fit the story into the space. I would finish each story with a professional looking "-30-" and go home, late but happy. I felt that I could even pursue a journalism career and I enjoyed the practice interviews that our school editors were invited to conduct and the "press conferences" that were arranged for our benefit.

When I got to Amherst, I continued to write a few sport stories for the *Amherst Student*, but my interests were more in science than in journalism, and anyway, I was never going to be another Red Smith, or even Jimmy Cannon. The *Riverdale Press* would continue to arrive weekly in my mailbox at Amherst. If Eric Radin, my frat brother, could get to the paper first, he would write in large letters "English Edition." -30-

1952-1955: Amherst College

Because of the year-and-a-half I had skipped in elementary and junior high school, I entered college at age sixteen-and-a-half. The college campus in Amherst, Massachusetts, was beautiful and bucolic. The air was clear. The Green was green, the rows of tennis courts were red and the red brick buildings were—well—very collegiate.

The 220 or so members of Amherst '56 were almost all white. The substantial number of preppies, from Deerfield and Andover and the like, seemed to have already read most of the assigned books. My single room in Stearns included the services of a "biddie," who made the bed daily and cleaned up once a week, and Gordon Linen, which supplied clean sheets and towels weekly for a small fee. The Stearns Tower carillon chimed out on Sunday mornings. We wore our green beanies, avoided walking on the grass, and dutifully greeted all upper classmen—as required. We had Friday night bonfire rallies before the football games and mixers at Smith and Mt. Holyoke. The meals in Valentine were tasty, including ice cream every day, and the cigarette companies gave out free sample mini-packs. The guys on my floor all bonded, and any differences in background were either non-existent or hidden from me. We ate together, studied together and played together. They were smart enough. I was the math and science pro on the floor. We wore khakis and white athletic department sweat socks and white buck shoes, appropriately scuffed. And never a coat and tie—unless we had a date and wanted to eat in the downstairs dining room at Valentine Hall on Saturday, where guests could enjoy a steak dinner for about $1.

I went to work on WAMF, the college radio station, and briefly on the student newspaper. By the winter of freshman year, I joined the ski team and learned a bit about racing. I had good friends and discovered the beauty of the hills. By spring, the buzz was all about fraternities and who would be recruited where. We had 100% rushing, which meant that nobody was left out. I went to Theta Xi—the only place that asked me—a rather geeky frat way past the football fields. And there I developed some of my best friendships, including Sandy Chaitovitz, Eric Radin, and Art Leff. We were an "intellectual" house, but not too presumptuous (at least in my view).

1955-1957: MIT

I came to Cambridge in 1956 as part of a 5-year combined Amherst-MIT plan. The look and feel of Massachusetts Institute of Technology (MIT) in Cambridge, Massachusetts, were being modernized in the 1950s, and the architecture showed it clearly. The graceful curves of Baker House contrasted with the stodgy look of East Campus, Burton and Graduate House. The new

Hayden Library was a delight to see from Memorial Drive and inside. Its Map Room and the Music Library were there for diversion. Kresge Auditorium and the Chapel made major architectural statements about MIT's changing face. The Alumni Pool with its glass brick wall was another modern touch. I believe the men swam nude for health reasons, until the view from the upper floors of Building 16 brought in a requirement for suits.

The dominant color of MIT in the 1950s was gray. The Infinite Corridor said it all. The path for an undergraduate to achieve professional standing in science, architecture or engineering was going to be long and arduous. With not many places to step aside.

McCarthyism and the Red Scare made us cautious about speaking out or attending demonstrations—at least until the 1960s. Drugs were not yet in general use, although alcohol was commonly abused. Our favorite places to eat included the House of Roy in Chinatown and Durgin Park with its long common tables and slabs of roast beef. A steak dinner at the Newbury Steak House on Mass. Ave. cost 99 cents, since any meal over a dollar incurred sales tax. Many of us lived in Back Bay and faced the brisk walk across the Harvard Bridge each morning, counting our progress in Smoots. For folk music we could hear Joan Baez at the Club 47 on Mount Auburn Street or, if we were lucky, we could catch Tom Lehrer at Harvard as he lampooned Werner von Braun as well as "Hahvahd"!

As to social life, MIT in the 1950s looked like an all-men's school. Our class started with about 900 freshmen, of whom only sixteen were women, and few or none were people of color. Foreign students were limited by quota to 5% of the class. About 10% of the class were commuters, most belonging to the 5:15 Club, with a grubby room in the basement of Walker on Memorial Drive with lockers for their clothes and brown bag lunches. Social life and dating opportunities, as described in "The Tech," were misogynistic, to say the least. *VooDoo* magazine was a college-level *Playboy* without the centerfold. Most women undergrads, known as "Co-Eds," were housed on Bay State Road. Women were not yet housed on campus. My girlfriend at Wellesley joked about the availability of so many men at MIT by saying, "The odds were good—But the goods were odd!" Not funny then and not funny now! At least to me.

Only two of us made the switch from Amherst, and we were clearly outside of the bonds and friendships within the class of 1957. Besides the ski team (which was almost all Norwegian veterans—nice but separate), my only friends were within the Pi Lambda Phi fraternity. Steve Freedman, a friend from Science, arranged for me to be a social member so I could have dinner there, but once again I was an outsider. (I was not going to join the MIT Chapter of Theta Xi, since Jews were not welcome.) There was no room in the dormitories for a transfer student, so I rented a furnished room on Marlboro Street in Boston's Back Bay, and walked or hitched across the bridge each morning.

For me, the saving grace in this grind in the spring and fall was the sailing pavilion where I would regularly sail a Tech Dinghy between MIT and the Boston shore—and race one afternoon a week, but never win. Bill Widnall, a couple of years behind me, was already one of the top skippers. In the winter my relief valve was the Alpine Ski Team.

Boston seemed gritty and small—neither as vital as New York nor as beautiful as Amherst. I never, ever thought I would stay beyond the two years to get my bachelor of science. In the spring I joined three others from Pi Lam in an apartment on Mass. Ave. and Beacon Street, above a Chinese restaurant. I learned to appreciate jazz (at Storyville in Copley Square) thanks to Arnie Langberg, who was by then a grad student avoiding the draft.

By my senior year at MIT, I was in my fifth year as an undergraduate and pretty streetwise—at least in academia. I knew which rules could be bent. I shared a large apartment with some other Pi Lams on a tree-lined street in Brookline. The ride to MIT by public transit took about forty-five minutes, so I bought my first car: a 1950 Plymouth two-door coupe. I was very pleased with it. (It really is true—you never forget your first car—or your first love.)

By the spring of 1957, I moved in with three Williams guys I knew from classes, to a duplex in Allston that most resembled the set for *Porgy and Bess*. I was tickled to be invited for job interviews in California, at JPL and Hewlett-Packard, and to say good-bye to Cambridge. My social life turned into a steady romance with Eric Radin's cousin, Pat Adel, who was at Wellesley. That correspondence continued all through the next year. Pat came to Paris in the summer of 1958, and our romance led to our engagement—which didn't last past Thanksgiving. My fault, I'm afraid.

1957: Paris

When I was in college, a trip to Europe was a very big deal. Some of my wealthier Amherst classmates had taken the "grand tour" as a prep school graduation present. The more I learned, the more I wanted to travel myself. I had never been out of the USA—or even on an airplane! My chance came when I was twenty-one and about to finish my second junior year at MIT. My roommate, George Marks, and my old friend from Science, Steve Freedman, were planning their European trip and invited me to join them. I asked Dad for the money and was turned down. Then I tried once more, arguing that it was a far better deal to travel then, and give up only some low-paying summer job like the tech writer job I had done the past two summers. Then, after graduation the next year I would get a REAL engineering job, at a high salary. (In fact, after graduation, my first job was as an engineer at the Sperry Gyroscope Company earning $100/week. It did seem like a lot.) Anyway, I soon received a telegram from Dad saying that I had won my case and he supported the three-month trip.

Most of the arrangements had been made by Steve's father, who had connections with the travel industry. Everything was new and interesting. We took an Italian ship from Montreal to Southampton in England. My cousin Evan was already studying at the London School of Economics and he hosted me during that first visit. I was amazed to see the dock workers in Southampton, and the speakers in Hyde Park, all of the London sites, and Oxford and Cambridge, and then the overnight ferry to the Hook of Holland, with raw herring, and wooden shoes, and all those other exotic things I had only read about. I was delighted by the museums, the sites, the food! And that was only the beginning.

Our three months, mostly tootling around in a Simca we rented in Paris, included the Riviera, Monaco, Genoa, Pisa and Rome. The time in Austria included concerts in Vienna and Salzbrg. Switzerland included touring the Swiss Federal Institute of Technology (ETH) in Zurich, skiing in shorts in mid-summer, and staying overnight in the youth hostel on the Jungfrau. My very first plane ride was from Frankfurt to Berlin and back through Belgium to Paris.

I wanted to find a way to live in France—preferably Grenoble, so I could ski. But my high school and college French courses were consistently my worst ones. C's at Amherst and a high school teacher who had given up on me. Nevertheless, I looked into graduate possibilities and applied for a Fulbright to do research at the College de France in their Laboratorie de Physique Atomique et Moleculaire. I knew very little about it, but my MIT lab partner, George Rubisow, had been there and recommended it. I heard nothing positive from the Fulbright office and forgot about the dream of living abroad. I had several nice job offers, including two in California (Jet Propulsion Laboratory in Pasadena, and Hewlett Packard in Palo Alto). The biggest coup was an offer from Bell Labs, in Whippany, New Jersey, which would also support me for a master's degree at Columbia. But I went for the Sperry Gyroscope position in Great Neck on Long Island instead. Then, out of the blue, came that famous letter from the Institute for International Education (IIE) informing me that my Fulbright application had been approved as a Bourse du Gouvernment Français, and would include a Fulbright Travel Grant. I was ecstatic—until I saw that the letter was addressed to Jerry Rosenberg, and not to me. That was simply a mix-up in the IIE, however, and we both got the fellowships. Happily, Jerry and I ended up as brothers-in-law.

I took an evening course in conversational French at Columbia and—lo and behold—did well and enjoyed the challenge. What a little motivation would do. Most of the Fulbrights sailed from New York to LeHarve on the *SS Staatendam* that fall.

In Paris, I was assigned or applied for housing in the Pavilion dés États Unis of the Cité Universitaire, one of a large collection of student houses, each sponsored by another country, on the southern edge of the city. There was a gym and a large student restaurant on the campus. I got to play basketball for our house and wear a uniform that said USA on it—but I was pretty bad. The food was ample and cheap (about twenty-five cents with the student meal coupons), but poor. Nonetheless I ate in one or another student restaurant most of the time so that I could afford to have a good meal every weekend.

I shared a generous duplex on the top floor with Harry, an American abstract expressionist. Harry was gay, which he never mentioned, nor did it become an issue until one awful night in the spring. I made plans to travel to Poland with a small French student group and made the classic mistake of thinking that the departure of the Orient Express from Gare St. Lazare at 20:00 was at 10 p.m., not 8 p.m. I missed it and caught up with the others a day later. Meanwhile, when I got back home, I found the door bolted. Harry and the boy who was staying with him were clearly disturbed and didn't expect me. Harry, some time later, told me that he thought I, too, was gay, because I hung out with my old friend David Kornreich. David, Harry explained, was just too handsome to be straight. (He is.)

I dated a fair amount in Paris that year, including a German au pair girl (which seemingly upset Mom and Dad) and an exciting couple of weeks with a co-ed from Smith, at her apartment near Gare Montparnasse.

Money was an issue. My fellowship was paid in francs, but I had to supplement it each month with dollars. There was the official exchange rate, which nobody used, and the unofficial rate, which was published in the daily papers and could be obtained from any of the well-known black-market exchanges. They were particularly busy on that day each month when the GI Bill checks for veterans came out. To keep from being robbed, and since I was not permitted to open a bank account in France, I kept my cash for the month in a money belt. I noticed that the belt was getting looser and looser each month, but, since I had not bothered to get comfortable with the conversion from pounds to kilograms, I never weighed myself. I just assumed I was losing weight. Until I finally got on a scale and found that was not the case. Only the money belt, and not my waist, had been changing size.

From my experience in France, I suppose most of all, I gained a measure of self-confidence and maturity that assured me I could get around in a foreign country by myself. That was the year de Gaulle returned to power and there were rumors of a civil war within France. But *c'est la vie*. I fell in love with Paris and remain so to this day.

1958-1959: Boston

Boston and Cambridge, Massachusetts, were very different in the 1950s, when I first came to MIT, than they are now—although it seems some of the same guys are playing the guitar in "the Square." I went to the Club 47 to hear the relatively unknown Joan Baez, and had a meal ticket to use at Elsie's diner on Mt. Auburn Street. I had three close friends from Amherst, Sandy Chaitovitz, Sam Liberman and Art Leff (who also went to Bronx Science), all at Harvard Law School, and that meant both intellectual diversity and also many good meals with Sandy and his wife, Lynn.

As I was finishing my graduate year in Paris, I asked Cousin Howie for suggestions on where to live. He was completing his first year at medical school and said he would work it out somehow. Indeed he did. After a short stay in his apartment on Beacon Street, I moved in with his classmates who had an amazing old house in the South End of Boston. Then the next year I shared a remarkable duplex on Pinckney Street, just down the street from the elegant Louisburg Square on the good side of Beacon Hill in Boston, with Howie, and my friends, Jim Vernon and Herb Benson, as well as Fran Avantagio, all Harvard Med students. I enjoyed a level of elegance unmatched by all my later residences. I worked hard at MIT and the others even harder at Harvard Medical, and we learned something from each other.

Later, Howie arranged for me to rent a room from another of his classmates, Alan Hobson, and his wife in Lyndeboro Place in the South End of Boston. The neighborhood was seedy but the house was classically colonial and the dinner conversations felt more like Amherst than MIT.

1960: Cambridge, Massachusetts

In 1960, just after we married, Jody and I lived in Cambridge at 329 Harvard Street, near "the Square." (I maintain that it is okay to say "the Square" but not to refer to New York City as "the city" or, even worse, to the Hamptons as "the country.") Our ground floor apartment consisted of just the ballroom of the old Dana Mansion with its high carved ceilings, window seats, and French doors opening onto a side porch.

1961-1962: Puerto Rico

Puerto Rico came into our lives by accident. Jody and I had spent our honeymoon in 1960 at Laurence Rockefeller's Caneel Bay Resort in St. John, with a brief stop in San Juan, and were charmed by it. I had never put on a mask and snorkel, let alone seen tropical fish outside of an aquarium. Jody and I loved it and I bought "beginner" masks for us, equipped with two snorkels built into the mask, but we didn't really get a chance to use them in the cold Atlantic waters of New England.

Then, when the joint grant shared by Larry Stark and José del Castillo permitted an exchange of scholars, in 1961-62, we swapped houses and cars with Victor Sanchez and moved into his faculty apartment in La Finca, in Rio Piedras, on the outskirts of San Juan. We had the use of his Morris Minor, which I drove daily to the old School of Tropical Medicine, near the Hilton on a site bordering the Caribbean. I often took my snorkel and fins to the local beach for a lunch swim. José's favorite place for lunch was a dive of a bar, which he frequented because "no other doctors ever come here."

The Puerto Rican infrastructure was a shambles. The only way to tell whose electric bill was responsible for whose apartment was for someone to stop paying and eventually someone else's power would be cut off. I knew where to stop in a bakery on the way home for the fantastic "pane aqua" (water bread) that accompanied our gin and tonics on the balcony. Our neighborhood had tree frogs, which made a racket at night, and painfully skinny wild dogs left behind by GIs who returned to the Mainland. We lit a foul-smelling spiral (a "cobra") to keep away bugs. José and his wife June kept a pet monkey in their apartment in La Finca. We had a favorite cove, just beyond the airport on a bumpy dirt road, with a beach all to ourselves, which we called our "shell beach." It had a little grass shack that served a sort of blintz of fried dough enclosing chopped beef, which would get washed down with a perfect half-size India beer.

The women students at the University of Puerto Rico were gorgeous and dressed for class in high heels and tight skirts. But their mothers showed the effects of a diet heavy on rice. The academic standards were miserable, and reflected the governor's desire to have "every son of every dishwasher" obtain a college degree. A friend of José's and ours was fired from his position as a law professor because he gave out D's.

Puerto Rico was a US Commonwealth, with big tax breaks for industry. The debate over independence or statehood was vigorous at the time, apparent in New York City from the banners and floats in the enormous Puerto Rico Day parade on Fifth Avenue each June. When JFK came to visit San Juan, the route was cleaned and painted, but only that route. Jody and I became friendly with the man who ran the local International Paper Company cardboard manufacturing facility, which used the leaves from sugar cane to make the product. He and his wife hated Puerto Rico and sent their kids back to the Mainland when it was possible.

At Christmas, we took a big cruise to the US and British Virgin Islands. The British island of Tortola was right out of Kipling, a sad reminder of the excesses of British colonialism. The white minority ran everything, under the government of a Brit who lived at the end of the power line in Roadtown. They all gathered to drink their cheap gin at the hotel most nights, and bought their essentials by mail from Selfridges back in London. Young blacks mostly left the island and were missed by their relatives. Jody and June went surreptitiously to do our laundry in the governor's bathroom when we visited for dinner. Later, we found out that the lights dimmed every time the power surged for the electric water pump and their secret was out. Another visitor, on the make, offered to let Jody shower in his cabin—but she countered that her husband probably needed one too. At first, Jody wanted to cut the cruise short because of her seasickness, but I assured her that she would get over it. Well, I was wrong. It was morning sickness, and Eliot was born that summer!

I enjoyed the half year tremendously. When I got back to a good library at MIT (remember this was way before electronic libraries or search engines), I found that most of what I "discovered" in the lab had been published years earlier by a group from Bermuda's Marine Biology Lab. Our work with crabs on the visual-vestibular interaction was not worth publishing. But my interest in visual-vestibular interaction was launched there and continued for my whole career, with studies on humans and monkeys, but never again on crabs. And I never returned to Puerto Rico—except for that one brief trip when Leslie managed to get lost on the beach and we found her riding on horseback with a policeman.

1962: Back to Cambridge, Massachusetts

After our first apartment in Cambridge, with Jody pregnant with Eliot in 1962, we followed our friends, Linda and Jerry Elkind, into renting the second floor of an old house at 8 Irving Terrace, just down Cambridge Street from the wonderful Memorial Hall. Mrs. Flint, the landlady, was so Old Cambridge. She related one day how she had three nephews, "Two of them went to college and the third went to Dartmouth." We had a small yard, and a splashing pool for Eliot, and neighbors who were all seemingly bright and energetic young professionals.

We got rid of my broken-down Plymouth stick shift and bought our first new car. We campaigned in favor of fluorinated water. Eliot splashed around the Cambridge Common in his red boots and I biked into MIT every day to begin life as a young professor. We made plans to meet in the tunnels under Harvard Law School in the event that the Cuban missile crisis brought bombs raining on Cambridge. There were movies at the Brattle Theatre and plenty of local theater.

1964: Newton, Massachusetts

Life in Cambridge was wonderful, and we didn't want to move away, even when Leslie was expected. But even then, Cambridge was too pricey. The classy parts we liked, near Brattle Street, were hopelessly out of our price range. And the less expensive places around Central Square (including the East Cambridge area that I now live in) were not our idea of "our house." Finally, taking into account the reputation of the local Cambridge public schools, we knew we would be sending children to Buckingham Brown and

Nichols and that was just too expensive. (My first year's salary at MIT was $7,000, and I earned $50/day at Bolt Beranek and Newman as a consultant on some NASA manual control work.) So we looked around at the contemporary split level and ranch houses with lot of acreage in Lexington, where most of our senior faculty colleagues lived. We found one and realized there was not enough room to stow all of our "stuff." So, we changed our goal and located a thirteen-room Victorian house in Newton Centre (only the Post Office insisted on spelling it "Center"), complete with a carriage house. My father–in–law helped out with the down payment and we bought 141 Grant Avenue for $30,000.

We moved into the Newton house in late 1964. I did as much of the repair and maintenance as I could. Now, recall that I had MIT degrees in electrical engineering. Along with the Sears booklet (50 cents) on home wiring I felt confident. I hung light fixtures from the gas lines that were serving as conduit for the electric wiring. And I rewired the electric control switch to our coal burning furnace. When I switched it on—all of the lights went out. Not just in the basement, but in the rest of the house too. And on the whole street. And in fact, the whole Northeast. I was afraid that I had single-handedly caused the famous Northeast Blackout of 1965. (But I hadn't.)

We wired in a communication system. Although Leslie was put to bed in a nursery at the far end of the second floor so that we couldn't hear her crying, we kept the speakers turned up so that we *could* hear her crying. We had three fireplaces and used them regularly. The upstairs sitting room was my favorite one. We quit smoking when the Surgeon General's report on smoking and lung cancer came out—but Jody regressed and kept on cigarettes. She only stopped when we came back from a walk to find the upstairs couch smoldering, and Leslie in the adjoining room.

In 1967, *Life Magazine* decided to do a story about what it is like to be a modern, high-flying faculty member in an elite engineering university. The reporter came to see the famous Doc Draper, my department head and supporter, who gave him my name to interview. A reporter and Leonard McCombe, the well-known *Life* photographer, followed me all around the country. They came to MIT and photographed me playing squash with our friend, David Feingold. They joined Jody and me for our annual lab picnic at our house in Newton, and took pictures of Jody and me, with Eliot and Leslie in our back yard. This was about the time Larry Stark and I were negotiating to sell our little company, Biosystems Inc., and our attorney, Ben Arac, thought that the *Life* pictures would greatly increase its value. The story was supposed to appear in the early summer, and the idea was to show the excitement in a career like mine. And then it was pulled. The Six-Day War in Israel occurred, I think, and that story bumped many lesser ones, including this one. McCombe then sent me a number of prints from his shoot. I ran into McCombe a little while later when he was at MIT to photograph an anti-war rally. He told me how lucky I was to have the story withdrawn. *Life*'s working title of the piece on me was "Academic Bonus," and according to McCombe, the intention was to show how young, bright, faculty technocrats were taking advantage of the "system."

The big Victorian house was on a quarter-acre corner lot. After the local politicians succeeded in making the other north-south streets into opposing one-way lanes, more and more traffic started coming our way. We found Grant Avenue too busy and we couldn't afford a house up on the hill across the road, so we just changed the address and main entrance around the corner to 8 Devon Road. I loved our house, together with its wonderful carriage house that still smelled slightly horsey (hay and manure) and was also home to mice and a family of raccoons that occupied the second floor. It was built in 1895, and we still see it on an old engraving of Newton, which hangs in our Cambridge apartment.

At first, we were afraid that there would be no intelligence west of Cambridge, and that the suburbs would be full of Babbitts straight out of Sinclair Lewis's novel who could only talk about insurance or golf or their lawns. We were so wrong—and so ridiculously snobbish. Our neighbors were just fine and I made good friends. I loved the Newton house. Jody, years later, surprised me by telling me that she never enjoyed Newton and that she was run ragged by being chauffeur and mom. Maybe so.

My study felt like a professor's den and housed a big roll-top desk, which now lives in Leslie's upstairs room in Colorado. On snowy days I could enjoy looking out the window at cars slipping as they tried to make it up the hill across the street. I biked to work, beginning after the first gas crisis hit in 1973. The Newton Squash and Tennis Club was just down the hill, a five-minute walk away. After they admitted me, in the 1980s, I used it regularly, although I never got very good at either game.

We had an upright piano in the living room, and at one point, when I was about fifty, I decided to try to relearn how to play. The children were taking lessons on various instruments at the All Newton Music School and I was put in touch with a woman who specialized in teaching adults.

I had stopped after several years of lessons when I was a teenager. I would go to Ms. Violet's apartment on the Upper West Side on Saturday mornings and struggle through my assigned scales and real pieces. I recall endless hours trying to master C. P. E.'s *Solfeggietto*, and it was arduous. Ms. Violet pointed out that I seemed to have none of the talent of my cousins (probably Janet and Alan). It was degrading and I stopped. But then, playing "Bach for Beginners" in the Newton living room, especially if it was a cold day and we had a fire in the fireplace, created a romantic sense of culture and a marvel that I could actually make music. I hoped to get good enough to actually play music that would please my ear and not merely my ego. But, like so many other things, I didn't put in the required time, even though we had bought an electronic piano for Rumney, and I regressed. Maybe in my eighties I will get back to it.

Newton was a good place to bring up children. The schools were known nationally, along with Scarsdale and New Trier, as the best of suburban public education. The children walked the mile to the Mason Rice Elementary School and we never worried about anything other than their care to await the school guard's signal before crossing Centre Street. After our return from Zurich, Eliot reported that the Newton school was not demanding enough and we decided that, if he could be admitted to the private, highly selective and ancient Roxbury Latin School, we would send him there. He did and we did. The proximity to the Green Line of the T made it easy for the children to access Boston and Cambridge, and so they did. They used the Boston Public Library—and God knows what else.

Jody and I play with Eliot and Leslie, in our yard in Newton in 1967, with the carriage house behind us, to the left.   Leonard McCombe/Life/Shutterstock

How I Became a Liberal

Do Liberals Evolve—or Are We Born That Way?

Politics: it's an adult game that we all can play. Just like other games, we can have our favorite team. The Yankees or the New Deal Democrats, for example. Or our favorite heroes, like Joe DiMaggio or FDR. (Except that now, a few weeks prior to the Trump v. Biden election, it feels more like a struggle for our societal existence, rather than a game.)

In my school days, politics was always a topic for discussion around the breakfast table. My father was active in the Bronx County Democratic Club. Not that he spoke about the really important issues, like welfare or civil rights or the like. But rather, he needed to be a player in this game—a lawyer with a small practice who could be counted on to pay his dues and get his troops (me) to hand out leaflets on Election Day. What he was really interested in, of course, was getting the Democratic Machine to put him on the ballot for a judgeship. That entailed buttering up the Irish leadership of the club. The leader, Dan Sullivan, was a frequent special guest for dinner at our house. Since Dad represented the hotel and restaurant meat suppliers in the New York area, we always had prime beef to offer. If the dinner was on a (meatless) Friday, Dan or another of the Catholic friends would dig in and turn to Mom with a smile and say, "Best fish I've ever tasted."

The real power in the Democratic Party in the Bronx was Congressman Charlie Buckley. Dad was in awe of him and seemed to enjoy their relationship. On a few occasions I would tag along when Dad went to visit the Congressman at his horse farm across the Hudson River in Rockland County. And at the top of the Democratic food chain, in Washington, was the handsome and influential Gael Sullivan. He was Second Assistant Postmaster General under President Truman and became Executive Director of the Democratic National Committee in 1947. I recall the shock in Dad's voice the morning he read us the story in the *New York Times* reporting that Sullivan had been stopped for drunken driving. "That's the end of him politically," lamented Dad.

With all of these contacts, and the friends who were judges or held political appointments in New York, one might have expected that I would learn about government, about the rights and responsibilities of the elected and appointed officials, or even about serving the needs of the people. But no. All I ever heard about was political influence—who would get which job.

Dad did contribute his time, of course. During the war he was the Selective Service Appeals Chief for the local draft board. I assume this involved tough decisions about which young men would be granted a deferment for family or financial reasons and could sit out the war out of harm's way. But

I never heard a word about the cases—as might be expected from my very straight-arrow father. As to the judgeship he sought and thought was in the cards, to his great disappointment, it never came through.

With my childhood friends, we also talked about politics, although we didn't know what we were talking about. In grade school, beginning around the fourth or fifth grade, we argued about political philosophy as though we understood the differences between the parties. Our neighborhood included the apartment block of the "Amalgamated"—the buildings constructed for the Amalgamated Clothing Workers of America. The residents were mostly Jewish, middle class, and patriotic. Their children, my classmates, were serious about studies, well-behaved, and responsive to the demands of their parents for achievement. Our folks were the "Tiger Moms" of our day. We were all ardent supporters of FDR and then of Truman, with no Dewey Republicans. We cheered when FDR was re-elected in 1944 and cried when he died. He was the friend of the little guy, a patrician who could still understand what it was like to be hungry or homeless. (We knew nothing at that time about his inaction with respect to saving the Holocaust victims in Europe.) A few of my fifth-grade classmates proudly announced that they were socialists, and explained about government ownership of the means of production, and one of my classmates said he was an ardent communist—the same as his parents.

For small grocery shopping, we went to the local co-op. Everyone read the *New York Post* in the afternoon and most also read the *New York Times* in the morning, except for our Protestant neighbors, who read the *Herald Tribune*. We rooted for the Yankees and the Knicks. If we even noticed that the teams were all white, in those days before Jackie Robinson joined the Dodgers, we never commented on this or other aspects of overt racism. We went to the movies on Saturday afternoons and once in a while we went downtown to hear the New York Philharmonic in one of their Young People's concerts at Carnegie Hall. There was never any question about our political choices. Everyone voted a straight Democratic ticket.

Riverdale—A step upward

Then, in 1950, my family's lives changed suddenly. Dad had left his government job with the Office of Price Stabilization. He went into private practice in Manhattan, first with a prestigious firm in the Empire State Building, Nemeroff, Jelline, Danzig and Paley—and then by himself. His income mounted enough so that he bought a suburban house with a quiet yard in Riverdale. To keep his political hopes alive, the house he bought was in the Bronx, two blocks from the Westchester line. It was an upper-middle-class region, bordering the Hudson River. A formerly restricted region, it became more integrated post-war. Jews and Catholics lived beside the Protestants.

There may have been Black neighbors, but I don't remember any. My only Black friend of color, the high jumper Avery Johnson, got off the subway at 145th St. with the other Black passengers. We belonged to a Jewish country club, Briar Hall in Briarcliff Manor in Westchester, and we drove a Buick convertible.

We were so suburban that our house had no sidewalk, only a sloping grass strip border that ran down to the street. Our dead-end Spencer Avenue was the last street plowed after a snow storm, and we could take a short-cut through the woods toward the Neighborhood House, with its library and sledding hill. On Friday night I would go to the community basketball game and dance at the Fieldston School.

Mom and Dad belonged to a circle of traditional, well educated Jewish members of the new Riverdale Temple. That was a "Liberal Synagogue," which meant you could pray as you wished, with or without a head covering or *tallis*. In its early years, Rabbi Charles Shulman led High Holy Day services in Ben Riley's night club on the Palisades and Bar Mitzvahs in the local church. My sister, Ellen was the first Bat Mitzvah of Riverdale Temple. Soon the congregation built a striking new building designed by Simon Zelnik. Its stained glass windows and fine choir helped create the ambiance that was intended. Jewish or not, it was often spiritual. Sermons were as likely to be about contemporary books or civic affairs as about the Talmud. Except for the Star of David on the bima, it might have been hard to tell we weren't Unitarians!

And our neighbors were WASP and Italian *and* Jewish—nice and friendly, but we were never in one another's houses. One Italian family, the Parisis, had a small, well-tended garden, and kept us supplied with fresh veggies. They also raised chickens and we could sometimes hear the rooster crow. Hard to believe that we were still in New York City. The other Italian-American neighbors, the Fortunatos, considered themselves of a higher class and had neither chickens nor vegetables, but they did have athletes. One nephew was Doug Ford, a top golfer who won the PGA championship. Dad hired him to give me a golf lesson on the playing fields of nearby Van Cortland Park. Another Fortunato nephew, Ralph Branca, pitched for the Brooklyn Dodgers. He lives on in our memory as the pitcher who delivered the walk-off home run pitch to Bobby Thompson of the New York Giants to give them the pennant in the critical 1951 playoff game. In recent years, it has been revealed that the Giants were using a spotter hidden in the scoreboard in center field to steal the catcher's signs and signal the next pitch to their batter. But that didn't seem to relieve Branca, at least according to the *New York Times*. Anyway, he never gave me any pitching lessons.

So what does all of this Riverdale experience have to do with my political evolution? Well, I'll tell you. By the time I was a high school senior, I developed a sense of social justice and concern for the disadvantaged. I read all of John Steinbeck during the summer of 1952, and most of Sinclair Lewis the next summer. I devoured Lincoln Steffens and thought I might become a muckraking journalist like him. (I was, after all, making money as a freelance sports writer for the *Riverdale Press* and had been the sports editor of the *Science Survey* in high school.) I was moving further and further to the left—but not too far. I agonized over the trial of the Rosenbergs and I was livid about the anti-communist actions of the House Un-American Activities Committee and that ogre, Sen. Joe McCarthy. I became interested in the plight of the small farmer, of all people, and of the differences between government subsidies and maintenance of parity for agriculture. The rights of labor and the treatment of Blacks during the Jim Crow era became my issues. I worried about the Taft Hartley Act and its effect on unions. But all I did was stew over these issues. I never demonstrated or wrote letters. Dad was emphatic in warning me to never sign anything or to get my picture in the paper.

The next step in my political evolution came when I went off to Amherst College in 1952. It was already highly selective, so everyone was pretty smart. Many, if not most of us, had turned down Ivy League colleges to attend Amherst. But somehow my preppy classmates, straight from Andover and Deerfield and the like, didn't all share my left-wing ideas. In fact, in a student poll in the fall of 1952, the majority favored Eisenhower over Stevenson. The golfer, over the intellectual! The faculty survey went the other way, favoring the articulate and witty, though divorced, Adlai over the friendly though inarticulate Ike. How could so many of my fellow students be so wrong? Simple. They were, at age seventeen, still repeating the opinions of their parents and probably also of their prep school buddies. To further complicate things, we were fighting a war in Korea—although it was called a "police action." Truman had difficulty keeping General MacArthur in line and Eisenhower seemed to have the necessary military experience to keep the conflict from escalating. We were all worried about being drafted and sent off to Korea. Most of my class joined ROTC to delay their service. I didn't, but had to make sure to keep my grades up high enough. And I counted on being able to get a deferment for working in the defense industry.

In fact, I did just that. I worked for two summers in Manhattan at Drake Merrit, a large government contractor. The first summer was spent estimating the plumbing supplies required for construction of a US Air Force base in Thule, Greenland, to become part of the radar DEW Line. The second summer was slightly more interesting. Still in Manhattan, I spent most days at the Engineering Library near Bryant Park, summarizing the key technical articles concerning telephone switching systems and rewriting manuals to make them understandable to an army installer with an eighth-grade education. Politically I was getting a broader perspective each summer. I saw up-close the life of a dreary office worker, just a small cog in the American industrial machine. I wasn't going to change that—but I didn't have to be part of it. Only years later did I recognize that what I was observing was the plight of the workers, as depicted in Charlie Chaplin's *City Lights*, or in Fritz Lang's *Metropolis*. I went to a lot of theater in New York and saw most of Shaw's plays during one summer. They all resonated with my growing leftist feelings. Not everyone was getting a square deal in our complex society.

After graduating from MIT in 1957, I took a job as an electrical engineer working for the Sperry Gyroscope Company in Great Neck, New York. I used the newly introduced transistor to make temperature compensation circuits for flight control amplifiers on the modern B-58 bomber, the Hustler. At last I had a job that justified my defense deferment!

Paris and Poland

The next step was a big one—across the ocean to Paris, thanks to a French Government Fellowship and a Fulbright Travel Grant. The technical, educational and cultural aspect of this first of many years in Paris was fantastic. As to politics, I received many surprises. "Yankee Go Home" was written on walls on the Left Bank. Why weren't the ungrateful French bowing down in thanks to the Yanks who saved their lives and their country? Could the realization that they had to give up the dreams of a French Empire be so strong as to blind them to the post-war reality? Didn't they realize that the real threat came from the USSR? Slowly it dawned on me that pride is just as important to a people as it is to an individual. I began to understand how a nation, a tribe or a religion could resent the presence of a "big brother." Was that why some in France resented the Americans, who had rescued them from Nazi occupation? Furthermore, the presence of American tourists and corporations could be a constant irritant.

As to the French student left, marching to the beat of Jean-Paul Sartre and overthrowing the government every few months, they seemed naïve and dangerous to me. I saw, up close, the chaos of France in the late 1950s, only quelled somewhat by the return of de Gaulle to power. He brought his own brand of unrealistic rule centered on one man instead of on true democracy. My illusions of the utopia of the left were being chipped away.

And finally, there was my spring break trip to Poland. Since I had spent the Christmas holiday skiing at Val d'Isere, I felt I should do something more adventuresome and cultural in the spring. I signed on for a French student trip to Poland. There were only three of us. Jean Paul went because he wanted to see what life was like in a real communist state—and not the sort of weak socialist government he saw in France. I wanted to go skiing in a new and exotic region, behind the Iron Curtain in the Tatra Range on the border of Czechoslovakia. And Michel wanted to find out if the Polish girls were really as sexy and easy to make as he had heard. Each of us was disillusioned. None of the three reasons to travel to a communist country were validated. At the ski area, Zakopane, I was warmly welcomed by a group of students and artists. They were intensely curious about America and just as intensely unhappy with their own government. Did we really all have refrigerators in the US? Cars? And so on. The People's Paradise had very little to say for itself. Even the skiing was limited because of the long lines for the cable car. Only the vodka seemed to flow freely!

Back in the USA in 1958, I was immersed in research and graduate courses. In Draper's Instrumentation Lab, I was in a classified area and working on the Air Force's DynaSoar project, which was a manned lifting body to go into space and return on a runway—somewhat of a predecessor of the Space Shuttle. The military applications neither occurred to me nor bothered me. Other parts of the Instrumentation Lab were working on weapons systems, especially the Polaris submarine-launched ballistic missile.

I was happily doing my master's thesis on error propagation in the inertial guidance system. At one point I was assigned to test our guidance system programs on a Digital Differential Analyzer computer at Rome Air Force Base in upstate New York. I never got close to working with military projects that make things go boom in the night. Then DynaSoar was cancelled, just when I had discovered my interest in biological control systems. With Doc Draper's approval and support, I left the Instrumentation Lab to move to MIT's Research Laboratory of Electronics to work under Dr. Larry Stark. And from then on, my only military-related work was as a consultant or as a member of the Air Force Scientific Advisory Board .

The next big event affecting my political evolution was the 1960 presidential election. John Kennedy was so perfect—so witty, charming, intelligent and even handsome. He was one of us, or so I would have liked to think. He relied on a number of eminent professors from Harvard and MIT. And Richard Nixon was such a sleaze. Of course I supported Kennedy, and woke up the day after the election to find that he had really been elected. Utopia, here we come!

Well, things didn't work out all that well. There was the Cuban missile crisis and George Wallace attempting to bar school integration. The Russians were beating us in space. Apollo was announced but it didn't seem doable—especially within the decade. There were riots in Detroit and in Watts. And the assassination. My God, what a terrible thing. Although Lyndon Johnson was far more effective than we had hoped, especially regarding civil rights, he was not Jack Kennedy, and Camelot was already becoming a memory.

By the mid-1960s, the misadventure in Vietnam was tearing our country apart. At first, I supported our involvement. The "domino theory" espoused by John Foster Dulles, that one country after another in Asia would fall into communist hands, seemed reasonable. And Ho Chi Min was leading some really bad dudes. Even though the French had failed back at Dien Ben Phu, the US could protect our grateful brothers in democracy in Saigon. Only slowly did I change my mind about the unwinnable war.

I never marched in a protest or wrote any letters. I was opposed to those of my faculty colleagues who were hurting the cause by their irresponsible support of sit-ins and threats to burn down the ROTC buildings. I believed in the principle of free speech and discussion of opposing views, but not in bullying or silencing the opposition. Since I was chair of the MIT Committee on Discipline, I was seen as part of the academic establishment. We were supposed to represent rational thinking and civilized debate, and were ill-served by shouts and demonstrations. I was outside the military but was eventually opposed to our military misadventures in Viet Nam and its spilling over into Cambodia.

Newton and the Nation

After JFK, my work and my family kept me distanced from politics. On the local level, in Newton, where we lived, Jody became involved in transportation and planning issues and worked part-time for the city. Local government was clean and effective. At the national level, following Viet Nam, we had our good periods (Johnson, Carter, Clinton and especially Obama) and our weaker periods (Reagan, and W.). And we hit bottom with Trump. I was unhappy with the removal of the welfare floors and the military consequences of "Star Wars"—the Reagan era anti-missile defense proposal. I was opposed to the fabricated excuses W. used to justify the second Iraq war. I was pleased with the maturing of the nation's attitudes towards LGBT+. (Two of my favorite relatives are gay. Both are witty and talented.) I celebrated the end of the Cold War and enjoyed working on space research with my Russian colleagues.

My excitement about national politics was revived with the election of Obama. At first it was just his color that made me proud. But after a while it was his character and his style, along with his speech and his charm, that turned me on. And then came Trump. Still in office as of this writing—morally corrupt and truly a danger to the very fabric of society and to world peace. But enough of that—this is MY memoir.

So, to return to the opening question: "How did I become a Liberal?" Surely home and environment, especially the views and actions of my parents, had a lot to do with it. But as time went on, my reading and observations strengthened my increasingly liberal views. I oppose the Ayn Rand, libertarian (and often Republican) view that we each bear the responsibility for our own destiny. Sure, individual hard work and dedication can elevate our standard of living—just as exercise and healthy diet can help to ward off disease. But certain things are beyond our individual control. And society does indeed have to help out the needy. We are all part of a broader community and we need to look after those who need help—for health care, for education, for housing and for security. Are we our brother's keeper? You bet we are. We affirm this commitment not just by paying our taxes, but also by contributing to charity, by carrying our load in the community, and by caring for our neighbors. And that, in short, is why I remain a liberal.

1968: Rumney, New Hampshire

For city kids from the Bronx and Manhattan, Jody and I had a deep-seated love of the countryside. We bought our land in Rumney, New Hampshire, after a long and very deliberate search. We began looking for a weekend place in the mountains in the mid-1960s. We decided we needed a place that was only a two-hour drive from Cambridge, on or near a clean river where we could canoe and swim, and near but not in a first-rate ski area. I didn't know if I would get tenure at MIT, though I didn't really worry about it, but we did know that the region suited us. We looked at places near Freyburg, Maine, and New London, New Hampshire, but found that the Baker River Valley in New Hampshire would suit us best. Mountains, a river, Tenny Mountain and Waterville Valley ski areas, Plymouth State University, great hiking, and Rte. 93 from Boston was just about completed to the area. We looked and we looked and were tempted by a huge old fixer-upper that backed on the Baker. Then, one spring weekend we drove through Rumney on our way to Vermont, where we had chaperoned an MIT weekend at the Rockefeller House and had enjoyed skiing at Killington Saturday and hiking the Long Trail on Sunday. (Eliot reported that he slept in the bunk room with "the other bachelors.") That weekend did it—we needed to buy or build a house. When we stopped for gas at Aaron Shortt's Mobil Station, I explained our quest to Aaron. He pointed to an elderly farmer and said, "Rupert (Ray) over there, he has land on the river and I expect he would like to sell some."

Well sure enough, he said he did (I think) and he said to follow him up to the Buffalo Road (I think), except that he was too arthritic to walk all around his hillside and meadows. Jody was pregnant with Rob and not ready to walk much either. But I did get to see the marvelous swimming hole. And, anyway, we sort of knew the land from a time earlier when we camped in Herb Hillman's neighboring meadow during another land-hunting weekend. Forty acres for sale. Way more than Mr. Ray needed for his diminishing herd of dairy cows. So, we bought the land for $5,000 and spent a year or so getting the deed cleared.

Here is Jody's corrected version of the land purchase. "We were on our way up to Suicide Six in April, the newest MIT lab members and therefore the lowest on the list for a weekend at the endowed cabin Laurence Rockefeller had given MIT. We stopped for gas at Aaron Shortt's and you apologized for me. I was wearing an appropriate wife-of-the-director wool maternity dress and hiking boots. Remember 'Your mother wears army boots'? You told Aaron that we had been looking for land to buy and that's why I had on hiking boots. That's when he sent you to Rupert's car—he was waiting for the school bus—and we followed him home and stood on the bank and looked over the meadow through the pine trees. We continued on to Vermont and skied on Saturday, but there was a terrific thaw, and Sunday was a washout. We left Vermont talking about the land, and decided to stop and buy it. You said we would never travel again. We did it anyway, put down $50.00 earnest money and Rupert drew a map on the back of an envelope. We were so happy, couldn't be any happier, and on the way home in the car we heard over the radio that LBJ was not going to run again. We were happier."

The land had a really nice swimming hole, complete with a mini-beach and a sort of rapid, and a large meadow. We could see that, after removing some trees, the view from a site on the Buffalo Road over the Baker River Valley would be great. In fact, we had everything—except money to build our dream house. Jody asked Kathy, her Radcliffe classmate and then an architect in San Antonio, Texas, to design a simple cottage to our specs. Which she did, except that they don't allow for big snow loads on the relatively flat roofs of Texas. Or, for that matter, the need for air space below the roof to prevent the build-up of ice dams. We contracted with Malcolm Ray, the owner's nephew, to build the house, leaving the interior to us to finish. He was in constant dispute with us as we changed the roof pitch, added a full attic, and so on. When the shell was completed we ran out of money, but it was livable.

By 1969, we were spending weekends in the house. I bought a chain saw and continued to clear our view over the valley. We had a five-foot-high stack of 4x8 plywood siding in the middle of the living room, waiting for me to put up the interior walls. By myself, using homemade T's to prop up the boards, including those on the cathedral ceiling. I never fell off the ladder, but it was a really dangerous and foolish thing to do alone. We heated it largely with a Morso air-tight wood stove—all the rage in the 1960s. Even with fans blowing down the hall, the bedrooms were more than a bit chilly. Our one luxury was the large butcher block counter in the kitchen. Jody made wonderful dinners, and sitting around the counter island made for lots of family bonding. Plenty of LPs, heavy on folk (Baez, Christie, McLane, White, Bickell, Mitchell, Seeger—Peggy and Pete and the Weavers, etc.) and comedy (Lehrer, Flanders and Swan, Sahl, etc.). No TV but lots of games.

We cleared a path to "our beach" and spent long afternoons there. The kids were not allowed to go there alone until they could pass the "swim test" of swimming to the little island and back. The camp site across the river sometimes had families who stayed over, and sometimes they were noisy, but we had our side (the north bank) completely to ourselves. We moved rocks in the little rapid to make a slide and played "king of the mountain" in the swimming hole. There was plenty of water for swimming all summer long. Each spring would lead to a change in the location and size of the beach.

Early in the fall semester, when the leaves had begun to turn their incredible colors, we would host a lab outing. It included soccer in the small meadow, swimming if it was warm enough, later on softball in the large meadow and even later a hike up Mt. Stinson, or once up Mt. Cardigan. The Mountain Day activity would finish with a barbecue back on our lawn and a wonderful feeling of camaraderie. I am sure we were inspired by the similar activities my MIT Mentor, Y.T. Li, and his wife, Nancy hosted back when I was a grad student and young faculty. I suspect these fall outings were one of the things that led to the remarkable sense of community that still pervades the Man Vehicle Lab.

The town of Rumney was definitely not a ski resort, although we had good cross-country on our meadows and were only a fifteen-minute drive from the small Tenney Mt. The only other weekenders were the Hillmans. Herb owned the Pangloss Bookstore in Harvard Square and was a would-be mountain man. I liked Herb and his wife, but Jody once took offense at some comment and we ceased to see them, or to borrow Herb's rototiller for my small vegetable garden. Otherwise there were woodsmen, some teachers from Plymouth State, the owners of a local bookstore and a mixture of tradesmen and professionals. Our immediate neighbor was the son-in-law of the man who mowed our meadow in return for the hay he used to feed his sheep, and was also a New Hampshire Supreme Court Justice. And then there were rednecks. Not far down the road was a log cabin with "Keep Out or Get Shot" or some such signs. I made the serious error of knocking on their door for something during a bike ride with our closest neighbors. One of these neighbors happened to be black and gay (and also an MIT planner.) We got away unharmed and not really threatened, but not welcomed either! Further down toward Plymouth was the garage belonging to the head of the John Birch Society of New Hampshire—a sort of Tea Party of its day, but worse, if you can imagine that. We had our car serviced elsewhere and were otherwise not bothered by him, except for reading his letters to the editor of the *Plymouth Record*.

We once got to see the daily journal of a neighbor's grandfather from Rumney written in the early 19th century. Every day concerned wood. Trimming or cutting trees, bucking and splitting firewood, burning the wood for warmth and emptying the ashes. Well, it hasn't changed that much. We had a lot of trees we took down for the building lot, but most of it was soft pine. We bought an old chain saw, which was a bitch to start and whose vibrations nearly broke my back. Then came the big family event: a weekend in the fall when we would rent a hydraulic splitter and work as a team. I would load a large piece on the splitter, Jody would pull the handle and the log would get split in two. Leslie and Rob would carry the split pieces around to the back of the house and Eliot would stack the wood ever so carefully so that it would not fall over in a high wind. Then, that winter, we would enjoy the heat as we burned the wood and enjoyed the smell as well. Except that I sneezed—all the time—until, many years later, when Jody changed over our heating system to gas, and my nose and my disposition both cleared up, at least somewhat. Life and my backaches got easier when we bought an electric chain saw and a very long extension cord. Each day spent on the hillside further expanded our open area and our view down toward the river valley.

When we first settled in Rumney there was no clear path down the hill and out across the meadows to our swimming hole. Nor was the boundary clearly marked. Over the years, we marked a path, cut down the brush, put a small plank walk across the stream, and began to mow the path. It all seemed very civilized and I took pride in how easy the walk had become. (Years later, thanks to the expertise of John, Jody's second husband, a real bridge and a proper path appeared.)

My attempts to grow raspberries on the hillside didn't succeed, but, like Beatrix Potter's Farmer McGregor, I did enjoy my little vegetable garden. We tried all of the standard veggies. Most failed—in part because I would have to take off for Houston just at the time that either the weeds were most aggressive or when the rabbits and raccoons had managed to dig yet another access to the garden, under my fence. But, when the tomatoes were ripe, or the green beans fresh, they were really delicious. Only one season did we ever get the corn to properly cross-pollinate. But, then again, the very fresh corn from the vegetable stand down the road was unbeatable—especially when plopped into boiling water within an hour or so of being picked.

Jody had much more to do with the local residents in Rumney than I ever did. She was active in weaving and book club and bird counts and the conservation bog. Most of my local buddies were involved in skiing and many of them lived or worked in Waterville Valley.

When Jody and I split in 2000, at the end of a mostly blissful marriage, she suggested that I buy a place in Waterville to fulfill a long-held desire to live at the base of a ski trail. She was right, as usual. Jody and her second husband, John Williams, spend the warmer months of the year at the Rumney house on the Buffalo Road. The house and the land have been immensely improved and are a credit to their vision. I have many fond memories of that place and hope it will serve future families well.

1972-1973: Zurich, Switzerland—
My First Sabbatical

Our sabbatical in Zurich (1972-73) was the first one I took, and it was terrific. I had been on the MIT faculty for ten years at that point. Sabbatical leaves were still pretty unusual, and I applied for one with low expectations.

When it came to finding a place to spend a sabbatical, I looked for an interesting place to live and a research lab that would allow me to learn something new and was related to expansion of my field. By that time (1972), I had extended from eye movements to vestibular function. I wanted to go abroad, and most of the challenging work was being performed in Germany or Switzerland. Dr. Kornhuber of Ulm ("Please, Larry, I'm a clinician!" he insisted as he reached for the dinner check) sent me to see Dr. Baumgartner, in Zurich, who arranged for me to work with an unknown: Volker Henn, who was about to return from a research stage at Mt. Sinai, in New York. Jody approved of Zurich and we made arrangements to move to Switzerland for a year, beginning in the summer of 1972.

Thanks to Volker, we rented a "chalet" in the upscale Gold Coast town of Küsnacht, on a country lane, "Geissbühlweg." Volker lent us some minimal furniture for our arrival and we bought the rest from Globus department store, a sort of Ikea of its day. Our house had five bedrooms, on three levels, and included a large open terrace that looked way down over the Lake of Zurich. All day and much of the night we would see the magical parade of ferry boats and tour boats making their way back and forth on the lake, from Zurich out to the castle at Rapperswil at its end. There were some very Swiss things about the chalet, which was actually the summer house of Herr Lehmann, who lived in the town of Küsnacht and ran the TV store. Nobody Swiss would live in a wooden house in the winter, except in the mountains. It was well equipped, but with a tiny refrigerator. But that didn't matter to a Swiss housewife, who was expected to shop each day for that day's meals. The large meal at mid-day was followed by a nap. Big debates raged over whether

Leslie and Rob stacking wood in Rumney

children should be allowed to stay at the school over lunch time or if they should be fed by their stay-at-home moms. And of course, that reflected on the question of working mothers. Hardly acceptable at that time!

Most of the taxes in Switzerland are paid directly to the Gemeinde, the town, which, in turn, provided most of the services except for the ever-present Swiss Army, with their knives, their watches, and most of all their rifles, which every reservist kept at home, to be ready for a surprise invasion. Since the taxes were based on real estate, this led to a very regressive situation, somewhat akin to that we have in New Hampshire. The rich towns, like Küsnacht for example, had rich residents, with large houses, and therefore a low property tax rate, which attracted high income residents who bought large houses, and perpetuated the feedback. One of the advantages for us was that the wealthy neighbors were generally people who had lived abroad—often working in the US, UK, Australia or Scandinavia. They were open, friendly and helpful to our naïve family of Americans abroad, not at all like the Swiss caricature of a dour, unfriendly bank official. For example, after a few weeks in residence, when our trash was left uncollected on the sidewalk, our neighbors explained patiently that we needed to put out the trash in a certain colored bag, in a certain place, on a certain day of the week. (Not so strange—we do that in Massachusetts, but it explained why our trash remained uncollected.)

And then there was the mysterious case of our seven-year-old daughter Leslie, who never really learned German and therefore got little out of her local school, which was taught in German. She was lost and would dawdle along the path through the woods to and from school. Our neighbor pointed this out to us and we were concerned about her intellectual ability until we guessed that it was the language that was getting in her way. After she switched to the International School, an English-based private school up the hill in Zumikon, she was fine. Jody and I were the ones who couldn't keep up with her "maths." One day she wanted to check the answer to her homework, which was something like, "If you go to the greengrocer's and buy a packet of crisps, and they cost 3 and 10, what change do you get from 6 quid?" (This was just after the UK switched to decimal currency.) She was far from being intellectually lacking; back in the US, and speaking English in school again, she later graduated from Harvard, earned a PhD from MIT, and went on to become a world leader in planetary science. Eliot, meanwhile, had a much more sympathetic and understanding teacher at the local school—and seemed able to get along both in High German, in the classroom, and in Swiss German, for recess. He found, however, that his Newton soccer skills were not up to the level of his Swiss classmates. Five-year-old Robert, meanwhile, attended an "International Nursery School." It apparently operated very well by having each child speak in his or her own language. They played together and shared the toys, with none of the bickering we would expect from a nursery school. The most serious language student in the family was Jody, who regularly attended classes at the German language school in Zurich and became friendly with her classmates. Interestingly enough, she had the best grammar in the family, and knew when to use "der," "die," or "das"—but was slower and more careful in forming sentences in conversation. I, on the other hand, had the advantage of daily German conversation (and only German) with Volker. I could blab rapidly in some language that sounded vaguely Germanic—and was full of errors! But I was usually understood. Our American au pair girl, Bonnie, was useless in language and not much better as an au pair. She returned home in the fall. We barely noticed her absence.

That Zurich year was full of great trips. We bought a US standard Mercedes ($4,000 for the 180, at a rate of 4DM/$) and used it freely, although my daily commute to the Kantonsspital (now the Unversitaatspital) could be done by bus, or by train, or best of all, on nice days, by boat from Küsnacht to Bellevueplatz. Eliot had school on Saturday mornings, so many of our outings were on Sundays. We would select a castle, read about its history and defenses, and drive out to visit it.

Our fall trip, during the potato harvest season, was to get as far south as possible by car. We spent it in Sicily, where Leslie wandered away and was found by the police—again. In the spring we drove to Greece, going by ferry from Bari (Italy) to Bar (Greece). By that time the Swiss franc had been revalued relative to the dollar, so we had much less money to spend, but the Greek travel agent near the hospital insisted that we must visit his homeland. He sent us to Kalamata, a small fishing village, and we visited Olympus and crusader castles. We stayed in a marvelous little pension. The cooking was done by Philippe, the Belgian-born husband of the manager. (They met when he parachuted from his airplane, shot down by the Germans, and her family hid him out all during World War II.) We learned some Greek songs. We climbed up a goat path to a mountain village, where the women were washing their laundry in the stream and the men were gathered in the town square, drinking ouzo. Our common language was German. They invited me to drink with them, but gave me a collective frown that could have frozen me in place when I asked if Jody could sit with us.

Of course, one of the advantages of Zurich was its proximity to the Alps. All of us hiked, and were delighted to find, near the top of almost every climb, one or more of the following: a café with a large Swiss flag and a terrace, a cow, and two older women in black skirts descending the path we had just struggled to climb. Day skiing was easy, often at Flims or Andermatt or even Davos. It was an easy train ride there, with the lift ticket included, and a relaxing train ride home with a good beer. When I drove Leslie up the hill to school in Zumikon in the morning, I could tell if it was going to be a good ski day and sometimes rearranged my schedule accordingly.

In about 1978, I was back in Zurich for a two-week stretch to work with Volker Henn on extensions of our earlier research on monkey eye movements. I was staying at the famous "Dependence," an affiliate of the larger hotel known for its low rates, lack of service, and proximity to the Kantonspittal, but little else. This story involves Uncle Isidore's fine German cello, which Eliot was learning to play. The cello was protected only by a flimsy corduroy case—not at all sufficient to protect an instrument of that quality. The cello teacher was emphatic in insisting on a better case. In fact, she could sell Jody one. She had a couple to show her, one from England for $1,000, and one from Hug, the major music store in Zurich, for $400. Brown fiberglass, nothing as fancy as the English one, but only $400. Because the dollar was stronger than the Swiss franc, buying it in Switzerland for 400 francs or so would be a bargain if it could be had for that figure. A day or two before I was scheduled to fly back to Boston, I got a call from Jody at the hospital, asking me to go to Musik Hug, the large music store down near the Lake of Zurich, and see about buying a cello case. We were really busy, but on my last day there Volker and I went to the music store and found that, yes indeed, they had cello cases., all sizes. Off we went, looked them over (all very well made and very Swiss) and I bought a nice one. Volker gave me a lift to bring it back to the hotel and I settled down for a last night's sleep before my return trip.

That was when I began to worry. Many things could go wrong. As I tossed and turned in the lumpy bed and resolved to stay in a more upscale hotel on my next trip, I wondered if I would be able to get the new case onto the tram and the train to get to the airport in the morning. And would the airline make me buy a separate seat if I were unable to check it in baggage, like real musicians do with their fine instruments. And was the price that I paid really a bargain? Did Jody say 400 dollars or 400 Swiss francs? And, most worrisome of all—did I buy the wrong size case? There are bigger cellos and smaller ones and I guessed at the size of Uncle Isidore's. The possibilities were limitless, and all were fraught with danger.

I decided to call Volker and ask him to pick up the case at the hotel the next day, after I left for the airport, and to return it to the store. I looked at the clock. At about 2 a.m. it was too late to call him, and I would have to leave at about 7 a.m. to make my flight. I was cornered. I had made a big mistake and was about to compound it. But if I came home without the case, I would let down both Eliot and Jody. So, I finished my packing by throwing all my dirty laundry into the case and decided to try to bring it home and hope for the best.

Well, it was no problem getting the case on the tram, which ran regularly down Ramistrasse, near the hotel, and then to carry it onto the train at the Hautbanhof. Even at the airport, I merely checked it with my suitcase, and boarded a direct flight to Boston, with no questions asked.

The real drama didn't occur until I was going through the customs check at Logan Airport in Boston. The setup there was that visitors, including friends or family who had come to meet you, waited in a hallway outside the customs hall, and could only peek into the hall for a few seconds at a time when the doors swung open to disgorge another arrival. Jody saw me waiting in line, then approaching the customs agent. I was there for an unusually long time. Finally, I emerged, with the case and a big grin. Here is what happened.

The agent looked at my suitcase and the cello case and asked me, "Do you play the cello?"

I said, "No."

"Are you a musician?"

I said, "No."

"Did you buy a cello?" she went on.

"No," I answered, truthfully, but offering no further details. All in keeping with my principle, learned from Dad, of not lying but not saying too much. The case was obviously brand new.

"Open the case," was the next demand.

And so I did. And she saw that it was filled with my dirty laundry and not a cello.

"What DO you do?" asked the agent.

I replied, "I'm a professor at MIT."

The agent burst into laughter and said only, "That's all right, then," and sent me on my way.

The cello and the case live at Jody's house in New Hampshire now, except for the glorious outing it gets each summer when Walter Grey, the exceptional lead cellist for the New Hampshire Music Festival, plays it in a way that surely would have delighted Uncle Isidore. And I never did pay any customs fee on the case, or on the laundry either, for that matter. Nor did I lie.

1979: Road Trip to Galveston

It was the summer of 1979 when NASA's schedule began dictating my family life. This time we had planned a summer vacation somewhere, when NASA let me know that I was expected to be in Houston, Texas, for some flight simulation or equipment checkouts. It doesn't matter—they all run together after a while. So Jody suggested that we turn it into a family trip—to Houston in August! We really didn't know what that meant, but off we went: Leslie (fourteen), Rob (nearly eleven), Jody and me in our Dodge station wagon. We had a CB radio and Leslie would contact the drivers of the big eighteen-wheelers on our route. They would respond to her signal of pulling down a handle as if it were on a steam whistle by giving her big blast. (She was pretty cute—as the drivers surely noticed.)

Our first adventure was a canoe trip of several days on the Buffalo River, a "wild and scenic" river in the Ozarks of Arkansas. It had been written up by a Spacelab colleague and sounded marvelous—no houses or roads, high bluffs, and clear water. In our two rented canoes we soon found the water to be bathtub temperature, and the air wasn't much different. We started paddling up the little brooks flowing into the river in search of cooler water. We dunked in the main river water and skinny-dipped when we made camp. We would have liked to set up our three tents on the grassy bluffs to catch some breeze, but we had been warned about snakes there—so we camped on one of the warm, sandy beaches found on almost every bend in the river. One night, after bedtime (Jody and me in a larger tent and Rob and Leslie each in a one-person pup tent), it began to rain and then to blow, and then blow harder and harder. I got out in the rain and pulled the canoes up further on the beach and tied them to a branch. And it blew harder still. Then our tent flap was opened and there was a soaking wet Leslie. Her tent had blown over and she was scared. Of course, we recovered her tent and made room for her for the night. I don't remember hearing from Rob. But the rest of the paddling was quiet and scenic indeed.

When we got to Texas, we headed right for Galveston Island, where I had arranged to rent a condo at "By the Sea" Condominiums on the Seawall, overlooking the Gulf of Mexico. It was gorgeous at night. Early in the morning I picked up a rental car and headed up to the Space Center to work. Jody, Leslie and Rob went off to play on the beach. Well, that was a shock. By about 10 a.m., the sand became impossible—too hot to walk on, even with sneakers. We did some fun things, saw some birds, spent a lot of time in the air-conditioned condo (where we also broke a glass coffee table and spent some time tracking down a replacement) and drove back to the lovely cool White Mountains.

Just to be fair, we had some other great times in Galveston, but in the winter. Dickens recreation weekend with Victorian entertainment was terrific, and so was the birding, biking, and the crawfish étouffée. But mid-summer is not its high season!

1980s and Beyond:
To Russia with Love (sometimes)

Russia, of course, was the enemy in the Cold War. In my first job after getting my engineering degree from MIT, I worked for Sperry Gyroscope Company in Great Neck, New York, on transistor servo amplifiers for the B-58 Hustler. Back at the Instrumentation Lab at MIT, I was involved in the guidance system for DynaSoar, the Air Force manned spacecraft that never was built. Defence work was driving high tech in those days. At no time did it occur likely to me that we would get to the end of the 20th century without a big war—bigger than Korea or Vietnam—maybe even nuclear. So it was with surprise and excitement that I started going to Russia, beginning in 1965 or so, on trips having to do with peaceful cooperation in space. The first trip

was to an International Automatic Control Congress in Yerevan, Armenia.
The Armenian researchers I met were quick to explain that they were not
Russian, and then to ask if I knew their relatives in Watertown.

The space-related trips began in 1980, when I got a call from Gerry Soffen,
then the head of Life Sciences for NASA. He asked me to join the NASA
delegation to a meeting of the US-USSR Joint Working Group on Space

The Soviet Lunar Lander at the Moscow Aviation Institute. Myself, Prof. A. Efremov, and Prof.
Mednov (the head of the lab of the "Space technology dept.).   Jack Kerrebrock

Life Sciences (or something close to that) in Moscow. "Come on, Gerry," I pleaded. This was the year in which the Soviets had invaded Afghanistan and the USA withdrew from the Moscow Olympics. But it was okay with NASA, and a curiosity for me.

Before going for the first time, I went to see Grandpa Young in his nursing home to ask him what he missed about Russia, and what I should look for and bring home to him. "Laurence," he asked me, "do you really HAVE to go? Do you know how hard it was for us to get OUT of that terrible place?" No longing for Mother Russia there.

The first thing that happened after checking into the Hyatt-style hotel (one of many built for the Olympics) was a call from Gerry, asking to talk with me. Not on the phone, but outside. And not in the lobby (microphones everywhere), but on the street, in December, without a coat, trying to look as though I had nothing to hide. In fact, Gerry had heard that I was bringing some gifts for a couple of Jewish academic "Rufuseniks," those Russians who had been denied employment or even their apartments when they applied to emigrate to Israel. That was true, although I don't know how Gerry and NASA found out.

I was carrying a still camera for a cousin of the MIT provost, Francis Low. The Russian cousin has been a professor in one of the universities in Moscow and lost his job when he applied for a visa to emigrate to Israel. He was scraping along teaching tennis. The other gift was a tape recorder, which would be useful to a translator whose plight was known to one of the Jewish organizations near Boston. That all seemed innocent enough and I brought them along. Gerry insisted that I accompany him to the US Embassy and meet with the Foreign Service Officer charged with US relations with the Refuseniks.

There followed a tense and anxious week, in which I was warned not to embarrass NASA or the US, let alone myself, and not to break any laws, even though there were no laws against giving gifts. My week was filled with anxiety as I contemplated how to get rid of the gifts without getting arrested. Finally, at the end of the week, a rendezvous was arranged at an embassy apartment. I was welcomed warmly to a Friday-night gathering of the Refusniks in an apartment filled with jubilant Russian Jews, all of whom spoke English. The air was filled with the familiar smells of Jewish cooking. On the host's advice, I proceeded to a bedroom down the hall where I met the intended recipients and got rid of the burdensome gifts. I also passed on some rubles I wouldn't need, as well as a stack of Russian cash Gerry suggested I put to good use! I was relieved to get the hell out of Russia the next day.

Alexander (Sasha) Efremov, now Professor and Dean at the Moscow Aviation Institute, had first come to work as a post-doc in my lab in the under funding from the Institute of International Education. Over the years, my friendship with Sasha grew, and I was interested to see him become more and more appreciative of our American way of life. When the Shuttle-Mir program began soliciting bi-national research proposals, we put together a project called "Pilot." It would take advantage of both the Shuttle for exposure of crew to weightlessness and the Russian Buran to test manual control during re-entry. It passed peer review and it was on its way to experiment definition, with details to be negotiated between NASA Johnson Space Center (JSC) and Roscosmos, the Russian Space Agency. At that time, I was full-time in Houston as an Alternate Payload Specialist. But at the Moscow meeting, NASA cancelled the experiment because I was not really a NASA researcher, but an MIT professor in disguise! However, having renewed our friendship, I gladly accepted an invitation from Sasha to visit Moscow, speak at the Moscow Aviation Institute (MAI), and visit the major air show outside of town.

That was amazing! Not only did we see formations of jet fighters performing their vertical climb aerobatics, but we got to see their Buran space shuttle up close. Apparently, earlier the Buran would get wheeled into a hangar to avoid being photographed by US spy satellites when they passed over the region. When I visited the Dean's Office of MAI, I was pleased to see that Sasha had my astronaut photo displayed along with two other heroes who influenced him, his professor and his father!

A story that appeared on the front page of the December 18, 1989 issue of the *New York Times* describes how the Russian Lunar Lander was shown to us Americans for the first time. My good friend, Prof. Alexander (Sasha) Efremov, identifies the figures, reading from RIGHT to LEFT as: Prof O. Alifanov (Dean of the Moscow Aviation Institute Aerospace School), Prof. Ivanov (Deputy head of their department of Space Technology) and me.

The most recent of the Russia adventures began around 2010, and are still going on. New international science and technology university and research centers, called Skoltech and located on the outskirts of Moscow, was started in an apparently generous partnership with MIT, all aimed at creating a Russian "Silicon Valley" to encourage home-grown innovation. Five areas for concentration were identified, and space was one of them. I was designated to lead the MIT effort. But alas, it came to naught after several years! [*On February 27, 2022, MIT president Rafael Reif wrote, in an open letter to the MIT comminty, "In light of the Russian government's violent invasion of a peaceful neighbor, we have determined that we must not continue the MIT Skoltech Program."—LAY*]

I was treated royally when I visited, put up in the finest hotels opposite the Kremlin, and was the beneficiary of the MIT reputation. At first the idea of taking a leading role on MIT's behalf seemed challenging, and spending half time in Russia seemed exciting. However, the more I saw of Russia, the less I liked it. Too crowded, too rude, and too little charm once past the tourist sites. Horrendous traffic. But most of all, a bureaucracy that made it nearly impossible to count on any agreement, and as a result I became discouraged, almost to the point of turning my back on it after four years of broken promises. I went so far as to resume studying Russian, as did Vicki. (That's as hard as I remember from my grad school days.) We'll see how this plays out.

1988-1989: Stanford

When I was a kid, I thought of California as heaven. It had surfing (even though I never surfed), starlets strutting on the beach, skiing in the Sierras and sunshine all the time. I didn't actually get to step foot in the "Golden State" until 1957, my senior year at MIT, when I went out for job interviews. That was when I realized "golden" was another term for scorched. I interviewed at the Jet Propulsion Lab in Pasadena (JPL) and at the then-small Hewlett Packard in Palo Alto. I turned down both offers, but I enjoyed the beautiful hikes and the flowers blooming in February. The JPL offer was to work on guidance for the Voyager satellite. I felt that twenty years to wait for its launch was much too long, in those days before I learned the realities of space. In fact, the amazing Voyager 1 and its twin are still gathering interplanetary data over forty years after their 1977 launch—at a distance of 13 billion miles from Earth.

Two things put me off at Hewlett Packard. First of all, each engineer's little office also contained a workbench where circuits could be assembled and tested. And secondly, a bell rang to announce the arrival of the cart with free coffee and doughnuts. In retrospect, I was so wrong. They were way ahead of their time, and even ahead of the rest of what we now call Silicon Valley. I was recommended by my former MIT advisor, and taken to lunch by the VP, Bernie Oliver, but I turned down the job opportunity before getting a formal offer. Maybe it was a mistake, but things worked out anyway. And I had a soft spot for the Bay area. I satisfied it thirty years later, in 1988.

In January 1986, the Space Shuttle *Challenger* exploded following launch from Cape Canaveral, killing the crew and setting back the space life sciences program we were part of. I knew that it would be a long hiatus until NASA completed its investigations and implemented the reforms of its management structure to restore the required level of safety. There would be a long wait ahead of us before resuming in-flight vestibular experiments on spacelabs. Since I was due for another sabbatical leave from MIT, this was the time to broaden my horizons and learn something new. I decided to get educated in a field I had only dabbled in—Artificial Intelligence (AI).

I considered three leading academic centers for AI in the 1980s. MIT was very strong, of course, but I knew if I stayed in Cambridge I would never really break free of my ongoing vestibular research and wouldn't expand my academic horizons as I had earlier, in Zurich and Paris. Carnegie Mellon was another hot spot with leading faculty and an attractive combination of robotics and AI. But who wanted to spend a year in Pittsburgh? So that left

Stanford, in Palo Alto, California. It had a growing reputation in AI—both in engineering and in medicine. Its location fit into my long-standing travel wishes. All I needed was to define a topic, seek out a professional mentor, and come up with the funding. MIT sabbatical policy would pay half salary for a full year.

Off I went to overcome these hurdles. To arrange for a Stanford faculty appointment, I went to see Prof. Peter Banks of the Stanford Electrical Engineering (EE) Department, with whom I worked when he chaired the Space Station Users' Committee, later formalized as NASA's Space Station Science and Applications Subcommittee. I served as its lead for the Life Science discipline, succeeded by Chuck Oman. Peter managed to get me appointed as a Visiting Professor and arranged for a lovely office in Durant, the engineering building in the middle of the campus, and I convinced Peter Friedland, at NASA Ames, to fund my year, as a NASA Visiting Scientist.

By the time my wife, Jody, and I headed for Palo Alto in 1988, I had all of the pieces in place—a topic ("PI in a Box," a Knowledge Based System for advising astronauts on spacelab experiments), a team, funding, an office, and an appointment. Finally, there remained housing for Jody and me. By then, all three of our children were in college or grad school. Jody contacted her Radcliffe classmate, whose husband was on leave from Stanford to advise on economic matters in DC, and arranged for us to rent their house. It was in Barron Park, a funky throwback to the 1960s on the edge of the campus, with the requisite fig tree and hot tub. I would set the tub to be ready for me when I biked back home from Stanford in the afternoon. All local travel was by bike, even though I had bought a used Toyota Celica, which felt very sporty indeed. About once a week we went to San Francisco for dinner and theater, even though our neighbors assured us that we could do just as well in San Jose.

I consulted on Space Station facilities for Lockheed, down the road in Mountain View, and also went to NASA Ames about once week. Between weekly trips to Ames or Lockheed, I stayed up on space life science.

Stanford was very obviously a place for the privileged. Both faculty and students enjoyed life—differently than we did in Cambridge. Lunchtime conversations were more likely to be about hiking plans than about politics. Dress was neat. I had my choice of the indoor or the outdoor swimming pools. I signed up for tennis camp, organized by the coaches of the NCAA champions, as a faculty perk. There was a driving range on campus and everybody bicycled. At the end of the school year, dozens and dozens of almost-new bikes were left in a pile to be taken by students whose BMWs had broken down. The women students were California gorgeous—good complexion, straight teeth, shapely legs and beautiful bodies. Why? Were they all, I wondered, the offspring of model mothers married to wealthy Stanford fathers? Did they grow up eating healthy foods and being treated by orthodontists and plastic surgeons?

Classes were good, but without the intensity of those at MIT. Less like drinking from a fire hose, as Jerry Wiesner famously described an MIT education, more like letting the champagne fountain gently fill your open mouth. Somehow the quality was there, but without the pressure and intellectual curiosity I loved back home. Maybe the weather was just too nice to worry about science—or anything else for that matter.

I had some old and some new friends at Stanford, including the amazing Dan DeBra, who could bicycle forever and who tried to teach me about California wines. ("The trick is not in finding a good red wine, it is in finding a good cheap red wine.") My MIT friend and colleague, Ed Crawley, later my Department Head, was also on sabbatical at Stanford and found comfortable living in a separate wing of our house. We enjoyed numerous meals together and shared our observations of California and our views of the world around us. Our old friend Don Kennedy was Stanford's president and was kind enough to cook us dinner and lead us on bird walks. Sitting on the Faculty Club terrace for lunch one day in January, he warned me that after a winter in Palo Alto I might not want to return to Boston. But he knew about my love of skiing and ski racing, which we had done together.

I was invited by my Lockheed boss, Chuck Rudiger, to join their ski house in Tahoe City and ski the Sierras. After the first experience of being stuck in a multi-hour traffic jam on the way to the Sierras on a Friday afternoon, I changed my weekends to start on Thursday and end on Saturday. Squaw Valley was our usual destination and we had plenty of snow. I had the pleasure of skiing there with our son Eliot one weekend. It was gorgeous, with the fir trees and white snow as a backdrop to the deep blue of Lake Tahoe. At the end of the day, I asked Eliot how he could tell that we weren't in New Hampshire. "Well Dad," he said, "I guess it must be the cappuccino cart at the end of the parking lot!"

Between tennis, swimming at my choice of pools, hiking or biking in the foothills, and skiing in the Sierras (we were invited to be part of a condo rental in Tahoe City), it was a fun and athletic year. Jody, on the other hand, was less enthusiastic about the year in California. Although we were warmly welcomed by her Radcliffe classmates and the Stanford faculty wives, she was cut off from her challenging assignments to bring order to public transportation in Newton and to advise the MBTA. She didn't feel right about "just playing." When I accepted the astronaut training assignment in Houston a year later, she shared my excitement but refused to consider another move, this time to Houston. I'm not sure, but that may have been the beginning of the end of our marriage.

1992-1994: Houston

When I began my two years of training as a Payload Specialist (PS) for the Space Shuttle, I moved to Egret Bay, an offshoot of Clear Lake, just a mile from our offices at the NASA Johnson Space Center (JSC) in Houston, Texas, in an apartment I shared with Marty Fettman, DVM, PhD.

My bedroom had sliding doors opening onto a deck just one floor above the dock where I kept not only my wind surfer and my kayak, but also the small sloop belonging to my friend, Drew Gaffney. Drew was a physician and cardiovascular researcher who flew as a Payload Specialist (PS) on the shuttle's SLS-1 mission and stayed on in Houston afterwards. I taught him to sail better and he later altered his life to live on his (bigger) boat in New Zealand. If there was a good breeze I would wind surf around Clear Lake after work. If not, I would kayak into the quiet waters off the main lake and commune with nature, particularly the egrets and herons. We had an outdoor pool and a tennis court in our apartment complex. I belonged to a tennis club across the bridge in League City. In Clear Lake or Nassau Bay, I played tennis with a number of my astronaut friends and enjoyed their camaraderie. Marc Garneau was a Canadian astronaut who later became head of the Canadian Space Agency and then a government minister. Claude Nicollier was a Swiss astronaut who had been a friend since his earliest days as a European PS for Spacelab and then flew as a NASA mission specialist (MS). Wubbo Ockels, a Dutch Payload Specialist and dear friend, had been an alternate payload specialist (APS) on Spacelab 1, and later was one of my space subjects on the German D-1 mission. He taught me a lot about wind surfing. So did Jeff Hoffman, another astronaut, and a friend since his MIT post-doc days. He later became a colleague at MIT. I biked too, mostly on weekends because of the traffic.

I made substantial use of the astronaut gym, once our commander, John Blaha, had convinced management to allow PSs to cross that threshold. By informing my scheduler of my desires, I would be put down for a couple of hours there several times a week. Sometimes I shot baskets, but mostly I just rode the stationary bike. I felt "cool," dressed in the NASA exercise shirt and shorts. The gym gave me a chance to talk to some of the astronauts about their experience and to benefit from their advice. Charlie Bolden, who had been the pilot on one of our earlier Spacelab missions, was the most friendly and helpful. I was delighted years later when he was selected to serve as NASA's Administrator.

The two years included many non-NASA adventures. I biked or played tennis almost every weekend and paddled down the beautiful Guadalupe River. I was welcomed as crew on a sailboat that raced on Clear Lake—but the winds were too light and sitting on the gunnels all afternoon was too uncomfortable to make that very much fun. One weekend, at the invitation of our vestibular colleague, Dr. Helen Cohen, I crewed on a small sloop that, *amazingly*, won its regatta in Houston. None of the regulars in the Houston Yacht Club knew us, however, and suspected that we skipped a leg. Until the second race—which we again won, handily.

I managed to get together with Jody about every other weekend, either in Texas or back up north in Massachusetts or New Hampshire. Her visits usually involved a trip to see birds. Sometimes it was in Galveston or nearby at High Island, where the exhausted flock finally set down and nested after their long flight across the Gulf of Mexico. Other times it might be in East Texas, which reminded me of the dying town in *The Last Picture Show*. Probably our best trip—for birding and scenery—was all the way west to Big Bend National Park, an amazing oasis of flora and fauna raised hundreds of feet above the desert. There was always something to do with her, and I regretted the Sunday night separations for another fortnight.

As time went on, I got to appreciate some aspects of Houston itself. I took country dancing lessons at JSC every Monday night. I would forget the steps by the weekend and relearn them the next Monday. Jeff Hoffman sometimes had extra tickets to the Houston Opera and I went along. Other times I would go to hear the outstanding Houston Symphony, directed by Christopher Eschenbach. But most of all, I grew to appreciate the genuine friendliness and helpfulness of the average Houstonian I would run into, at least down near NASA in Clear Lake City. I received more than the fabled "southern hospitality." They were certainly not rednecks—even if they did say they were "fixin' to" do something—and then not get around to it.

Although I would not return to Houston full time, I did later serve as the Founding Director of the National Space Biology Research Institute (NSBRI). Our headquarters were in Houston at the Baylor College of Medicine. Late in my career I served as Head of Science Education at the Houston-based Translational Research Institute for Space Health. I have fond memories of Houston. Everything except the heat!

A Lifetime of Washington Trips

Dad used to travel to Washington, DC on business. It was often to meet with Congressman Cooley from North Carolina, head of the Agriculture committee of the House, who dealt with meat regulations. He and Dad grew close and respected each other. Dad would wear one of his many very neat grey suits and look as distinguished as I knew he was. I think he always traveled by train. But for me, growing up, a trip to DC to help the government run was always very special.

So when I began getting many such invitations later, mostly to serve on advisory committees for NASA or the Air Force or the National Academy of Sciences, I always accepted. Each time I look out from National Airport (I still can't call it Reagan) and see the Capitol and the Washington Monument, I get a kick out of walking in Dad's footsteps. I was invited to join the famous Cosmos Club in the early 1990s and usually stayed at the club and enjoyed the fantastic popovers they served for breakfast. For a while I helped to found and run a Boston chapter with monthly meetings but I dropped out and eventually left the club when the fees for non-resident members became excessive. Now it is still a day trip, usually by early and late planes, when it fulfills my three requirements for service on a committee: that somebody will actually read and react to our findings, that the others on the committee know more than I do, and finally, that it be held in a nice (or at least interesting) location.

I rather like Washington, except for the hot summer weather. I love the DC museums. The city is a joy to look at, from the Mall and the Memorials to Georgetown. And it is full of young people on a mission. And good restaurants. And plenty of theater. In fact, I was inclined to move there for two years, back in 1991. I was offered the temporary position of Chief Scientist of the International Space Station (ISS), and spoke to enough of my NASA friends to nearly accept it, when the Payload Specialist opportunity came along and that moved into first place.

2020s: Up and Down the I-95 Corridor

Nowadays, the weather bureau presents the synopsis about how storms or fronts move relative to the I-95 corridor. As though that were a geographic entity, like the Appalachian Mountains. But it's just a highway. For me, as I ride the Amtrak from New York back to Boston, it is a trip through time and life. Here's how:

I'll start in New York. Even though I was born in New York and went to its amazing public schools, I was never a real New Yorker. That is, I didn't live in Manhattan. And we had a yard with grass that needed to be mowed, and no sidewalks. Other than my subway trips to the orthodontist on 57th St., with a stop at the music store opposite Carnegie Hall to buy some sheet music, I rarely ventured there. Yankee Stadium was in the Bronx and our golf club was in Westchester. By the time I got to high school and started to hang out with some more hip friends I would, rarely, go to the Village or to hear the Weavers at Riverside Church, or go skating in Central Park. I was fairly comfortable using my subway pass to get around, although I NEVER went to Brooklyn. It wasn't until I had summer jobs as a technical writer way downtown, below Union Square, that I started to take advantage of off-Broadway plays and sometimes even a jazz club on 52nd St. with one or another of my college friends.

And now, in my seventies, I spend four or five extended weekends a year there with Vicki in her office apartment. That is the REAL New York. Located on 55th Street, near the University Club, just west of 5th Avenue. With lots of people on the street, speaking everything but English, and horns blowing, and parades nearly every Saturday, and lots of restaurants of every ethnicity, and just a ten-minute walk to the half-price ticket booth in Times Square. Though I am still not a REAL New Yorker, I can appreciate the city and enjoy it now. And I am somewhat of a novelty among Vicki's literati friends, who have never met a scientist—let alone an MIT space cadet. They are fine and seem to really want to know about space and this side of C.P. Snow's Two-Culture divide. I get a little tired of hearing the meta-commentary about what this or that op-ed writer in "the paper" (guess which one) wrote about this or that politician. A real pleasure is accompanying Vicki to the galleries and getting her to try to explain why some bizarre assembly of spare parts is really art and why anyone would pay so much for it and even want it on display at home (or NOT, as she often says). It is fun to visit the photography galleries and to hear her treated with such respect and warmth—and then the discussions usually lapse into shop talk and I just appreciate the pictures.

As we head north (well, actually east) we pass New Rochelle, where I first learned to sail, and then the Westchester public golf courses, where I played with Dad and had so many meaningful discussions, without having Mom there to explain what he really meant.

Then into Connecticut. That was associated with ex-urbia. And big lawns (Gatsby-esque) and stone walls and the Aryans from Darien (remember *Auntie Mame*, the 1958 film with Rosiland Russell?). When Jody built a stone wall around a quiet area of our yard in Rumney, we named it Connecticut. Now I think of Connecticut in terms of the views out over Long Island Sound, and the ferry from New London across to Orient Point in Long Island, which was part of our trip to Sag Harbor when Vicki still had a house there. We spent a relaxing and beautiful four hours on the train, with the views flitting by, the sunset topping off the background, power and Internet and a cold beer available. As Concord Trailways advertises, "Why would anyone drive?" But drive we did when I was in college—the traditional drive down from Massachusetts, with traffic building all the way. Except for summers, including the brief time I worked for Sperry Gyroscope on Long Island before going to France to study, I never moved back to New York, and never missed it. I wonder if our friends who fight the traffic to head off to the Hamptons for the weekend really appreciate how spectacular the real country can be—and what a tonic the mountains can be for the nervous system. Well, maybe the art scene is somewhat limited in New Hampshire. But the fall foliage is unbeatable.

Finally, we get to South Station. I have become so fond of Boston that it is hard to recall my original impressions in 1955. It is Goldilocks perfect. Not too big and not too small. A high enough population of intellectuals and enough of us who were not "natives" to keep it stimulating. Few skyscrapers and the charm of the Charles River or the harbor never too far away. Plenty of small theaters and not too hard to get affordable tickets. A walking city with left-leaning politics. Easy to get to the White Mountains or to the Cape. (I had to relearn that "the Cape" could mean "Canaveral" when I changed states for a couple of years.)

What don't I like about it? Not much.

My Travels

I would never have imagined that my technical profession as an engineering professor would allow me to travel the world—or that I would so much enjoy the international contacts. I have friends with far more money who are frankly jealous of the way we are welcomed into the bosom of foreign friends and colleagues—and so they should be! It is one thing to see a world-famous site and to check it off the bucket list, and quite something else to be part of a vigorous dinner conversation or of a ski-hiking outing with a group of foreign friends and colleagues. I have made so many such friends, many of them through international conferences and visits. Sure, the travel can be tiring and frustrating, and as I get older the stress and strain get more evident. But it has still been part of my life adventure.

Places and Sounds

Just as Proust inhaled the aroma of a madeleine and expanded it into a world of remembered experience, I do that with certain sounds. Not songs or symphonies, those are too obvious. But I mean momentary acoustic bings or bongs that remind me of how I felt or what I experienced. For example:

Scraping of snow off the driveway. When we returned from an extended ski trip and there was a foot of heavy, wet snow on the driveway in Newton, and I was too tired to shovel it clear—suddenly we would hear that marvelous reprieve that told me that a plow was getting down to ground level and doing the job for us. (Sure, we paid for it, but that was well worthwhile.)

Then, on the subject of sweeping snow, there are the sounds that only a skier may understand. The first is a gentle swish, almost like whispering, "Shh," to a crying baby. This swish happens when we are making a clean turn in deep powder snow and our skis never touch the hard base underneath. It feels like flying, or like dancing on down pillows, and it sounds like—well—"Shh."

On the other hand, when you make a hard, edged ski turn on an icy surface, of the kind all too common in the East, you hear a very different sound—sort of a "crack, crack, crack, hiss" as the ski skips slightly down the hill (bad) or as it slices around in the direction of the carved turn sought after by all who race. You can hear, as well as feel, the difference between a slip and a carve, and feel bad or good accordingly.

Some other sports sounds are unmistakable, and bring back numerous games, played or watched. The sound of a wooden bat making good contact with a baseball. (Not an aluminum bat—please!) Or of a driver hitting a golf ball cleanly, especially the click of the modern super large head club. How about the hiss when you (or more likely a partner) open a new can of pressure-packed tennis balls? That sound brings out the (unfulfilled) hope that today will be different, and all the topspin backhand shots will stay in the court!

On a sailboat every sound means something. My favorite is the "flap—flap—flap—hiss" as the luffing sail is sheeted in, stops flapping, and the boat heels and accelerates forward.

Back at home there is the reassuring sound of the dish washer, doing its job after the dinner cleanup when I am too tired to spend any more time in the kitchen.

And how about the sound of "nayumm, nayumm, nayumm BARUP, putt, putt putt," when your car engine turns over and finally starts on a very cold morning?

Or the "whoop, whoop, whoop" of a police car, which makes me check the speedometer and wonder what I did wrong. There must have been something back there.

Late at night, around midnight, the horses, which stand opposite the Plaza Hotel until the guide finds some tourists to drive around New York's wonderful Central Park, finally get to go home to their stable. From Vicki's apartment on 55th Street I can hear the slow but steady "clop-clop" rhythm they make as they head west to their stable. Do the horses know they are headed home? Are they bored with the regular circular tour around the park? Do they listen to the guide repeating his stories of New York? Or the tourist comments? Do they understand the Russian exclamations? Or are they just glad to be heading back to the stable and some oats before bedtime? Like me.

And, of course, there is the sound of a key in the lock of the door that signals the return of my wife. My heart beats faster as I go to greet her!

Sports

Home Sports

Close to our house on Saxon Ave., we kids would play "stoop ball," which involved throwing a small pink "spaldeen" ball, slang for Spalding, a branded handball with many knockoffs, against the front stoop and trying to get it to bounce past the opponent who was fielding. When she was working for Spalding in Springfield, Massachusetts, years later, my niece, Liz Rosenberg, tried to get them to re-issue the pink ball, which she said came from reject tennis ball cores.

After-school games included stickball (with a "strike zone" chalked onto the schoolyard wall), dodge ball and "punch ball" (a kind of baseball in which the "batter" would punch the ball instead of swinging a bat). And marbles—at which I once lost so much and went so far into debt to a bigger kid that I thought I would never recover. My parents advanced me the money to repay the debt, but it taught me not to gamble.

And biking—everywhere. With Howie in the summer and on weekends—what a wonderful sense of freedom and independence. More grown up sports, like tennis and golf, started around age thirteen. Howie said recently that we would have been better off starting those sports earlier, but I would never trade those days.

In baseball I hit pretty well. As a leftie I got to play first base (farther reach for the ball while still facing the oncoming batter). However, I never overcame my fear of the throw from third or short bouncing in the dirt and hitting me in the face. Consequently, I let too many throws sail right past me.

My lowest softball moment came in junior high school. I was captain of our class softball team, and, as in Gilbert and Sullivan's *H.M.S. Pinafore*, I was "a right good captain too." At the championship game, we were leading by a run or two in the last inning. I was playing first base. With two out and two runners on base the batter hit a high pop fly—up and up and spinning—over toward our pitcher. To be sure to get the out I waved our pitcher out of the way and moved over to make the catch for the final out myself. And the spinning softball landed right in my glove—and spun right out again. Both runners scored. We lost the championship. Does that little bit of hubris still bother me? You bet it does!

Then there was lots of schoolyard and backyard basketball. In the days before the jump shot became popular, we all shot a hook shot to lift the ball over the outstretched arms of the defender. I was briefly called "hooks" because of my ability to sink a hook shot from out near the foul line. My hero was George Mikan of the Minneapolis Lakers, with his ambidextrous hook shot. My hook shot was only left-handed, which further cut into my scoring ability. Foul shots then were two-handed underhand tosses, starting with the ball between the knees. Later on they were two-handed set shots, but not yet the one-hander, which is standard today. No jump shot, no dunking, and, most amazingly, no Black players in our neighborhood. We would root for the Knicks and play in all seasons, indoors or outdoors, full or half court. Howie was clearly the most talented of us.

Back in the Bronx, our home field was "Pine Island," a strip of grass dividing Mosholu Parkway near DeWitt Clinton High School. It was an odd size, possibly 200 feet long and eighty feet wide, ending in a little hillock with pine trees on it, but it served us for football in the fall and baseball in the spring. We had orange and black "Blackjacks" uniform shirts, with shoulder pads but no football helmets, supplied by the local sports store under the elevated railway, or "El," on Jerome Avenue. No league, no referees, and amazingly no injuries. Just lots of fun. I was neither the best nor the worst athlete—but I sure did like to play.

Biking

The earliest bike misadventure I can recall took place when I was about nine years old and living in the rented house on Saxon Ave. in the Bronx. Mom and Dad were out. Why did they leave me alone? ALL THIS WAS THEIR FAULT! I was riding my tricycle around the living room when I searched for a more adventuresome obstacle course. They had a pair of delicate "ladder back" chairs which, when turned over, made for a perfect barrier for my expedition. So, I tried to ride the tricycle up the ladder back and SMASH—I broke right through and ruined the chair. I don't remember the consequences, or punishment if there was any. But I never tried that trick again.

Bikes led to independence and adventure. Especially with my cousin Howie. During our summers in Long Beach, we would take our fat-tire, one-speed bikes, with their coaster brakes and fenders, and start off in the morning. We would be armed with everything two ten-year-olds needed for the day. Peanut butter and jelly sandwiches, a spaldeen ball and broomstick for stickball, and a promise to be back for dinner. We could ride the length of the boardwalk, all the way to the Lido end. The boards in the middle section lined up with the boardwalk, and made for a smooth, fast ride. But those toward the side gave a bounce I can still feel.

Biking to school or to work has been a morning delight as long as I can remember. When Jody and I were first married, we lived in an elegant apartment carved out of the ballroom of the old Dana Mansion at 329 Harvard Street in Cambridge, between Harvard and Central Squares. It was an easy ride to MIT, where I was first a grad student and then a young faculty member. I remember regularly seeing an old I-Lab engineer who still rode his bike to work and I marveled at his ability to do so. He must have been sixty at the time. I have long since surpassed that age, and keep on riding.

When the gasoline shortage appeared, in about 1973, I had been working at NASA Ames in California and learned of the Odd-Day/Even Day rationing and the long, long lines to get gas in Massachusetts. On my return, I decided to try biking to work, from Newton to Cambridge—a distance of less than ten miles, over a few steep hills (think of Heartbreak Hill on Commonwealth Ave., famous in the Boston Marathon), and then through Brookline and over the Charles River. It was possible, but hard—and led me to buy my Raleigh ten-speed bike and to keep on experimenting with routes. Eventually I discovered and began using the bike paths along the Charles, from Newton all the way to Cambridge. It took me about thirty-five minutes into work and forty-five minutes to return home, against the west wind and somewhat uphill toward Newton Centre, and I loved it! No traffic. I would see the ducks and the geese on the river and pass the same scenes on the bike path as the seasons changed. The color of the leaves served as my calendar and the half hour cleared my mind and allowed me to think through that day's lecture or research meeting.

I skipped the bike ride if there was snow on the ground, but otherwise it was there as a treat for me. I rigged up earphones and a cassette recorder (in the days before the Walkman was popular and everyone lived in a private world accompanied only by the music playing through his ear buds) and carefully selected the symphony or the folk music for that day's commute. I was in no great hurry. At one point I installed a speedometer and kept track of my distance and peak and average speed, but it was only distracting and the competition was interfering with my solitude. I kept a change of clothes in my locker at the MIT Alumni pool, swam, showered and changed when I got to work, and the whole commute took less time than showering at home, then driving and parking. Sometimes the ride home seemed daunting, especially after daylight savings time was gone and it became hard to see the potholes in the dark, but once home, with a fire in the fireplace and a drink in my hand, it all seemed like Nirvana.

I never thought of racing or going on organized bike rides—except once. My old skiing buddy and MIT classmate, Art Albert, talked me into entering a hospital fund-raising twenty-six-mile race starting in Plymouth, New Hampshire, and going up past Rumney. It seemed low-key and casual—at least until I got to the parking lot of the Hannaford Mall. All these trim guys in their lycra suits and very light bikes. It seemed as bad as a Masters ski race. And they were pumping their racing tires to over 80 psi. When I borrowed a pump to do the same, I blew out my tire. What now? One of the gang was shocked that I didn't have a spare tube, and gave me one of his and got me going—on my commuter bike. When I was awaiting my starting time, the official starter looked me over and commented on my bike's accessories. As to the light, he allowed as how I might need it if I didn't finish before dark (it was then about 11 AM). But he couldn't figure why I need a kick stand! I resisted the strong temptation to convert the race into a "half Marathon" at Rumney and pushed on to finish the race. I beat only one person, my friend Art, and ended my bike racing career then and there. Why spoil such a fun sport?

I continue to bike all the time. From our Cambridge condo to MIT takes me only about five minutes now, and I look for other errands to do to lengthen the trip. I bike across campus and I was delighted when, about a month after my knee replacement, my surgeon gave me the green light to bike and my physical therapist added easy biking to my recovery program. In New Hampshire I just simply love to go down the trail to town to get the mail, whether on bike in the summer or on cross-country skis in the winter.

My latest biking find is the new "stationary bike" in the Z Center gym at MIT. With its computer graphics screen, when I select an Alpine Terrain route to follow it takes me, along with other riders, along a mountain road, up and down hills, passing lakes and hills, shifting gears, steering to stay on the road while looking ahead, coasting down steep hills and pushing along—all the while with a realistic sense of self-motion and slight fear of falling off the cliff. "Way cool," as some of the kids might have said. But, then again, isn't the whole point to make me feel like a kid again myself?

I accompany Vicki to New York periodically. It is a far different place from the city I grew up in, but Riverdale was far from Manhattan. Her apartment is on 55th Street—so near Central Park. That, too, has changed incredibly. It is safe, beautiful, full of kids playing games, bikers and joggers, tennis players, skaters, boaters, musicians and street artists. Amazing that a public movement could bring Olmstead's dream back to life, from the mugger-filled, drug dealer place of fifty years ago, though I still would stay away after dark. The biking is the big lure for me. Park Drive is closed to traffic in the middle of the day. It takes me about forty minutes to circle the park, from 59th Street near the Plaza Hotel, with nary a sighting of Kay Thompson's Eloise, to 110th Street on the North, bordering the newly gentrified Harlem apartment houses. The setting and the characters seem right out of a musical, and the mixture of all sorts of foreign languages makes it clear what an international attraction it has become. And I coast along and drink it in—with gusto!

Running—Track and Cross Country

I only began to run in high school because my cousin Evan said I was fast, and I believed everything he said. In order to run in the indoor season, including the exciting carnivals, we had to also run on the cross-country team. That was probably my first exposure to the pleasure of running through the woods. We practiced and competed at Van Cortlandt park. We started with a mad dash across the flats for about a half mile, and then entered the hills on a narrow path where it was hard to pass anyone, finally emerging onto a brief finishing sprint. We trained "over distance" five miles on Mondays and took off Friday to rest for the Saturday meet. When I groused about the long distance to Mike Levenson, our coach and our neighbor who would drive me home after practice, he pointed out that it would not seem so long if I ran faster! Our best runner was my friend, Dick Range. I liked the feeling of tired legs and the hot shower and oil of wintergreen that followed. I liked the look and feel of the sweat suits and admired the uniforms of the Manhattan College team that trained in the same place. I liked the spring in the track shoes (no heels) and the sound the spikes made when they ground into the cinder track. And I liked the feeling of being on a team, and a good one at that. We won the Bronx High School Cross-Country Championship in my junior year, although I probably didn't finish high enough to count.

In the winter we trained on the flat concrete floor of the Kingsbridge Armory and competed in the indoor meets on banked wooden tracks with eleven laps to the mile. I ran the quarter mile (440 yards), which was a paced run with a slow pace on the back stretch—not like the all-out sprint the 400m is today. Mom and Dad came to see my first indoor race, where I was nearly lapped by the faster guys, and Mom may have said to Dad, "Make him stop." I don't think I ever ran the 440 in much less than a minute—but improving was a constant goal. In the summers at Long Beach, I would run between the jetties on the hard sand near the water. It is a feeling I cherish to this day, when my running has been reduced to a walk by my knee issues. I still love to walk along the water's edge at the beach and look out over the waves. These old delights keep going "around and around!"

Then in my last year in high school, I was diagnosed with a heart murmur and withdrew from strenuous athletics for several years. (Now only the more skilled cardiologists can detect the murmur and I ignore it.) After that forced me out of running, I stayed with the team for my senior year as manager. We traveled by bus to Philadelphia for the famous Penn Relays. Our other big event was a weekend meet—the state championships in Schenectady, New York. I ran one leg of the 4x220 relay. We didn't win, but the sense of trying and belonging was marvelous.

Golf Clubs and Country Clubs

Mom and Dad had played golf before they were married, and in their poignant letters to each other during the summer of their broken engagement, they refer to their golf games. Dad had a very chic mauve suede golf suit, with knickers, that I admired and later inherited. I started to play back when we summered in New City, New York. We belonged to "Zukor's" country club, later renamed "The Dells in Rockland County," where we went during a few summers (1945-47), and where Jody and I later had our wedding dinner. It had been the estate of Adolph Zukor, the famous movie producer at Paramount, and was populated by others of the original Paramount or Warner Brothers' crowd. I never saw him, but his partner's daughter, Cherry Blossom Balaban, would show up from time to time and be admired by the hoi polloi. I began to play golf right-handed because there were rightie clubs around. Pretty soon I was hitting the ball far—if not straight.

When we were around fourteen, Cousin Howie and I began caddying at the nearby local Oceanside Golf Club in Long Island, not far from our summer home in Long Beach. Howie's brother, Bob, was three years older and could drive us to the club. We would wait in the caddy pen, along with the other boys, and hope for the caddy-master to call us up. We might get a nine-hole loop (about $4) or an eighteen-hole loop (about $8, or more with a tip if you didn't lose any balls). Bob would often be given a double, which meant carrying two bags around the sandy hot course. I was too skinny to ever be called on for a double—and just as well. It was hard work. I learned to look for slices and hooks patiently and to listen to the grown-ups discussing all matter of things—and to keep my tongue. On Mondays, caddies could play the course ourselves, but I wasn't very good at that time.

We also belonged to the Lido Beach Club from 1948-52. It was a rather fancy hotel and beach club at the East End of Long Beach, complete with cabanas, tennis courts, and formal dress requirements for the Saturday entertainment. We had a cabana there and took full advantage of its entertainment and social life. From time to time one of the Lido guests would look at me and recognize me as his caddy, but no words were exchanged.

In addition to swimming in their Olympic-length pool, we played a fair amount of tennis. Although I never developed much skill in tennis, I still enjoy the sound and the sight of a well-hit top-spin cross court forehand or a well-placed backhand down the line. The weekend night-life at the Lido was a big deal, with guest stars from New York City and Los Angeles. When the entertainment was appropriate—a famous ventriloquist or hypnotist, or Jerry Lewis—we kids would get to go along too. As we got into our teens, we learned to dance starting with the famous "box step" and progressing to the mambo, samba and tango, as well as the rhumba, foxtrot and waltz. There would be two bands—a lead one like Xavier Cugat (with his beautiful and sexy wife, Abby Lane) and a backup. The bands rotated on a turntable stage at the break, with nary a step missing for the dancers.

The primary purpose of the membership, I later learned from Howie, was to try to find a suitable man for his mother, my Aunt Minna, the beautiful recent widow. I don't recall any of the suitors for Minna—although there were several, including a successful communist stockbroker. She did, in fact, remarry a kind and charming man—but not from the beach club.

By the time I was in high school and we lived in Riverdale, we belonged to the Briar Hall Country Club in Briarcliff Manor in Westchester, New York, a half-hour drive north. Briar Hall Country Club was the next step up socially for my parents. It was a "pay by the season" golf club, as opposed to the more exclusive "membership owned" ones like Elmwood where the Greenburgs belonged. Briar Hall was a "Jewish Club." There were few, if any, mixed couples. Most of the friends of my parents were members, as well as co-congregants at Riverdale Temple. We went there for the day every weekend. Sometime Dad would entertain colleagues, like the New York City Chief of Markets, or clients, and I would tag along, but mostly it was only Ellen, Mom, Dad and me. I was good at golf but others were better. Dad and I won the Father-Son trophy in our class one year and I still have it. I loved the smell of the newly mown grass and the beauty of the course.

My fondest recollection is of an afternoon, playing with Mom, at a fairly long par three hole. There was a foursome of men on the green, and normally we would wait until they putted out before driving. But one of the men waved to us disdainfully, to go ahead and hit—we would never reach the green! Mom whispered to me that she would give me a dollar if I hit the green. And so I did! The sweetest dollar that I ever earned. I liked the golf and the pool but not the Club. Too materialistic. The cars were parked by the valets, with the Lincolns in the front row, then the Caddies, and finally the Buicks, Olds and others. (We graduated from a Buick to a Caddie after Mom convinced Dad that it would not be taken badly by his clients.) I had a few friends there, and would usually go to the Saturday night dance. I even had a steady date all one summer, but the Club wasn't my cup of tea.

A highlight of my discussions with Dad occurred early one Saturday morning, as he was preparing coffee before we took off to the Club. I confessed my discomfort about the money and shallowness to Dad early one morning before heading to the Club, afraid that he would criticize me for being scornful of something he had worked to attain. I was a sophomore in college then, and going through the typical "I know more than my parents" stage of post-adolescence. I will never forget how he turned to me with his big smile and said to me, "Good boy, Larry! I feel the same way!"

Although I may never have broken ninety at our course, I had enough really good shots to keep me going. At that time, Dad represented Wilson Meat Packers, and used that connection to take me out to the Wilson Sporting Goods dealership where he bought me my own fancy set of matched Bobby Jones irons and Kroydon woods.

I joined the freshman gold team at Amherst. (Well, the truth is, I wanted to play freshman baseball, but after one or two practices the baseball coach said that I looked more like a talented golfer.) We practiced on the beautiful course at Mt. Holyoke and sometimes at the Amherst Golf Club, behind my fraternity. I never got high enough on the ladder to play in an intercollegiate match. But I am in our team picture at Amherst. I liked my stylish white golf cap with the Amherst A on it. I continued to play a little bit over the next years, especially with Dad when I visited New York. He enjoyed the game and the friendships it entailed. I have a happy picture of him and the rest of his Briar Hall foursome hanging in New Hampshire. I found the game frustrating and it took a lot of time while giving me no real exercise. In grad school I essentially stopped playing.

After his heart attack, Dad gave it up (they did that back then) and therefore so did I. And I didn't take it up again until I was seventy-six. With my bad knee limiting tennis and eliminating climbing, I was left with only biking and swimming as summer sports in Waterville, New Hampshire. Since the course there is right in our back yard, I decided to give it a try. My beloved Wilson clubs were a laugh, so I got some modern ones and—lo and behold—within a short time I was playing better than I had in college. It is a pretty walk in the woods. But it remained a boring and frustrating game—a game for old men. Am I there already?

All that changed as I approached eighty. I bought new clubs and took a few lessons from the pro at Owls Nest, a nearby upscale golf club. I straightened out my drive and began to feel good about hitting long fairway shots. I got more pleasure from a good shot than pain from a bad one. I limited my competition to the Waterville Valley Golf Club Thursday evening "scramble" and the Plymouth Senior Center weekly contest.

Diving and Swimming

I nearly drowned in the surf of Long Beach when I was about ten. Uncle Herman led a bunch of the cousins into the surf and then out beyond the breakers, where he would famously float along on his back smoking a cigar. (I don't know how he kept it lit.) I was running out to join them when, suddenly, I was in over my head. I didn't know how to swim. My cousin Alan saw me in distress and carried me back to the beach. Somehow it didn't dampen my love of bodysurfing and I looked forward to doing it each time I visited the Hamptons.

Diving was ugly. I gave up diving at the swimming pool at Zukor's. In addition to its very pretty golf course and its handball court, it had this gorgeous pool, with crystal-clear water and a blue-and-white tiled pattern. Unless there were ripples on the surface of the water, you could see down to the pool's bottom from the diving board, and it looked a mile away. I needed to get someone to swim first and ripple up the surface so that I would no longer see the bottom before I could manage the courage to dive. Even then I was timid about the three-meter board. One day I tried a flip and landed flat on my back—Pow. It hurt, and left me with a lifelong fear of diving, at least from anything higher than a one-meter board. I can make a racing dive from the side of the pool, and I didn't mind jumping off moguls on skis (actual ski jumps were another matter, however), but diving off a diving board into a pool is a fear I have never overcome.

But I really began to swim well in the summers we spent in Long Beach. Swimming out beyond the breaking waves, I could float on the gently rising and falling surface and let my mind wander all over the place. I could finally swim well enough by the time I got to Bronx High School of Science and made its swim team to swim back stroke, but wasn't fast enough to compete. Our practice was in a small, musty, over-chlorinated pool in the basement— sort of like swimming inside of a Clorox bottle.

During the summers we spent at the Lido Beach Club, I would swim a lot in their pool. Ellen was the promising star there and the life guard/coach tried to convince her to swim competitively at the New York Athletic Club —selective, elitist, and restricted. But upon learning that Jews were not very welcome at NYAC, Mom and Dad quickly squashed that.

But now I love to swim outdoors in pools or lakes or beyond the breakers in the ocean. Once in a while I come back with a really good idea for a new experiment. But mostly I just veg out.

Sailing

I fell in love with sailing the first time I was exposed to it. The Rotners bought a sixteen-foot Cape Cod Knockabout, shortly after Uncle Phil died. I was around thirteen and Cousin Evan was about nineteen. The boat was kept in New Rochelle harbor, in Westchester, on Long Island Sound, and Howie and I learned the fundamentals for tacking and jibing. On windless days we would swim alongside and hope the boat didn't get too far away. We kept at it for years, although I don't think we ever sailed all the way across the Long Island Sound to Huntington. I delighted in the feeling of gliding across the water, and seeing the sail billow out, of imagining the flow of wind between the jib and the main, and of feeling the pull on the main sheet that in turn was propelling us forward.

Except for one or two days using some old dinghies that Amherst kept on a lake, I didn't sail again until I got to MIT in 1955, where I delighted in the sailing pavilion on the Charles, right in front of the 'Tute. I would rely on the tech dinghies on the Charles River to give me peace and time for contemplation. The feeling of acceleration and control that came with a wind shift and the sudden pull on the sheet was marvelous. They were so much fun that I never went beyond to the larger boats. By the time I got to grad school, I began racing them in the Tuesday evening racing series, around the buoys between the Harvard and Longfellow bridges. I learned the racing rules, how to get a good start, and how to look for the little wind changes that would come down the streets of Back Bay. I never won a single race, but I only tipped over once. And I sometimes took girls out on a sailing date. But mostly I just went back and forth from Cambridge to Boston on a series of broad reach tacks, letting my mind drift over the events of the day and the joys of life. As I think it over now, it is close to the way I feel out back of our condo in the White Mountains, gliding on cross-country skis, by myself in the woods watching the firs and birches pass me by. Once more I find that I am the center and the world moves by me—a foolish bit of relativity. Probably that is my own "zen" experience.

In Puerto Rico, where I was studying the eye movements of crabs in 1961/62, I was asked by my boss, Dr. José del Castillo, if I would sail with him on their double-ended Carroll Ketch, which he kept in Fajardo, at the eastern end of the island. Since José was Spanish and his wife, June, was English, they needed an American to be licensed as a radio operator. Sure, why not? I could be an AM radio operator (in the days before VHF). At Christmas we had a big two-week cruise, to the US and British Virgin Islands. On many weekends, Jody and I would accompany José, June, and their two young twins on day trips, diving for Caribbean lobsters. We would sail out of Fajardo—usually only as far as Culebra, being careful to stay out of the Navy bombing range beyond Roosevelt Roads. The sailing was beautiful in those days, long before it became a tourist mecca. I managed to fail as a lookout on the bow by letting José run us aground on a shallow reef at Beef Island out toward Virgin Gorda. The helpful other boaters were all slightly loaded. It was just after the "Children's Hour" when yachts exchanged news and gossip on the AM radio, before VHF or wide use of short wave, and the crews drank. We attempted to have everyone hang off the boom while it was extended out, to roll the boat and raise it. We failed. Finally, we went below, drank and ate, and waited for the tell-tale bump as the rising tide came in and lifted us off the reef.

Cousin Evan's wife, Sheila, was quite pregnant when we spent a week sailing in Great Britain's Solent, between Southampton and the Isle of Wight, being blown back and forth with little control. I kept scanning the chart, looking for "Byew-Lee" as a safe harbor, only to have Sheila point me to "Beaulieu" on the chart! But we survived and enjoyed some good English ale once we tied up and dealt with the high tide at Yarmouth.

Jody and I bought a sixteen-foot sloop, a Rebel design, sight unseen, around 1976. Our dentist told Jody it would be the perfect boat for our family—and at a price of $600 for the boat, outboard engine, two sets of sails and the trailer, how could we go wrong? It was a marvelous investment. Like Ratty in *The Wind in the Willows*, just "messin around in boats" kept me occupied and happy for years and years, from re-decking and scraping, to getting a new compass, to rebuilding the rudder, which was lost one day in Newfound Lake when our guest refused to move back into the cockpit and away from the foredeck. We turned over and the unsecured rudder went straight to the bottom. We kept our boat on Newfound Lake, a short drive from our house in Rumney. On one of the very first outings, with children and our cute but stupid dog Sherman on board, Sherman slid off the foredeck into the water—even though I had clearly shouted "hard-a-lee." When we didn't pick him up after two tacks, Eliot took matters into his own hands and dove in to rescue the little guy.

I named the boat *Orbiter*, and joked that my secretary could inform callers that "Professor Young was working on the *Orbiter*." But she never did. Over a number of years, all the children learned to sail and we often dropped the anchor off the beach or on the sand bar, and swam or built sand castles.

There followed several years of keeping the boat at a mooring near Mal and Sylvia Green's house on Newfound Lake, and then several more years on Squam Lake, courtesy of Bob and Lorraine Kingsbury. But nobody else in the family was interested much in going out with me. The children married and moved away, Jody found it boring, and so did Vicki, whose limit for time spent just "having fun" was much lower than mine. The boat needed repairs, and I couldn't even donate it to a charity. I finally gave it to the kid at the garage where I had been storing it over the winters, sails and motor and all, for him to give it to his father. I understood that his father filled it with sand and kept it on the lawn as an odd sort of exhibit. I still miss it, especially the exhilaration of feeling the boat accelerate when I made just the right adjustment in sail trim or center board. All that remains with me is the thought process of going through all of the steps of getting the boat ready to push off from the dock and letting the breeze do its work.

Meanwhile, I got into wind-surfing some time in the late 1970s. Our friend, Bud Corkin, who did nothing in halves, ordered a board after trying one on vacation and then couldn't wait for it to be delivered, so he bought another one in New Hampshire and talked me into taking the first one off his hands. Together, after watching an instructional video, we learned a bit about how to start, come about, and even jibe—but mostly how to swim back to the board, in full view of both of our families on Loon Lake, New Hampshire. It was exhausting, but very enjoyable, and somewhat exhilarating—especially when the wind and the mast and the sail were all in concert and I could feel the power of the wind through my tired arms and hands clutching the wishbone. Wow. Now it turns out that windsurfing was becoming popular among my astronaut buddies, especially Wubbo Ockels (the "flying Dutchman") and Ulf Merbold. I bought a Magnum board, which Wubbo imported from Holland. He and Ulf attempted to cross from Naples to Capri for their arrival at the final Investigators' Working Group of the Space Shuttle's First Spacelab Mission (SL-1), but they only made it partway over. Fortunately, the accompanying boat picked them up. Wubbo taught Jody and me a lot about how to windsurf in the bay in front of Jeff and Barbara Hoffman's house in Seabrook, Texas, near Johnson Space Center (JSC). I never got very good at it, but I always enjoyed the feeling of control over the elements as I skimmed along on the water.

I never did any offshore sailing until my old Amherst friend, Eric Radin, who kept his Tartan 34 in Marion, Massachusetts, asked me to join him on a cruise to Nova Scotia. I was to be the navigator, and Eric showed me how to operate the analog radio direction finder (to point toward a shore beacon identified by its Morse code signal). I studied navigation from a book—mostly coastal navigation dealing with estimating distance and speed by observing lighthouses or towers on the shore. Our first big trip was to Nova Scotia. The crossing from Portland, Maine, to Yarmouth, across the Bay of Fundy with its big tides and currents, overnight, in dense fog, tested my limitations. In the morning I told the crew that I calculated that we should be near the Yarmouth lighthouse and, when we looked up through the fog—there it was! Eric has credited me with great navigation skill and only I know how lucky I was. The next week we came back from Marion with a handheld "Whistler Radar" that you scanned back and forth until you heard the return echo, from land or from a buoy. Except that most of the buoys in Nova Scotia harbors were wooden without any radar reflectors. We got better at it, and in a couple of years Eric entered us in the Marion to Bermuda race in 1979. I was to be the navigator—and only celestial navigation was permitted.

Chuck Oman, my MIT colleague and an experienced ocean racer, told me it would be easy—just an application of spherical trigonometry—and I need not take a course. He got me to buy the book by Mixter used at Annapolis, and Eric bought a modest sextant. I read and practiced much of the spring. Since we didn't have a clear horizon visible from our yard in Newton, I practiced with a pseudo horizon using vegetable oil in a soup bowl and "bringing down the stars" for my sightings. I could locate Newton as being somewhere near Wellesley. I was even worse on the water off of Cleveland Ledge in Buzzard's Bay, Massachusetts.

But, nevertheless, we set off for Bermuda, only to be met by a full gale, for almost a day and a half, while crossing the Gulf Stream. It pulled our mainsail track right off the mast, and we rigged some sort of repair and proceeded toward Bermuda. The racing rule was that you could only turn on any electronics when your celestial navigation calculation put you within the 100-fathom line approaching Bermuda. At dawn on the fifth day, I said that Bermuda should be dead ahead, some thirty miles or so. I switched on the ADF and heard the Bermuda radio beacon, as I hoped. It was dead ahead. I felt like Magellan! We got to the Yacht Club, cleaned up, slept, and located a replacement mast track. I was hoisted up the mast and installed it with pop rivets, and a week later we started back. Once again in a storm. We were knocked over on our side. The engine quit and wouldn't restart. Then the wind died, and for a couple of days we drifted toward Ireland in the Gulf Stream. One particularly depressing day was when the trash we had tossed overboard at breakfast drifted past us at lunch time. (This was well before current environmental awareness.) When Eric asked me where we were after I took the "noon sight," I refused to tell him. We finished the trip by being towed by a fishing trawler the last twenty miles into Woods Hole. I swore I would never sail the Bermuda race again—but I did, once more with Eric, once with David Feingold, and once with Chuck Oman on the more serious Marblehead race. None was ever as exciting or threatening as that first one.

Almost every summer, for a decade or more, I would spend a week cruising with Eric and some of his friends. We started the first years on the coast of Maine. Navigation up and down the New England coast was a challenge, using a handheld Whistler radar and a radio direction finder tuning into AM radio stations and navigation beacons for crawling up the coast of Maine and eventually crossing over to Nova Scotia. Later we upgraded to LORAN and eventually to GPS. By that time, however, the thrill of actually sighting the buoy or lighthouse we aimed for was gone. It became too easy.

Eventually we extended our cruising to the Canadian Maritimes. Eric left the boat in the Bras D'Or (pronounced Board Oar) at Baddeck, Nova Scotia, over the winter. We would fly up for our trips sailing to Newfoundland or the Gaspe Peninsula in Québec, or even up toward Labrador. It was always an adventure: new harbors, different people in "out villages" and sailing challenges. The thrill of actually making the desired destination and the feeling of swiftly cutting through the water was what I needed to recharge my batteries—by working very hard at something I didn't have to do.

Several close friends joined Eric on the summer cruises. Amherst classmates Jay Jacobson, Sandy Chaitovitz and Mike Ritter, as well as the orthopedic residents Eric drafted onto the crew, all contributed good stories, good music and friendship. Jeff Hoffman and I nearly mutinied one summer when Eric was about to cancel our anticipated sail to the French islands off the coast of Newfoundland. Eric was afraid that his boat would be impounded because he had a shotgun on board, for protection against polar bears if we had gone all the way to Greenland. Finally, I bought the shotgun from him and we toured and dined in Saint Pierre and Miquelon. We had a fine French dinner without arrest or incident. One day, with a gale forecast, we made for the deep harbor at Lunenburg, Nova Scotia, and carefully tied up to the protected dock alongside the fish cannery. Well protected. Until, after dark and with the wind already picking up, Eric insisted that the fish smell would never get out of the boat, and we motored out into the middle of the harbor where we somehow anchored or picked up a mooring and rode out the gale.

Sometimes Eric became the excessively opinionated surgeon and captain, and we disagreed about everything, from the advantages of jibing downwind rather than running directly before the wind, to almost all aspects of politics and the roles of women. But he remained a funny and thoughtful friend—one of my oldest. Amazingly, we remained close friends for all those years. Eric was an esteemed orthopedic surgeon who passed away, a victim of COVID-19, in 2020. I miss him.

When I was living in the Houston condo I shared with Marty Fettman, during my two years training as a Space Shuttle Payload Specialist (PS) in the early 1990s, my bedroom sliding glass door opened on a little balcony overlooking the dock where I kept the sailboat I had borrowed from Space Life Sciences 1 PS, Drew Gafney. Also at the dock was my kayak and a wind-surfer beside Drew's sailboat. Most afternoons, with NASA JSC essentially closing down at 4 p.m., I would take the windsurfer if the wind were up, or the kayak if it was a calm day, and ever so quietly explore the shallow inlets off Egret Bay, an arm of Clear Lake. I could sneak up on the birds, especially the egrets and sometimes the herons, and silently observe them while they observed me. It cleared my head like nothing else, and I often stayed out on the water until dusk. Somehow, at age fifty-seven, the experience of sailing alone after work was as peaceful and meditative as it had been during my MIT student days thirty-five years earlier.

Snorkeling and SCUBA

I was first exposed to the beauty of life underwater when Jody and I went snorkeling on our honeymoon at Caneel Bay, in St. John, Puerto Rico. I was overwhelmed by the conches and tropical fish, the multi-colored coral and the quiet of it all. We bought some snorkeling gear but couldn't really use it in New England. The desire lay dormant until Rob was about twelve and said he wanted to learn SCUBA. Although MIT had classes, the easiest for him was the YMCA in Newton, but that required a parent to be present. Both Jody and I signed up for the pool sessions. I did the open water qualification in Key Largo, when I was already in Miami for some work with Eastern Airlines at their simulator facility. It was terrific, and of course Rob and Jody soon got their certificates in the Caribbean too. Over the ensuing years I tried to tack on a SCUBA dive or two when I could. Probably the best was on Australia's Great Barrier Reef, with Volker Henn at a neuroscience meeting. It turns out now, at my age I need to get a special physical exam to be allowed to dive, so I satisfy myself with snorkeling, most recently in Bali in 2014. Nothing dangerous or fancy—just a pleasure to be immersed in the natural habitat of the fish.

Whitewater Canoeing and Kayaking

Whitewater canoeing and kayaking became a passion for both Jody and me. We each had done a little bit of flat water canoeing—and of course Jody was the daughter of a camp director, so that gave her a leg up (or into) a canoe. I'm not sure what got us started, but some time in the 1960s we both went to the Appalachian Mountain Club White Water tryouts at the Red Wing Boat Club near Needham on the Charles. I passed and Jody didn't! So, as you might expect, she worked and worked at it to make sure she would pass

I signal my triumph after a kayak roll in 1967.   Leonard McCombe/Life/Shutterstock

the flat water qualification test the next year—and off we went on a series of increasingly challenging weekend river outings in New Hampshire. We began on Class 2 (easiest) rivers in open Grumman aluminum canoes, and the experienced paddlers taught us to draw, sweep, pry, and especially to brace (lean) away from the current. It was a lovely, friendly, and well-educated group we enjoyed calling friends. Saturday nights were campouts with communal cooking and lively stories. As we got better at the sport, Jody came upon the MIT White Water Club, which was building their own fiberglass "banana boats," using a mold Tom Wilson made, starting with a prize winning (Yugo) C-2 (two-seater canoe). She threw herself into that as well, eventually building a C-1 (one-seater) for herself, and C-2 for the two of us and two kayaks. When our friend Ray Hanselman, an MIT PhD in organic chemistry, came over for dinner in Newton, he asked about the peculiar odor in the house. Jody explained that it was acetone and epoxy for the canoes she was finishing in the basement. Ray informed us that we were breathing poisons and to cut it out at once!

Our paddling together led to the usual blame game ("I got my end past the rock–what's wrong with you?") and eventually we went out singly. I got fairly good at ducking in and out of eddies in my kayak and was elevated to Class 4 by the AMC. The thrill of inspecting a difficult rapid, thinking through the forces and torques that would require manipulation of the boat, and then actually getting through without tipping over (usually) was amazing. Lots of similarities to skiing—the aesthetics, the planning, and the thrill of survival. Only one time, when I flipped over and got my hand caught in the

Eliot, Rob and I are pictured descending from the bare ledge on Mt. Cardigan near our house in New Hampshire.

painter loop as the kayak filled with water and shot downstream, was I really afraid. But then there was a drowning (on another trip, we didn't know the victim), and yet our children wanted to join us on later trips. The risks that seemed acceptable to us seemed to be too extreme for our kids. And so, when we were in our forties, we gradually stopped. The boats remained under the deck in Rumney, and would be taken out once a summer or more, for an easy Class 2 trip on the Pemigewasset River ("the Pemi") or a weekend on the Ammonoosuc. But nothing hair-raising any more. To this day, however, when I drive past a stretch of white water, I look it over and think about a route, and how it would feel to brace over and scoot into a big eddy. And I still get the thrill.

Hiking

All three children hiked with family and friends. I wasn't interested in bagging all the four-thousand-footers in the White Mountains, but I did love the views from my special places, and returned again and again with family.

Rob and I pause on a New Hampshire peak.

When we lived in Switzerland in 1972-73, we did a lot of hiking. The mountains were beckoning and I started the practice of telling long, long stories on the way uphill. The principal character evolved into "Harry the Hacker." He was a wise guy, but never as clever as he thought he was. He would come up with harebrained ideas, to rob a museum or counterfeit money (I really don't remember them any more), but he was both loveable and laughable. Anyway, to hear the story, the kids had to keep up with me—and so they did. Eliot has continued the tradition with his own children.

Wheels

All American boys can remember their first driving experience and their first car. When I was fifteen, Mom taught me to drive in our HUGE Buick, one size smaller than the Roadmaster, a convertible with white wall tires and a stick shift. Our dead-end street in Riverdale was very quiet and had a hill and a narrow track to practice making a U-turn. But the real test of skill was over the line in Yonkers. Caryl Avenue was steep and curvy and narrow, and usually had oncoming traffic. The trick was to parallel park, and then smoothly pull forward without either popping the clutch or sliding back down the hill.

One of my daring and very stupid moves I still shudder over involved the Buick convertible. It was parked in the narrow steep driveway alongside our house, and I was home alone when it began to snow, heavily. I decided it would be best for me to put the car in the very narrow garage, which involved backing it down a steep, icy and narrow ramp, with only inches of clearance on each side. I didn't yet have a license, of course. There was no way to put it into first and smoothly climb back up once I was committed to the descent. No scratches—but a very sobering experience.

After mastering Caryl Avenue, I got my license at age sixteen, but it was only valid outside of New York City and only during daylight. Those privileges came at eighteen. So my use of the car for dates was limited. One important exception was a date I had in the summer I was sixteen and working as a counselor at the Town and Country Day Camp in Yonkers. I got a date with Jody Fisher, the owner's daughter, a fellow counselor, and ten years later, my first wife. We all went to Rye Beach Playland—a very upscale amusement park near the Connecticut line. By "all" I mean Jody, myself, my mother and my sister, Ellen. We had a great day on the roller coaster, slides, paddling on the pond, etc. Ellen was instantly a fan of Jody, since my date didn't like whipped cream and offered it to Ellen. On the way back it was dark and required a trip into New York City—so Mom drove, of course.

The Buick was not a sports car, but it was very fast. One night, all alone on the straight road bordering the ocean on the way to Fire Island, I floored it and reached 115 mph. What was I thinking? But usually my driving was limited to going to Briarcliff Manor with the family for a day of golf and dinner in Ossining, New York, and home to Riverdale. Never in Manhattan!

I drove very little while I was in college. On some Saturdays, Eric Radin would ask me to drive my date back to Smith, while he necked with his date in the back seat of his Ford. But my first car wasn't acquired until the fall of 1957, as a direct result of my first trip to Europe that summer. It was a three month "grand tour" with MIT friends Steve and George. We drove our rented Simca from Paris to Naples to Vienna and all points in between. In those days, nobody took a short European trip. The ocean crossing alone took a week each way. We (I forgot who) dented the fender on the rental car by being sideswiped by a fire truck on the narrow balcony road outside of Livorno, Italy, but no serious financial damage was done. (It is never the fault of the fireman—don't even try to argue with the police.)

For my last undergraduate year at MIT, I shared part of a house on Tappan Street, near Brookline High School. It turned out to be a good forty-five-minute commute by T, the Boston area public transit, and I decided to buy a Vespa. All over Europe that summer I had seen countless carefree young people zipping along on their motor scooters and it seemed just right for me. Mom and Dad didn't think so. So, they reasoned with me and bribed me by advancing me $150 for a used car. We relied on Mom's cousins, one of the Rothbergs, who owned a garage in the Bronx, to select a reliable starter vehicle: a 1950 Plymouth. Two-doors. No dents. Stick shift and a running board. And mine. No problems, and I kept it until I left for my Paris graduate work a year later.

One problem, however, was parking at MIT. There was no student parking and the free street parking on Memorial Drive would fill up earlier than I wanted to arrive. But the MIT *VooDoo* published a "travellers' aid issue" with MIT parking stickers on the cover. They were perfect for me, although each had a distinct permit number. I waited until after the Thanksgiving break before proceeding to make an illegal color copy in the Instrumentation Lab. It looked fine, and I dirtied it up a bit before attaching it to my car window. The scam worked for almost two weeks—until I was contacted by Campus Patrol. The officer took me in to meet the head of MIT's police, a distinguished, middle-aged, very fit man in a dark gray suit and an ex-FBI agent. He had found out that my father was a lawyer, and asked me what he might have thought of my parking escapade. He told me that a student's record of offenses (he didn't say "criminal") would follow me all my life. He said that if I ever wanted to study law my record might make me ineligible to take the Bar exam, as well as endanger any possibility of a security clearance. He scared the hell out of me. I immediately scraped the counterfeit sticker off the window. And I never told Dad! Or boasted about my innovation, either.

When I got back to MIT in 1958, I bought another black Plymouth (four doors and no running boards) and kept it until Eliot was born in 1962. It had a tricky (or just worn out) clutch. When Jody was driving it up a long hill, on our way back from skiing in Vermont, she would have to nudge me awake to shift into second while she operated the clutch and steered. The timing was off, and to start it I would sometimes have to open the hood, turn the distributor cap a little (to advance the spark, of course), let Jody start it and then rotate the cap back for driving. I wasn't much on maintenance, except for flushing the radiator and putting in anti-freeze every winter.

There followed our first new car, a 1962 Plymouth Valiant. (Professor Y.T. Li thought I should buy the more modern rear-engine Chevy, despite its many technical glitches, because engineers should do that.) And from then on, our cars followed our stage in life. With a move to the suburbs and three children, we went up to a full-size Dodge station wagon, with a third seat that faced backward, and so on. When we lived in Switzerland we had a Mercedes 190—very luxurious, and it made it back to the USA with us. For my year at Stanford, I bought a Toyota Celica that looked sporty but had little performance. And then, inevitably, the switch to Japanese cars—Toyotas, Subarus and a Nissan. They are amazingly reliable, start in all weather, and get through the snow. But dull, dull, dull.

A friend in Waterville Valley, even older than me, offered to take me to the race track in Connecticut and teach me to go around in his Porsche 911. I declined. I don't need another hobby—or any additional risk in my life.

Flying

But onto the air—and airplanes. Like most of the other ten-year-olds in my school when World War II broke out, I learned a bit about war planes. The enemy planes, just in case the Germans or the Japanese decided to bomb New York, and I would need to identify the Junkers, Fokkers and Zeroes. But more so the American planes. I could draw the rough shapes of the Grumman Tomcat and especially the P-52 Mustang, with its sleek lines and bubble cockpit. I built model planes with balsa wood from kits and I can still recall the (probably toxic) smell of the airplane glue. On flying models, with their rubber band-powered propeller, I played around with trim and balance, using paper clips to adjust the position of the center of gravity, although I really didn't know much about what I was doing.

And then, as a grownup, I got to play around in some amazing real flying machines! I never did get a pilot's license, even though, as a professor teaching a course in aviation human factors I probably could have gotten MIT to pay for the lessons. But there were always other demands on my time. I did learn the fundamentals of flying, however. I had a small Link (GAT-1) Trainer, the famous "Blue Box" used to train so many new pilots during World War II, and a moving-base flight simulator in my lab, which we used to study motion sensing and air traffic displays. It could simulate a single engine basic plane like a Cessna 190 and, with a little bit of instruction, I managed to "fly" some routes, maintain altitude and attitude, take off and sometimes even land. I passed many happy hours by myself in the simulator down in the basement of the MIT Space Center.

I got so interested in the subject of pilot training that I introduced a graduate course in Flight Simulation. We discussed math models of the airplane for computer simulation, vision and the presentation of realistic scenes projected on the windows, movement of the motion base, and pilot training. Along with Mark Connelly, we made ample use of another flight simulator in the department—a Boeing 707-era model in the cockpit of a fixed-base transport simulator. We could add Air Traffic Control and Traffic Avoidance Displays to the piloting task. With all of that exposure, I began to feel at home in a cockpit—as long as I didn't have to take control of a real plane.

For a while I had some government funding to study pilot training. That allowed me to obtain an FAA-approved Cockpit Pass, which permitted me to fly in the jump seat of commercial flights with the captain's approval. I had to have a paid ticket. I was never turned down, and for a number of years I took advantage of the privilege and looked forward to riding along, observing the crew's actions and discussing flying with the crew. I was always welcomed and was very careful to obey the rules, like observing the stricture to avoid any conversation when below 10,000 feet. Usually, I was not allowed up front until well after takeoff, but often I could stay for landing.

The crew was often curious to know about MIT and our research, and then to hear any new stories I could tell them, as they had generally heard all that their fellow pilots had to say. I learned a lot about commercial flight operations and the stresses of being a pilot. All of that came to a halt after 9/11, when the FAA withdrew jump seat privileges.

And then there were the astronaut training days. Flying had nothing at all to do with my job as a Payload Specialist Candidate for the Space Life Sciences 2 shuttle mission, but the NASA system insisted that our indoctrination include the rudiments of flight operations and procedures. My one official "dollar ride" in the wonderful T-38 that was used for astronaut proficiency training was conducted by our Spacelab commander, John Blaha. I was seated in the back seat behind him and I marveled at the sights of southern Texas as John flew us from Ellington Field, near the Johnson Space Center (JSC), out to our assigned maneuvering space over the Gulf of Mexico. And then I was given control of the plane. John, of course, could take over at any moment. After reaching our desired altitude over the Gulf of Mexico, he let me fly as much as I wanted. Climbing and diving, turning and leveling out. He took us supersonic and back.

John would instruct me to establish a desired heading and altitude. I wasn't very adept at the task and wandered back and forth around the assigned compass heading. When he saw me oscillating in roll, back and forth, he suggested that instead of concentrating on the little artificial horizon on the instrument panel, I would do better by looking out the windshield at the big horizon all around us. It was a clear day. And he was absolutely right. Suddenly, on that blue sky day, with a clear horizon in view, everything became much easier.

There were other flying opportunities in the astronaut training period, including a number in the twin jet Cessna nominally used for Mission Specialist training—but no more hands-on flying for me. Somehow the idea of going back to learning to fly a small single-engine turbine plane seemed less appealing and I never followed up.

On another day, just for fun, Dave Wolf took me up in his little plane to show me the acrobatic maneuvers he performed during competitions. That was illuminating, but once was enough!

The astronauts were also able to use NASA's new Gulfstream, acquired, supposedly, to allow Mission Specialists to maintain their piloting abilities. It was used whenever a good excuse could be found. We flew in it from JSC to Kennedy Space Center (KSC). And we flew to North Carolina for the funeral of Bill McArthur's mother. Nothing wrong with that. I was interested in the steep approach of the Shuttle for its landing in Florida, so I was allowed to sit in NASA's modified Gulfstream's cockpit while Rick Searfoss practiced the 28-degree approaches to the landing strip at KSC. It looked and felt like falling out of the sky each time.

In front of "our T-38" with our JSC trainers on another fun day. It was used on occasion for transport and more for pilot recency (a general term relating to the amount of flying time in recent months). It was a treat to go supersonic and to be "in control," from the back seat, while John really remained in command.

Even before I began any astronaut training, I flew on numerous parabolic flights. After each 2-g pullout there followed a zero-g path for about twenty seconds, allowing us to practice some of our experiments in weightlessness— and to have a lot of fun as well. The parabolic flights played an important part in the development of equipment and procedures for our Spacelab experiments. Chuck Oman, Bob Renshaw and I from MIT, Doug Watt from McGill, and Ken Money from Toronto, all accumulated a lot of time in weightlessness— twenty seconds at a time. I always enjoyed the chance to observe my own spatial orientation when moving around in a zero-g parabola.

I would avoid motion sickness on the so-called "Vomit Comet" by limiting my head movements during the 2-g pullout phases separating each of the forty or so free fall periods. I also took the medication "Scope-Dex" (Scopalomine-Dexamphetamine) before takeoff. For one of the fights during our crew training, I decided to evaluate my reaction to the in-flight medication being prescribed for astronauts. The intramuscular injection of promethazine was supposed to eliminate motion sickness symptoms, although it might bring on side effects, including drowsiness. I told the on-board flight surgeon that I intended to produce symptoms by making head movements during the early parabolas and then to have him inject the larger than usual 50 mg dose of promethazine in my arm. And so we did. I made head movements, got nauseated almost to the point of vomiting, and he gave me an injection. So far so good. Except that the symptoms didn't really disappear. An hour later, after landing back at Ellington I could barely find my car–and driving the five miles back to home was like trying to drive after a week without sleep. Fortunately, I made it, and crawled into bed—dead to the world for the rest of the day. And convinced that I would avoid that drug—at least in that dosage—if I ever got space sickness.

Skiing

Early Skiing

I loved to ski ever since my cousin Howie Rotner and I got our first pair of wooden Northland skis for our twelfth birthdays in 1947. They came from Sun Sporting Goods in Manhattan. They had no steel edges, were sized to the reach of our outstretched fingertips, and had rat-trap toe pieces and fat cable bindings, which could be attached toward the heel for "downhill" or toward the ball of the foot for cross-country. Best of all, they came with a booklet from Northland on how to ski, and Howie and I taught ourselves to ski over a couple of winters on the hill in the Van Cortlandt Park golf course in the Bronx. We worked our way through all the lessons in the Northland Ski Instruction manual. We began with lesson one, side-stepping and packing out the hill, and then proceeded to the herring bone for climbing. Then on to straight running, snowplow, snowplow turn and then to the stem turn and the stem Christiana. The parallel Christiana was an "advanced technique" that we did not attempt until we were thirteen.

I had so much trouble getting into the cable bindings that usually I would put the boots into the bindings in the warmth of our front hall, and then put my feet into the boots and slide down the six steps to the snow-covered street and ski down Saxon Avenue to the golf course, where we could squeeze through a hole in the fence. There we learned to ski and to make a desperate hockey stop to keep from tumbling down an embankment into the road. Fifteen years later, a rope tow was put into Van Cortlandt Park, and it opened for skiing on Dec. 11, 1964. I put these recollections in a letter to *Skiing History* magazine, where it appeared in September 2014.

As we got better, my older cousin, Evan Rotner, would take us up to Fahnstock State Park where he was a patrolman, just to the north of their home in Westchester. And, oh boy—was that fun! He showed me how to go up the hill holding onto the wet and slippery rope tow.

The biggest excitement involved going off to ski with Evan on real mountains. Later, Evan went to northern Vermont and worked on the ski patrol of the newly-developed Mad River Glen, which was, and remains, the most macho of all mountains. "Ski it if you can" is its motto. We stayed at Mad River Glen in the attic of a farmhouse for a dollar or two a night, including breakfast. The trails were narrow and turny, and the glades required skill to avoid hitting the trees. No grooming and no padding. My ski clothing included my high school varsity track jacket and double lace-up boots. I loved every minute of it. Despite the cold wind I would eat my sandwich while waiting on the long line for the chair lift. At the single chair lift you could borrow a blanket for the ride up.

Nobody took lessons and we could leave our skis against the lift shack overnight without fear of their being taken. I never thought of racing, only of the next way down and of the beauty of the Vermont hills and valleys. The "beginner hill," with its own T-Bar, was steep and challenging, as Jody was to discover when I steered her there for lessons many years later. Entertainment was provided by the ski school band, led by the school director, Bud Phillips (mostly for the older folks—twenty or more years of age). I began a long practice of staying at the marvelous Mad River Barn where Alice Billings and her husband, Les, treated everyone as family, and seated everyone around the dining table or the fireplace. It may have been just too Norman Rockwell, but for a teenager from New York it was perfect.

College Ski Racing

College ski racing was a big step. Howie and I both raced for Amherst College. My freshman dorm room in Stearns was only about fifty yards from the top of Memorial Hill at Amherst, where they had a rope tow installed and ski lessons were offered by Coach Steve Rostas. He was an ex-Hungarian ski and motorcycle racer who ended up at Amherst by some circuitous post-war route and coached soccer and lacrosse as well as skiing. Unfortunately, his ankle injury in a motorcycle race kept him from actually skiing, so he was limited to giving us printed instructions and lots of shouted encouragement.

On the first day that Steve saw me ski, he asked me about my racing experience. Well, actually he asked me if I owned my own skis. When I said "yes," he invited me to try out for the Amherst Ski Team. That was a pretty snowy winter and the rope tow that Amherst had placed on Tinker Hill in Hadley ran most weekends, manned by the ski team. Apparently, Steve had traipsed through the hills in Hadley one winter and found lots of snow there, and convinced Amherst College to buy or lease the hill. The rope tow was, like so many of its time, just an old truck with a rope passing over a large pulley. We did have the Amherst Winter Carnival there one year, complete with downhill.

A few people had real racing experience, from prep school, and taught the rest of us to make our way down the courses. Alpine skiing had only two events: slalom and downhill. Giant slalom came into college racing later. The

Amherst College Varsity Skiing, Winter of 1954-1955. Howie Rotner is in the Rear, Center, and Larry Young in in the Rear, Right.

slalom bamboo poles were the furthest imaginable from modern "breakaway" poles, and had to be contacted by the back of the shoulder, leading to the "reverse shoulder" posture of the day. Downhill was top-to-bottom, with no control gates. You tried not to go off the twisting course and especially not to hit a tree—but in at least one race I hit a tree and still finished.

We were invited to some of the Winter Carnivals. Williams and Middlebury were the ones I recall, where we got to see the big guys in action and lost to some of the best. In the Winter Carnival races we also had to compete in Nordic events: cross-country and jumping. Cross-country was a challenge, but it was jumping that really spooked me. Steve handed out ditto sheets with jumping instructions on our way to our training at Gilford, New Hampshire, where Gunstock had three jumps of different heights. Steve explained that on the first jump we should just float off the little platform, and not jump. Well, I figured that if it were cautious to do that, then it would be even safer to slow down, so I threw in a snowplow to kill my speed on the in-run and then, as might be expected, I didn't even have enough speed to clear the flat knoll and landed on the out-run. Ooof! My knees went right up to my shoulders, but I survived. At the bottom the coach explained, "Larry, next time please try to jump—just a little." I never got much better at it and never overcame my fear. Finally, when we were training for the Middlebury Winter Carnival and jumping off their big wooden scaffold that swayed in the wind, I gave in to my fear and good sense, withdrew from the event, and stopped jumping entirely.

Meanwhile, I was slowly but surely getting better at slalom. I even was on the *New York Times'* list of top finishers at the Williams downhill, well behind my later friend, Olympian Tom Corcoran. I spent my two years at MIT competing against my former teammates from Amherst in the newly formed league of non-elite ski teams. No carnivals. No Nordic events. No Friday races. And reasonable competition. I had some good races—never winning but doing my best and benefitting from the experience of my new Norwegian veteran teammates. I was one of only two Americans on the MIT team and we enjoyed ourselves, win or lose. Maybe that was when I learned my life lessons, that it is the voyage and not the destination that counts. After college I entered one or two open Eastern races, and stopped that after losing by many seconds to a sixteen-year-old from Stowe named Billy Kidd, who later became a skiing legend and Olympic medalist. I only got back to it through Masters Racing many years later.

A week skiing Mount Katahdin, Maine

After college, when I shared a duplex with my cousin Howie and other Harvard Med students, we all worked long hours and we barely took any time off—except for an occasional ski trip and one adventuresome week at

Spring Break. Howie, Jim Vernon, a friend of Jim's, and I went off to climb and ski Mt. Katahdin, the northern terminus of the Appalachian Trail in Maine. It took two days on climbing skis to get in and to reach the unheated log cabins, which had been broken into by wolves sometime earlier. Every day was a climb to a peak, near the famous "knife edge," and then the high adventure of a slide back to the cabin, trying to avoid falling into any of the boulders. My effort to warm and to dry my ski boots by keeping them near the wood stove overnight resulted in separated soles and I managed to gingerly urge them into the "bear trap" bindings for each day on the snow. After Cuz fell and slid down on his back, narrowly avoiding the rocks, we became much more cautious.

Joining the Ski Patrol

After college racing for Amherst and for MIT, I did a little bit of USSA Masters' Racing, but it was getting hard and expensive, with a third child on the way. I thought I might someday try to get on a ski patrol as a way to get some winter exercise and avoid having to buy lift tickets. I took the First Aid course offered by the Red Cross in Boston.

That first winter in Rumney, New Hampshire, 1969-1970, I bought us inexpensive season passes to nearby Tenney Mountain. But they had no snow-making, and Christmas came and went with still no snow at Tenney. Adam, the Red Cross instructor, was a patrolman at Waterville Valley, New Hampshire, which had just opened its chair lift on Mt. Tecumseh, and he encouraged me to stop by. Waterville Valley was the area started by Tom Corcoran, whom I knew somewhat from the days when he and his buddies at Dartmouth would dominate college racing. Tom had told me a year earlier that they had no land for sale in Waterville Valley, but that they would be putting up "condominiums." Condo—what's that? I hated to reveal my ignorance, but it seemed like an unlikely plan.

I knew Mt. Tecumseh from college racing, where I had twice competed in the downhill race. It was probably straight down what is now White Caps and Old Tecumseh. We climbed up on Saturday for an inspection run and then once again to race it, with hand timing, on Sunday. In one of those races I crashed into a tree down near the bottom—but got up and still finished. This was before release bindings. Long thong leather straps stayed on! All of the teams stayed at the old Waterville Inn. The Sunday race started late enough to accommodate those who wished to attend Mass. The only lift skiing was on Snows Mountain, and consisted of two T-Bars in series. Not very interesting, and no comparison to Cannon Mountain, further up Route 3 in Franconia Notch. All of this was before the Interstate Highway System was extended by Route I-93, which cut an hour off the trip north from Cambridge. I thought that Waterville would be a great place to ski if it were ever developed.

Anyway, I went to Waterville and looked up my friend Adam, who recommended that I ask if I could be accepted onto the Ski Patrol. Al Emerton, the Ski Patrol Director, asked if I wanted a tryout, and assigned his assistant, Jimmy Roberts (later the Mountain Manager of Beaver Creek), to take me out on the T-Bar. The skiing test consisted of a few runs down what is now "World Cup," to show my strength in a snowplow—or at least enough to prevent a toboggan with an injured skier from getting away from me and flying down the hill. I passed, and, since I had the Red Cross training, I began patrolling the next weekend. I was hired as a weekend volunteer, and began a decade or so on the Waterville Valley Ski Patrol.

We were qualified by the National Ski Patrol System but were run under the Professional Ski Patrol Association. At first everyone was paid, but by the time I started the volunteers were just that. In that first year, 1969-1970, we patrolled out of a corner table in the Schwendi Hutte—that log cabin mountain restaurant at the summit. The previous patrol shack had burned down. All the skiers in the hut could hear our telephone calls from lift attendants as well as our other conversations. It was a big relief to get moved into our proper hut the next winter, complete with a ski preparation bench and rudimentary kitchen.

Ski Patrol was a blast. The group was friendly and spanned the ages from young twenties to late fifties. There were no other academics, and the conversations were wide-ranging. Other part-timers of about my age included Speed Walker, who climbed poles for the phone company, Dick Palmer, who worked for the New Hampshire Electric Co-op, Jerry McNally, who might have been in real estate from Boston, and Dave, a fellow who was a Williams graduate of my year and headed the North Country Economic Development Council. Among the full-timers were a logger, a house painter, several contractors and a recent college graduate taking some time off.

Some of the full-timers were really, really strong skiers. George Askevold taught me how to ski moguls by carefully picking a line and then working the two legs independently to soak up the terrain. George, along with Floyd Wilke of the Ski School, went on to compete in the early Professional Free Style meets, and the elegant Ross Farnham was doing graceful long leaps (geländesprung) long before terrain parks were imagined. Jason Wilkie, a strong skier and later Patrol Director, could power through any terrain, but was no match for a collision on his motorcycle on Route I-93. The current ski patrol hut is named in his honor. Once, Jason got so involved in throwing snowballs from the lift, aimed at his buddies on the trail, that he threw himself right off the High Country chairlift. Ross, Jimmy, and John LaPointe went out to Vail and ran the Race Department before climbing higher in management. Billy Cushing was a good-natured and very responsible, hardworking patroller who became the Patrol Director and served well for many years. His nephew, Butch Cushing, took over the patrol and later, for many years, remained at Waterville in charge of the lifts. The whole operation answered to the head of the clinic, Dr. Henry Crane, a general surgeon from Plymouth, New Hampshire. He was a master at closed setting of bones, without surgery. He was a graduate of Harvard Medical School but did his best to maintain his "country doctor" attitude.

From time to time the conversations drifted to politics. As the profes-

I'm posing with Eliot's son, Josh, one of the "Plus Guys" for Eldora, above Boulder, Colorado.

sor from Massachusetts, I was naturally labeled as the liberal in a gang of conservatives, but the arguments were civilized. Toward the end of one ski season I asked my buddies, all of whom said they were opposed to government interference in their lives, what they were going to do over the spring and summer. Their answer was "the same as always—collect unemployment and go fishing!" They did not see the irony in that or their continued opposition to government in their lives!

The day-to-day job of patrolman was rewarding, and generally great fun. I liked the prestige of wearing the patrol jacket with its large first-aid symbol (one of those "Plus Guys," Rob called us) as well as the camaraderie. I particularly enjoyed the quick sense of accomplishment. Someone was hurt (usually a broken leg back in those days), and five minutes later you were easing his leg into a balloon splint and tying him into the toboggan for the ride down to the clinic. Ten minutes later he was being examined, and maybe even treated by Henry Crane, the surgeon in charge, or one of the Harvard Medical School residents who had been assigned for the weekend. In twenty minutes the job was done—in contrast to my day job, where writing the grant, doing the research and awaiting the reviews took a couple of years.

We had an informal competition to see who would be logged in for the most accident calls. We would wait in the summit hut, and when the phone rang, the first two to be out the door, with their boots buckled and gloves on, would get to take a toboggan and rush to the site of the injured skier. We did not have radios in those days (let alone cell phones), so every call was answered as though it were critical—with two patrollers and a toboggan equipped with a backboard. We each carried an emergency pack with the usual first aid equipment. In addition, we each carried a plastic inflatable splint, kept next to our bellies so that it would stay warm and flexible. Most often the injured skier had a broken leg or a sprained ankle. Later on, as bindings improved and boots got stiffer, the number of lower leg injuries was cut down, but they were replaced by knee injuries. Snowboards came along later than my day, and brought their own pattern of injuries, mostly to the wrist and shoulder as the rider fell forward with an outstretched arm.

The skiing part was easy, except for bringing a loaded toboggan down the steep face of True Grit or Upper Bobby's Run (then known as Lower Psyched, before Bobby Kennedy's assassination). Those descents required two men (there were no female patrollers at that time), one with his arms pushing down on the handles in front and the other belaying the sled with a rope from the back. The only time I came close to losing an empty toboggan was after loading it onto a chair at the base—but I caught it in time and the lift was stopped to allow it to be re-loaded.

We had annual avalanche training, which was pretty much a joke. We also trained on evacuating skiers from the chair lift, which was no joke at all. This took guts, especially on the part of the skier who had to step from the safety of the chair out onto a slim step and pole, which could be lowered to the ground with a rope thrown over the lift cable. It was scary. One time, when Sunnyside, our steepest lift, needed to be evacuated and I was involved, we found that one of the first chairs to be unloaded contained Ethel Kennedy. She was well known in Waterville along with her family. She stayed around to help us out and shouted to the frightened skiers, "Come on! If I could do it, so can you!"

Getting out of the house in Rumney early in the morning was a constant battle—but the first run of the day, before opening to the public, made it worthwhile. And the ring of mountain peaks around Waterville Valley became very familiar. For one or two hours we would be assigned to High Country or to Valley Run, and we ran the lift at closing time. (During my first season as a patrolman, they played a prank on me by dressing a snowman on the descending lift and hosing it down to freeze overnight. I was supposed to turn off the lift after everyone was safely on the ground, but when I arrived the next morning, there was a figure, covered in icicles, and Al said, "Larry! You shut off the lift too soon!") The end of the day around 4PM in December was cold and dark—but the final sweep of the mountain lent a certain closure to the day.

The last time I mentioned my patrol experience was many years later, when I was going through my astronaut interviews in Houston in 1990. When I asked my friend and colleague what made them feel that I was qualified, Rhea Seddon said that it was not my knowledge of space physiology, which was taken for granted, but rather my service as a ski patrolman, which proved that I could work as a member of a team in critical situations. And I thought it was only a way to ski for free!

Perhaps the best part of patrolling had to do with the sight of a skier, down in the snow, cold and scared and hurting. And then, with care, he or she was splinted, placed in the toboggan, transported down to the clinic at the base of the mountain, and within about twenty minutes, was being treated in a warm and well-equipped setting and reassured by a confident nurse and a Harvard orthopedist. The grimace and fear were usually replaced by a relaxed state and usually the first question was, "When will I be able to ski again, doc?"

The patrol experience led me into a whole new career path—tracking the statistics of ski injuries, studying the function of release bindings and boots, investigating tower pads, studying the trajectories of skiers going off jumps in terrain parks, and even characterizing the friction characteristics of different materials in ski clothing. Somehow it seems very wrong to have a sport that brings so much pure pleasure and adrenalin rush also contribute to so many accidents—some of them very serious. Are we all a little crazy? Are we affected by the cold to the extent that we think we are immune from fractures and concussions? Or is it worth the risk?

Skiing Children

Skiing children came with the territory. Jody actually taught all of them to ski, passing on the lessons she had gotten from me or from the instructors at Mad River Glen. I was devastated when Rob broke his leg at about age six (a green stick fracture, but still a break). We sent him off to visit his maternal grandparents, Sam and Ruth Fisher, in Florida, with his little cast. What a trooper. Leslie was always up for one more run, and when she was a teen, she and I won the local father-daughter qualifying race and went up to Stowe for the finals. She stayed with it through high school, but neither she nor Rob took racing seriously. Rob switched to cross-country, probably as a reaction to the success that Eliot was having in Alpine.

Leslie learning to ski in New Hampshire.

Our children, along with some of the other patrol brats, were adopted by the ski patrol. If they needed anything it would be available from somebody on the staff, including hot chocolate at the restaurant. In the spring, Eliot and some others would settle themselves in chairs under the lift and, using the ten-foot-long steel avalanche poles as blow guns, would launch snow pellets at their friends on the chair lift.

In the 1970s, the pied piper was Wayne Wong, who introduced free-style skiing. Eliot joined the teen followers but, after a few seasons, he developed such bad chondromalacia ("runner's knee") that Henry told him to either switch to a more upright posture, as in alpine racing, or face a future in which he would be unable to hike. Eliot switched, of course, and by the time he got to college he had gotten very good—but that is his story to tell. To this day he is my best coach.

As the children got older, skiing was always a big part of our fun—and it sometimes included slightly crazy stunts.

Ski Safety

Around 1971, Henry Crane asked me if I knew anyone who had access to a computer and who might be able to analyze the ski injury data he and the patrol had been collecting. I recruited Chuck Oman, then a grad student at MIT in need of a statistics project, and we began our studies. By the next year, with encouragement from the National Ski Areas Association and the National Ski Patrol, we designed a control group (uninjured skiers) and an

Eliot still races, and coaches masters ski racing at Eldora near Boulder, Colorado.

experimental group who were interviewed in the Waterville Valley clinic. We found the usual relationships among experience, activity, gender and age, as related to the kind of injury. When we presented our results at the American Academy of Orthopedic Surgeon's Winter sports injury meeting in Aspen, Colorado, we were given the "Best Paper" award. And just like that—we were "experts" in a field composed largely of orthopedic surgeons and patrol directors. It didn't take much to become an "expert" among amateurs! Henry and I started getting invitations and acclaim.

We attended the organizing meeting that Ejnar Erickson, of the Swedish Karolinska Institutet, put together in Riksgränsen, on the Swedish/Norwegian border, north of the Arctic Circle in midsummer 1974. The meeting,

This picture, taken in Snowbird, shows Rob testing gravity and our sanity at the same time.

along with some memorable skiing and beautiful bikini-clad skiers, launched the International Society for Skiing Safety, which became the pre-eminent forum for ski safety. I made lots of good friends and associates, and attended meetings all over Europe and the US for years. I was able to get some research support from Salomon, the French binding manufacturer, to allow me to bring MIT students up to Waterville Valley for the month of January to video skier falls and analyze the needs for binding release and retention. During that period of the 1970s, the injury rate dropped dramatically as the equipment became functional and standardized. I became more involved with the American Society of Testing and Materials (ASTM) for setting ski equipment standards, first as Statistics Chair, and eventually in the early 1990s as overall Chair of the Ski Committee.

Leslie in Snowbird, sanely heading off a cirque.

My interest in bindings function, and especially the way they would need to operate to protect against certain kinds of falls, brought me to the attention of Salomon. Their research director, Gilbert Delouche, often visited the US and demonstrated his Gallic independence by cutting the wires to the seat belt alarm in his rental car. When I showed him how relaxed it was to wait in an orderly queue for the chair lift at Copper Mountain he agreed, but said it would never take hold in France, where maneuvering ahead in the lift line was part of "sports d'hiver." He and Claude Gantet, and his US counterparts, Jackson Hogan and Joe Campisi, supported my projects with MIT students. We would rent a house in New Hampshire and the students

Rob worked in Winter Park, Colorado, filming skiers during the winter of 1991/1992, and got very good at snowboarding. This photo hangs in my Cambridge condo.

would spend a week, skiing part of each day, video-taping skiers on the slope and hoping to record a fall, in which case they would measure the binding release and, that night, analyze the fall mode. My Salomon connection went on for about twenty-five years, through the introduction of their rear-entry boots and their series of low-friction bindings. My few visits to the factory, in Annecy, France, were always accompanied by skiing and good food. All that and free equipment!

The experience led to being hired as an expert witness. Usually for the defense. The typical case would be a rental binding that didn't release, or a skier who was injured crashing into a padded lift tower. I would visit the site, measure the slope and estimate the skier speed and trajectory, try to recreate the accident conditions, test the equipment and prepare a report. If the case was not settled, I would testify in court.

Some cases were non-skiing, like the case where the skier slipped and slid into the woods on a rainy day in Michigan. He sued the ski shop for selling him the garbage bag he was wearing because it did not meet ski clothing friction requirements (there were none). Or the several cases in which I defended the manufacturer of the plastic dishes or plastic sheets used to slide down the hill. They couldn't be steered. Well, of course not. You didn't need an MIT professor to show that—but I did it anyway.

I seemed to do very well in court, and attributed my success to solid preparation as well as to shamelessly trading on my reputation both as a patrolman and as an MIT professor who ran a weekly seminar on ski safety. Apparently, I was good at testimony. I was well prepared, and I treated the jury respectfully, the way I would a class, and explained the physical principles involved in binding release or in lift tower padding. The work took me all over the ski map, from Yugoslavia to the Sierras, and I enjoyed it thoroughly.

Ski-related innovations

The least successful of my business ventures was my invention of the "Pressure Plate." It is a plate to go over the ski binding for alpine skiing to make it easier for a skier to exert his force on the inside edge of the downhill ski, as required by modern techniques for turning. I went into preliminary design and evaluation with Rick Howell, an inventive though unpredictable ski binding colleague from Vermont. He built a couple of prototypes and we brought them along to the International Ski Safety Society meeting in Switzerland for our colleagues to help evaluate. It made for quick and powerful turns, but required the boot to be elevated to avoid an inadvertent release. It seemed promising, but we were unsuccessful in getting any of the binding companies to invest in it. Our first attempt to get a patent was turned down. It seemed that the racer technicians who were assigned by the binding companies to follow their World Cup racers on the circuit already know about this trick. After having invested $10,000, I declared it a loss. The two prototypes sit in the attic at home in NH.

Another unsuccessful attempt to turn an invention into something really valuable was the "Fluid Helmet Liner." This too came out of skiing, and my realization that ski helmets were, as of the turn of the 20th century, not widely adopted for several reasons. They were uncomfortable, hot, and un-chic. They messed up your hairdo. And they weren't effective against the most serious kind of injury—a concussion from hitting a tree or pounding down on the ice. I looked into an improvement in the helmet liner and got a series of our undergraduates to work out the details of a liner. It permitted a viscous fluid, like a water/glycerin mixture, to flow through narrow tubes when the helmet shell was impacted, as in a fall or collision. This would dissipate some of the energy before reaching the skull, and would distribute it around to a larger part of the helmet and make a skull fracture less likely. Preliminary lab tests looked good and I got an MIT Deshpande Center grant to work on commercializing it. The MGH and the Army picked up the project and it led to a substantial three-year grant from the Office of Naval Research.

The military was not interested in sports injuries, but they were very much concerned with traumatic brain injury (TBI)—the kind that is induced by the pressure wave from a Unidentified Explosive Device (UED), of the type so deadly to the military in Iraq and Afghanistan. Meanwhile, I got one major ski helmet company, POC, interested in cooperating with me on the design, and the test results kept getting better and better, although the blast protection was a tougher nut to crack (sorry) than the ski or bike problem. We went toward commercialization by using the MIT Technology Licensing Office and their outside patent attorney, Bruce Sunstein. Meanwhile the whole business of head protection and TBI, from skiing to football, became vastly hotter. But the first patent application was denied since we had neglected some relevant prior part. I was too busy with space activities to follow it any further and so it withered on the vine. Is it still of value? Who knows?

Masters Ski Racing

For me, the drive, and the satisfaction, comes from working hard to achieve a personal goal. Maybe that is why I always enjoyed ski training more than the actual racing. The masters ski racing program got better and better for me with the creation of our own race training program within Waterville Valley's "Black and Blue Trail Smashers." WVBBTS is the oldest competitive ski club in America. A genuinely compatible and friendly group emerged around masters ski racing, and I finally found a sport in which I was proficient and enjoyed the training. Undoubtedly the two were closely linked. We trained at

Waterville nearly every weekend. I travelled to the Nationals out west several times and trained in Austria a couple of times. I loved it so much, I would keep on until the lifts closed because of high winds or darkness. I progressed to near the top of my age group, although always trailing the really top racers,

Here I am, showing my not-so-secret pleasure at my skiing trophies. On March 7, 2018, the Silver Streaks hosted Challenge Cup but I no longer race. Each of the trophies was memorable, to me at least, but what will I do with them, or anything else? I have some of the mugs, and use these for hot chocolate on snowy days.

former national champions. I made good friends in Colorado and California. I went to the gym and rode my bike all year to keep in shape.

And I am secretly pleased to look up at the TV cabinet in Waterville Valley where I keep my rather large collection of trophies, awards, and mugs. Almost each year, when I attended the Winter Conference on Brain Research, I would win the ski race, except when Miles Herkenham, another ex-Amherst racer, would beat me. My strongest event, to my surprise, was Super-G, a speed event calling for daring as well as skill. I enjoyed the speed and won several times. At my best I tied for first place in the Eastern Masters championship.

I only "retired" from ski racing at the age of seventy-five—and then very reluctantly after several concussions. At age eighty, I have switched from

I now have reserved parking weekdays at Waterville Valley. Just for being 80 and still skiing! When I was in home hospice, Silver Streaks sent the sign to me in Cambridge, and I kept it in view in our living room.

ski racing to just easy cruising on the groomed terrain. And, beyond that, our ski club for seniors, the Silver Streaks, provides us octogenarians with a reserved parking spot right up next to the main lodge, and I still love it. Gliding past the snow-covered pine trees and feeling at one with the crisp white blanket is my own sort of zen experience. Even on days too stormy to go up the mountain, I love to strap on my cross-country skis and head into the Town Square with my backpack on to pick up the mail. Spiritual it has been called—and so it is.

Controlling Nature

My whole world seems to be based on using the forces of nature—for my glee, amusement, and even my profession. Well, let me explain that a little.

Nature has provided these strong forces for us to use, and to try to control. There's gravity, of course, and all I have to do is to point the tips of my skis downhill—and off I go, ready or not. And there is water power. Ah, what fun to body surf in the waves, or to float up and down in the ocean, out beyond the breakers, or to swim in a lake or river. And even more forcefully, to feel the whitewater nudge my kayak around into an eddy and to lean on my paddle and allow the river to pull me into the quiet of an eddy downstream from a boulder. And the wind, the way it pulls me along when my sail is trimmed right—the smaller the boat, the greater feeling of controlling the force. And then there is centrifugal force, and my half-century of spinning people on centrifuges to investigate their balance system and to probe the use of centrifuges in space to create artificial gravity.

I've never been into engines or fast cars or motorcycles or speedboats. Not even airplanes, that much. But when it comes to controlling natural forces to move swiftly and deftly—well, that really turns me on. Nearly all of the esthetic pleasures I enjoy seem to involve my ability to control my motion by manipulating an outside force. Take skiing, for example. Gravity supplies the force and I provide the control—by shifting my weight and edging the ski. Whether the sense of motion is enhanced by the speed with which the trees disappear behind me, or the racing gates rush at me on a course, or even the smooth, slow gliding through the woods on cross-country skis—I am turned on by turning myself.

Even before my first skiing adventure, on the local golf course when I was twelve years old, I loved the feeling of rushing downhill on my Flexible Flier sled. Belly-whopping (lying prone, with my head out over the front and my hands on the handles—what a dangerous thing to do!) or sitting up, two to a sled, I never seemed to get cold or tired. Just gravity and the snow and me in control!

Whitewater provided yet another great opportunity for attempting to control nature. Like skiing and biking, it allowed me to control my motion (and to keep my head above water) while the natural power of the river carried me along and toward or away from rocks and the bank.

Education

PS 95, The Bronx

I was jealous of the Rotners, since they went to a school with a name, and not a number. I wore knickers to school, and my knee socks would tumble down to my ankles before I reached there. It was a big deal to get my first "longies" and get away from those damn corduroy knickers. I had a bunch of friends in my class and we all used to play together after school. I always did well in school. There were several bright kids, both girls and boys. My report cards were strong and I stayed out of trouble—but mostly I was curious about everything. Arithmetic was easy and geography and history were like "story-time." I liked to draw maps and would try to sketch them from memory and put in all the states or countries I could manage to recall. In fourth grade I was skipped ahead by a half year, from the January term to the June term. The students were mostly Jewish and the kids were from middle class families that encouraged education.

My only real beef with school came in about the fourth grade when I was marked wrong for my exam answer to the question of the capital of Russia before it was Moscow. The answer Mrs. Katz wanted was "Leningrad," but I reasoned that it couldn't have been Leningrad before the Russian Revolution, and that it must have been still called St. Petersburg.

We didn't have girlfriends, although we did send out Valentine's cards to a few special ones. In around fifth grade we organized a movie outing and I asked Adrianne to go with me. Then I backed out because we were going as a family to Long Beach, but Adrianne told me she wasn't going anyway. Ah me—the first of many such disappointments!

After school, informal debates took place many afternoons. We were all products of our parents' political persuasion and firm supporters of FDR—the "man of the people." Some of the kids said they were socialists and one said he was a communist, and by sixth grade (around 1946) we understood the essential differences. I used to hand out leaflets, given to me by Dad, from the Democratic Party. The leader of our "gang," both as the best athlete and the best debater, was Arthur Cornfield, whose parents did not want him to leave the neighborhood school for the Special Progress (SP) program at Creston. (I ran into Arthur only once more, when I was in grad school and he was a classmate of Sandy Chaitovitz and Art Leff at Harvard Law School. We had nothing to say to each other.)

I used to be late getting to elementary school even though we lived only two blocks away. And I was late coming home from school, too, and would get reprimanded by Mom almost every day. But there was so much "stuff" to do on the way home, like playing marbles. The only thing I liked more than doing stuff was listening to the Yankees game with Mel Allen on the radio. One day, when I was pretty late coming home from school, Mom told me that it was really, really too bad—since she had bought two tickets for us to go to Yankee Stadium that afternoon. But, since I was so late, she had to give them away. I was crushed—but that was that. Did she lie to me in order to stress the importance of being on time? I suppose so, but I will never know. I continued to be late for almost everything for the next fifty years, however. (Now, in my dotage, I am insistent on being early for appointments, dinner, or theater. My punishment is that Vicki, in turn, refuses to hurry along in order not to be late. Maybe that is Mom's real revenge!)

Hebrew School

Hebrew School was boring and went on forever. The Van Cortlandt Jewish Center—or Synagogue—was orthodox and old school. The Hebrew lessons taught almost nothing of use in conversation or grammar. And the Bar Mitzvah drills were just rote memorization with no philosophy or ethics or even religion that I recall. The Saturday services were chaotic and foreign. (Just like the ones I now have seen at the Orthodox shuls from Paris to Lisbon.) Everyone went at his own pace, following his own prayer book. Men and women were separated and nobody cared about kids. What a waste of time, when I could have been out playing with my friends or even reading about religion. And then, to top it off, I saw the vastly different experience that Ellen had five years later when she was the first Bat Mitzvah in the (Liberal) Riverdale Temple. Rabbi Charles Schulman ran his synagogue more like a book club. Lively, relevant and intellectual. Maybe more Unitarian than Hebrew—but enjoyable and meaningful. I might have been less skeptical today if I had gone through that experience. I am pleased to have a Jewish heritage and to have a moral compass to guide me, but there was little or nothing in my training as a Bar Mitzvah to guide me in ethical judgments.

Creston Junior High School—Leaving the Nest

By virtue of standardized tests, New York City had a program for gifted children in which they were sent to the Special Progress program at a junior high school out of the neighborhood. There we would complete three years of study in two years and skip ahead. I was one of two boys and one girl selected from my elementary school. The junior high school for me was Creston, near the Grand Concourse in the Bronx. It required taking two city buses—and cut me off from my neighborhood gang. Creston was wonderful! Everyone was smart. Everyone was curious. Everybody had the answer to the teacher's question and raised his hand (Creston was all boys). I was in a constant competition with my good friends, Steve Rothman and Richard Hannes, as I was reminded by looking at my Creston graduation booklet of pages we signed for each other. I belonged to the Math Club and found that not everything was easy for me. Typing class was probably the most valuable one I had, and I am grateful to this day that I can touch-type. Our keyboards had the letters blanked out.

We all had to be in the chorus in music class and our parts were assigned to different birds. I was a Blue Jay (Blue Jays just mouthed the words). I played the piano and was pleased to be the pianist for the weekly assembly, for which I played a hymn (really). The lowest point came the week when we had a surprise. Assembly was on Tuesday, rather than the usual Wednesday. For non-assembly days I did not wear a tie, and that day I was dressed in my nice light blue short-sleeve shirt, open at the collar. After playing only three or four measures, the music teacher (Miss MacMurray, or something similar) shouted "STOP! You cannot perform before God with your undershirt showing." And that was that for my musical career! Alan Natapoff, my oldest friend, verified the story and how shocked he was all those years ago. He was at Creston with me, and recalls our basketball games played in the rooftop gym, covered with a wire cage to keep the ball on the court. Avery Korman, later a friend of Vicki's and author of books about growing up in the Bronx, was also there. Going to that program was probably the single most important step in my education, more than Bronx Science, Amherst or MIT, not so much for what I learned as for the attitude it instilled, that it was okay—and fun—to be smart.

At some point, probably when I was in junior high school (which modern folks call middle school), at age thirteen or so, we were given the standard IQ test in school. I don't recall seeing the results, but Mom told me I had scored up in the "near genius" range (165). Was that the truth—or was it a "white lie" which served her purpose in convincing me that I was capable of doing anything? Certainly my performance at Bronx Science (upper quarter, but not the top 1 percent) didn't square with any extraordinary intelligence. But I did have a certain confidence to take on almost any task. So, if it was a lie, it worked!

Bronx Science—the Big Step

Most of us took the single comprehensive exam which was used as the only criterion for admission to three of the New York City Specialized High Schools: Bronx Science, Stuyvesant, and Brooklyn Tech. Of course, my parents and I were pleased that I was admitted. By that time, I guess Dad was earning enough money in private practice, so private school was an option, and I heard that they might have had me apply to Horace Mann if I were not admitted to Science. But I WAS admitted, and off I went to my first year, in the annex across the Grand Concourse from the main building, in the fall of 1949. Again, it was a bus ride—the same route as for junior high school—and my life was tied up with that wonderful school. I took journalism instead of the regular English course and really enjoyed it—writing tight articles, interviewing celebrities, and so on. I worked on the *Science Survey* and became Sports Editor. I used that experience to get my part-time summer job writing the softball weekly column for the *Riverdale Press*. If it weren't for French, I would have had smooth sailing all through high school.

There were girls in class by now (that had only started a few years earlier), and dances and music and clubs. I fell in with a fantastic group of friends. We were competitive and enthusiastic. We studied hard and argued. We got together after school to listen to folk music and sing along with Eric Sackheim, who played the guitar. My closest friend was a girl—Joan Leopold. We went to hear the Weavers in Riverside Church, and went ice skating in the new Wollman Rink in Central Park. We occasionally went to Greenwich Village. I swam (poorly) and ran on the track team (slowly).

Of all of the honors I have received, I got the most joy and pride out of being invited to be the Commencement Speaker at the Science graduation ceremony in 2013, and again at their 75th gala at the Waldorf, along with other distinguished alums. The sea of eager faces was now largely Asian and Indian instead of white and mostly Jewish, as it had been in my day, but the energy and the pride of the families was just the same.

Amherst College—A Whole New World

I was admitted to college everywhere I applied (Columbia, MIT, RPI and Amherst). Things were easier then, and not so many kids were born in 1935. At age sixteen-and-a-half, I had no idea what I was getting into, but loved it from the beginning.

Our class of 1956 was bonded by the uniform set of courses in the "New Curriculum." Required math and physics bothered some, but I loved the imaginative teaching of Boris Arons, who had also just come to Amherst. He exuded an insistence on "understanding" beyond just solutions to physics problems, which I rarely found later in my education. English One was a regular challenge and puzzle until we finally learned to write carefully. Be precise, define your terms. The map you held in your hand: was it Amherst College—or was it a map depicting it? When the professor walked in through the window, did that make it a door?

Later on, our "house," Theta Xi, undertook a schoolwide curriculum review, and we had faculty visits from Robert Frost to mere mortals. I loved every minute of Amherst and did well scholastically in everything except French, once more. I never doubted my earlier decision to carry on with the five-year combined plan (aka the 3-2 plan), yielding a bachelor's from MIT as well as from Amherst at the end of five years. I majored in physics, along with five or six others, and after my junior year, I left for Cambridge, Massachusetts, and a very different sort of experience.

MIT—A Lifelong Attachment

I came to MIT in the Class of 1957, from Amherst under the five-year Combined Plan, and began my sixty-five-year journey as an MIT Lifer. Our Class of 1957 contributed at least four full professors to the Institute: Ed Roberts, Al Drake, Alar Toomre and myself. And one landmark building, thanks to Ray Stata.

All of us at MIT knew we were highly selected. Compared to Harvard, up Mass Ave., admission to MIT was strongly made on the basis of academic scores, as it still is today. Larry Bacow told some of us, after he went up Mass. Ave., that, in contrast to Harvard, at MIT he never had a student whose last name was that of a building on campus. (Bacow was Chancellor of MIT 1998-2001, and became president of Harvard in 2018.) I now proudly wear the pin Gerry Sussman designed—a button that proclaims "Nerd Pride." I was very proud to be at MIT, now as then. For my class's 50th reunion in 2007, President Susan Hockfield wrote, "MIT's physical campus may have changed, but its core mission has not. Our commitment to excellence is as strong as ever." I fully agree with that.

Undergraduate engineering education was changed dramatically by the role of scientists during World War II. Engineering science was replacing "handbook engineering." We were expected to be well-grounded in physics and chemistry. The MIT first-year requirements were rigid and tough. According to Ed Roberts, Dean of Students Fred Fawcett told the assembled freshmen class on their first day, "Look to the right of you. Look to the left of you. One of you three won't be here in four years!" Not quite!

All freshmen took full-year courses in chemistry, physics, calculus, and western civilization. Everyone seems to recall the physics demonstrations of Prof. Hans Mueller. Drafting, or descriptive geometry, was also required in Course 16 (Aeronautics) as well as in Course 13 (Naval Architecture). There was no biology requirement back then.

Since MIT is a Land Grant College, we were supposed to be in ROTC and take military science. For most students, the humanities subjects were taken less seriously than the technical ones, even though we had world-class instructors. We all had Saturday classes and that left the rest of Saturday to play and drink.

Every living group, it seemed, maintained an archive of "bibles," the solutions to homework problems and quizzes from previous years. We relied upon our worn copies of "Burrington's" for tables of integrals and other shortcuts. We could both see and hear the "slap-slap" of the leather slide rule case that held our slip stick. The marvelous Texas Instruments calculators were not yet in our tool box. Computation was done in Fortran or COBOL and our punch card programs with their "dimension" statements were batch processed overnight. Personal computers were unheard of. The student innovators in digital systems gathered in the Model Railroad Club, and relied on relays as logic elements.

As undergrads, most of us were far removed from the pioneering research our professors were doing. The 1950s were before the days of Undergraduate Research Opportunities Program (UROP) and before Independent Activities Period (IAP). The chances to get involved with research, or to get to know our professors out of class, were minimal. Except for the requirement for a senior thesis, and the "cookbook" lab exercises, we were largely left to imitation rather than innovation. The answers were often in the back of the book.

The prevailing attitude toward the 'Tute was tough love. Many dorm rooms displayed the MIT banner reading IHTFP. Go ahead and ask someone who was there!

We were highly in demand after graduation. We benefitted from the nationwide growth in technology and the rising status of engineers and engineering. Thanks to MIT's Vannevar Bush, government's support in the Cold War continued significantly. Just a decade after World War II and at the end of the Korean conflict, MIT was the recipient of massive infusions of defense spending, including at Lincoln Lab as well as the Instrumentation Lab and the Naval Supersonic Wind Tunnel beyond Briggs Field. Everyone knew that the Manhattan Project had been the key to shortening the war. Atomic energy was anticipated to be the answer to the world's growing thirst for clean, cheap energy. Radar too, with its development in Building 20, showed the power of engineering. Jets made their way from the military to commercial transport, and the Boeing 707 introduced "jet set" into the social lexicon. We broke the sound barrier and the F-86 was able to outfly the MiG 15. Computers were making their mark on everything from autopilots to stock market guidance. The Whirlwind computer filled a building up Mass Ave., and the Compton Labs, Building 26, would house the Thomas Watson Computer Center and 704 main frame computer given by IBM to MIT in appreciation for all MIT had contributed to computing, and to IBM! Life at home, where most women were still expected to toil now that "Rosie the Riveter" left the factory, was advertised to be revolutionized with electric appliances. When *Life* magazine did a story on our class, I was told, they asked for our class song. In a takeoff on the "M i c k e y M o u s e" theme song, we sang, "M I T, P H D, M O N E Y."

Aside from sailing dinghies and skiing, I did little except study. I was afraid I would fail to keep up with all the MIT geniuses. Only when I made Dean's List the first term did I begin to relax a bit. I continued to get good grades in electrical engineering and discovered the differences between the deep understanding demanded at Amherst and the problem-solving capability expected at MIT. Course "bibles," home problems, and all-nighters were all new to me.

I was lucky enough to land a part-time job in the Instrumentation Lab (now the Draper Lab) to do my senior thesis under Charles Stark "Doc" Draper. I designed and built a vacuum tube voltage to pulse frequency converter. This was a device to convert analog voltages, which might come from an accelerometer, to a string of digital pulses that could be entered into a DDA (digital differential analyzer) for inertial guidance calculations. It used vacuum tubes and was based on circuits in the back of the RCA handbook. Transistors were still over the horizon—and much too expensive to dispense to undergraduates. Besides, there were lots of 6s and 7s. My device worked only for the wrong reasons.

Doc Draper was another hero of mine. He must have seen some talent in me and, both as head of the Instrumentation Lab and the Department of Aeronautics and Astronautics at MIT, he supported and encouraged me. He had made critical contributions to winning World War II, with his inventions of the Mark 2 Gunsight used against air attacks by the Japanese. A firm believer in engineering, he perfected mechanical spinning wheel gyroscopes. He carefully and judiciously selected "his boys" for system developments, and is recognized for his firm belief that we could navigate to the moon reliably using inertial instruments.

1957-1958 Sorbonne

1957 was a pivotal year for me. After graduating from MIT, I sailed off to Paris on a Fulbright fellowship administered by the Institute for International Education (IIE). I finally proved that Mrs. Schwaegler, my high school French teacher, was wrong—indeed, I could learn to speak French, at least well enough to pass courses and have a French girlfriend. On October 4, 1957, Sputnik was launched while we were on the ocean. I turned to space research with a passion—a flame that burned through over a half century of space experiments, astronaut training and teaching.

I attended the Sorbonne during 1957-58, when there was still just one Faculty of the University of Paris, and it carried a mystical appeal full of the romance of the ex-pats of the 1920s.

Work in the solid state physics lab was merely tedious. I went in at the height of excitement around solid state physics and didn't have a real mentor.

I was given an assignment to calculate the secondary radiation involved in some particle collision, and I didn't have the background to carry it out. Most days I sat in front of a Geiger counter and recorded the radiation counts, in English and then in French. Stupid and boring work.

I registered for classes at the Sorbonne and took a week in Cannes to improve my language skills while staying at an almost-deserted little hotel. The owners' small children were happy to talk with me and find out about the cowboys in America. I tootled around on my rented motor bike, including one trip to meet friends in Nice that ended up with a failed motor and ride that took until dawn.

On my return to Paris, I went to the fellowship office and told them I probably should turn in the fellowship. The very French and very bureaucratic lady glared at me over the tops of her rimless spectacles and told me that it would involve far too much paperwork for her—and why didn't I see what else I might like to do at the Sorbonne? So I did.

I found a new course on the math of computers (Calcul Automatique) given in the Institut de Statistique by senior engineers from IBM and from Bull (later acquired by Honeywell), with a lab activity (Travaux Pratique) in the main show room of IBM on Place Vendome. That was a really good move, even though the material would be considered ridiculously elementary now. The text was in English (Birckhoff and Maclane) and the class was small. I teamed up with Roland Gozland to do our homework, and a lifelong friendship grew out of it. I took only one big non-science course that year, a political science overview by the conservative but brilliant Raymond Aron, offered to a packed house at the Sorbonne. After I found that the lectures were being broadcast, I tended to sleep in and listen to them at home.

The student body in those days, before the division of the Sorbonne into separate faculties, was heavy with "professional students," who received their government stipend and spent their days nursing a coffee or a beer in one of the cafes on the "Boul Miche" (Boulevard St. Michel) or the Blvd. St. Germain. I, too, had a café (The Old Navy) thanks to a friend from Bordeaux. I grew a thin beard and wore a black turtleneck sweater with a zipper up the neck that I doffed only on the days I was going to be at IBM.

Graduate Work at MIT

Graduate work at MIT, like most of the critical parts of my education and career, just sort of happened, without a whole lot of planning. On my return from France in 1958, I was offered a position at Bell Labs in Murray Hill, New Jersey, an incubator for information theory, the birthplace of the transistor, and the home of Claude Shannon and Nobel Prize-winning pioneers in the development of the transistor.

We all worshiped Bell Labs. It was the plum job to get filled. In the fall of 1958, I was looking for a novel PhD. Everyone else was studying inertial guidance—nothing left there. At this point, Shannon moved from Bell Labs to MIT. I couldn't just walk into his office. But I'd just read an Institute of Electrical and Electronics Engineers (IEEE) article on reliable circuits with unreliable components. I thought that was really neat because the human brain is full of unreliable circuits. I met Shannon in his little office full of books on the second floor of the MIT computation center, lighting and relighting his pipe.

"What can I do for you, Larry?"

I told him I'd been reading about crummy components.

He said "Yes?"

I asked, "Isn't it interesting? Should I be doing this?"

He said "Yes and no."

But love cast a long shadow. Since Pat was returning to Wellesley, I turned down the chance to be at Bell Labs and wrote to Jim Nevins, my old supervisor at the MIT Instrumentation Labs, to ask about a research assistantship for the fall. It all fell into place so easily compared to the stress and competition of today. He said yes, the Electrical Engineering department said yes (EE, not EECS, since there was no computer science then), and my cousin Howie arranged for me to stay with him and his med school friends on Beacon Street.

I was put to work on a new type of digital computing for control of a spacecraft, the Digital Differential Analyzer. I eagerly agreed when they asked me to go to Rome for the project, only to find out that it was Rome Air Force Base in upstate New York. (The local Air Force guys said there were only two sources of entertainment. One was to drive to the outskirts with your girl and smooch while watching the Revere horse, in lights, gallop on a billboard. The other was to go to the local Italian restaurant on Sunday nights and look at the girls in their sweaters returning from a weekend of skiing. I didn't have a girl, but I did have skis, So next trip I brought my skis and went to Turin Ridge. Not much vertical but it wasn't a total loss.)

In those early days of digital computers, programmed in Fortran, you would make up a program with its Dimension punch card and it would be left for the computer guys to run overnight. The next day you would review the printout, change a few punch cards and send it back for another night's run. Tedious business and not very much insight—until I noticed that all of the results concerning the buildup of errors in navigation were sinusoids with the period of the Schuler tuning, eighty-four minutes. Aha. A lot more thought and a lot less number crunching was called for. I found the analytical solution.

Around 1959, having finished my master's thesis and with nothing much else to do, I applied for Draper's instrumentation doctoral program. With Draper as my mentor and co-author, as well as the funder of my graduate studies, I had nothing to worry about except my new research direction.

In the meantime, our world of aerospace changed—beginning on October 4, 1957, with the launch of Sputnik and the dawn of the space age. MIT's ultra-broad academic track, invented by Doc Draper and administered by Prof. Walter Wrigley, was intended to provide the same sort of science and engineering insights which made Doc so successful—from his World War II airplane tracking gunsight to the reduction of inertial navigation to permit submarines, planes and missiles to navigate without emitting radio signals. Not only did the program require a wide range of courses, it also required you to pass qualifying exam questions from aero, electrical, and mechanical engineering. The oral exam day was especially grueling as the student rotated from one panel of three faculty to another throughout the day. My low point came after my second erasure of a poor attempt to draw the geometry of a two-degree-of-freedom gyroscope on the blackboard. Prof. Ober, who was quite hard of hearing, "whispered" to his neighbor, "This kid doesn't know what he is talking about!" A couple of years later, when I was a fellow faculty member and confronted Ober over the incident, he flatly denied it. I passed all the exams, but it left me with a strong sense of technical humility. I took the range of graduate subjects and particularly enjoyed those having to do with feedback control systems.

MIT's Aero Department under Draper was shifting away from the classical model that Jerome Hunsaker developed. Doc Draper directed both the Aero Department and the Instrumentation Lab where they were designing missile guidance systems and envisioning interplanetary travel. President Jim Killian was the key science advisor to President Eisenhower and, we later learned, he and Edwin Land introduced the concepts for the CIA to build the U-2 spy plane to monitor the missile buildup of the Soviet Union. In 1961, Jerry Wiesner, a faculty member in MIT's EE, and later president of MIT, became President Kennedy's Science Advisor. The Aero department was filled with heavy hitters who regularly moved from Cambridge to Washington and back, including Ray Bisplinghoff, Bob Seamans, and Guy Stever. Draper chaired the National Academy of Engineering. Long before Sheila Widnall became Secretary of the Air Force we had departmental faculty putting in their time at the Pentagon as Chief Scientist of the Air Force or Associate Administrators at NASA. Jack Kerrebrock, Jimmy Mar, Win Markey and Gene Covert all brought some of MIT to DC and, in turn, planted the seeds for Unified Engineering a decade or so later. Later Wes Harris, Dave Miller and Dava Newman continued the important exchange with NASA.

Aero had some great teachers in my student days. We had academic leaders like Holt Ashley and Robert Halfman, as well as teachers who had been active in aircraft design. Wally VanderVelde could somehow shed light in all the dark corners of modern control theory. He would start on the upper left corner of the blackboard and finish his lecture at the lower right corner just as the bell rang. He was by far the most effective teacher I was exposed to, and

I have tried in vain to emulate his organization and teaching skill ever since.

Dick Battin emphasized the underlying concepts behind orbital mechanics. He liked to remind us in public that he taught both me and my son, Eliot. Incidentally, Sheila Widnall succeeded Battin in teaching his orbital mechanics course. Jack Kerrerock assembled a dream team including Jim McCune and Gordon Oates in fields including magnetohydrodynamics and advanced propulsion. Eric Mollo-Chistiansen patiently taught fluid mechanics, and John Barlow and Al Shaw, the omnipotent technical instructors, managed to allow the clumsiest of us to build things that worked! In the emerging field of control systems, Draper competed with MIT's RLE (Research Laboratory of Electronics) and its Servomechanisms Lab—later the Electronic Systems Lab. Doc had hired Sid Lees and Phil Whitaker and my mentor, Y.T. Li, to carry on his own teaching, although they declined to use his arcane self-defining Draperian Notation. My tennis partner, Walt Hollister, and I taught Walt Wrigley's summer course in inertial guidance in Huntsville, Alabama, for a couple of years. Leon Trilling and Harold Wachman were known for their deep concern over the well-being of each student. And, yes, we had one professor, who shall remain nameless. He was sometimes referred to as "The Shadow." Like the radio character, he possessed "the power to cloud men's minds."

Another of my personal heroes, Professor Yao Tzu Li, was my mentor at MIT and the man with whom I developed the Man-Vehicle Laboratory fifty years ago. (Y.T.'s story is told in his autobiography, *Freedom and Enlightenment*, The Lexington Press, 2003.) Born into a privileged family in China, his academic record brought him to MIT in the 1930s to work on aircraft engines with Draper, the developer of inertial navigation and another one of my mentors and heroes. Y.T. returned to China when war broke out, and was assigned to build the factory to manufacture airplane engines under license from the Curtiss Wright company. His factory in Kunming was bombed by the Japanese. He rebuilt it and it was bombed again, and then a third time. Finally, he was told by Chiang Kai-shek to build a bomb-proof factory in a mountain cave. His trek to find suitable remote caves, erect a village, provide electricity and finally to manufacture engines, is the stuff of an adventure movie. He overcame enormous hurdles to equip the Chinese air force with engines. Returning to MIT after the war, he and his brother S.Y. Lee, also an MIT professor, started several successful companies.

Y.T. was the most innovative man I have ever met. Regardless of the technical problem, he would ignore previous solutions, start from scratch, and look for innovative approaches. Our laboratory was studying the human balance system in the inner ear and Y.T. applied that knowledge to build an automatic balancing system for narrow wheel base vehicles to deal with the growing traffic problems in Asia. When I took him skiing one day, he invented a bizarre-looking system of straps and cables, connecting the leg to a hook near the tail of the ski, so that all you needed to do to turn was to lean forward and to the side. That's the basis of modern race technology. Of course, he left it to me to try it out—and darned if it didn't work—preceding modern shaped skis by forty years! From this hero I learned to approach each new problem with a blank sheet of paper, looking for essentially new innovations, rather than beginning with the existing designs.

When it came to choosing a doctoral thesis area, a fortunate and entirely unplanned incident occurred.

My choice of a PhD (actually an Sc.D., because it sounded classier to me) was a complete accident. In 1959, when I was working on algorithms for inertial-optical guidance systems in the Instrumentation Lab and looking around for a thesis topic somewhat different from that of all the other graduate students, Jody and I were invited to Newton for dinner with Howard and Debbie Hermann. On the drive out there, she explained that Debbie was the sister of her ex-boyfriend, which did not seem to bode well for me. I imagined I would be compared to the ex, and not favorably at that. And what about Howard? "Oh," said Jody, "he's a psychiatrist." Oh shit! I resolved not say anything at all about myself or my interests.

As we sat in their wonderful Victorian house with good food and drinks, I kept shifting the conversation away from me and over to Howard's interests. It turned out that he was much less interested in psychiatry than in animal behavior, and in mathematical modeling of the apparently random movements of the crab. "Tell me more," I kept insisting. And so he did—all about the eye movements of the crab and how they were influenced both by the movement of the creature (through its vestibular organs) and the movement of the visual field. I continued the diversion. "Oh, just like the roles of radar and gyroscopes in the guidance system of an airplane." And by then I really was hooked.

Howard insisted that I get to meet his old medical school friend, Larry Stark, a neurologist investigating biological control systems, who was about to move from Yale to MIT. I did so, and we hit it off famously. I decided to do my thesis on the modeling of human eye movements, and convinced Dr. Draper to support the enterprise financially while I went to the Research Laboratory of Electronics to work under Stark. The new field of biomedical engineering was just getting started and MIT was full of dreamers like Jerry Lettvin, Walter Rosenblith, Warren McCulloch, and even Norbert Wiener. I was very lucky to be in the right place at the right time and my thesis and its follow-on into space applications worked out better than I could ever have imagined.

Larry Stark was another of my personal heroes. He was a neurologist who was convinced that mathematical models could lead to an understanding of complex neurophysiology. He came from Yale to MIT in the late 1950s, when cybernetics was born, and Norbert Wiener and colleagues attracted us like the Pied Piper. Feedback control theory, which had grown out of the military problems with gunsights during World War II, was finding applications in biology and medicine. Stark's insight enabled us to make sense of the human eye movement system. We could measure and predict how we jump our eyes between instruments in a cockpit and follow moving objects, even when they disappear momentarily behind trees. For Stark, science was an enormous jigsaw puzzle, and he felt privileged to work on putting at least part of it together. From that hero I learned to appreciate the fun of science.

To my delight, Draper hired me as faculty after graduation in Aero-Astro and I soon chaired the MIT Interdepartmental PhD Program in Biomedical Engineering. I then helped Irving London establish the Harvard-MIT Health Sciences and Technology Program (HST). Larry Stark and I established a small company (Biosystems, Inc). I accumulated all sorts of early honors, awards and promotions—and a lot of international recognition. But, you know, it all seems like luck, and I continue to feel like an imposter. One of these days I will be found out. That I really just fell into a new field to avoid an embarrassing discussion with the husband of my fiancee's ex-boyfriend's sister. And oh yes—as to the Hermanns. I love them. We bought a house in Newton as much like theirs as we could afford. Howard moved his neurophysiology work into my lab at MIT, and they became the godparents to Rob. They gave Rob an enlarger and everything he needed to set up a darkroom in our basement. All-in-all a nice story of how to turn a challenge into an opportunity!

Larry Stark engaged in biomedical analysis using an early computer. A rare photo that shows Larry in jacket and tie. His then graduate student, Larry Young, is second from the right. Figure and caption from Gauthier et al. 2007, Computers in Biology and Medicine 37, 898–902.

Science

Why I Became A Scientist

When my oldest grandson, Josh, was about ten, he asked me to tell him why I became a scientist. We were sitting comfortably in the living room of Diane and Eliot's home in Boulder, and I had to think fast. I could make up some inspiring story about benefitting humanity or unlocking nature's secrets, or I could tell him the truth. And the truth is that science was always a fun game for me. As a kid in school, I was competing against my classmates, and then as I grew into a real scientist-engineer I began competing to uncover some of the secrets of nature herself ("nature, the bitch" as I called her). It was pretty easy for me in school—certainly easier than French!

Engineering first became my choice of professions back in high school. My image was romantic and unrealistic. Would I be suntanned and marching around foreign mountains, with my Panama hat slightly tipped to the side and with my khaki shirt sleeves rolled up, taking sightings through a theodolite as we prepared to build a new dam? Or would I be maybe testing a new prosthetic arm to be controlled just by thinking about it? The wonders of technology were everywhere—and we were as yet unaware of the "law of unintended consequences." Cybernetics, as defined by Norbert Wiener, meant integrating computers (whatever those would turn out to be) with humans to eliminate tiresome repetitive labor. Atomic energy would supply our clean, safe electric power and low-cost private air travel would be a reality.

I wanted to be part of it. Not to copy old designs from handbooks. And not to merely repeat the tried-and-true bridges or circuits that worked before. But to be ORIGINAL. I wanted to be an INVENTOR! Money and prestige were of little concern. I knew that with the elite education I was afforded I would certainly be able to keep food on the table. Most of all I wanted to be recognized as an INNOVATOR.

My earliest innovation came at the stately Amherst College library when I was a freshman. My part-time job at the reserve book desk consisted of giving out and taking back books that were lent out for a two-hour period. Most of the rush was on the night before a big exam, like the freshman World History course, which I was also taking. I could hear the thump every time a book slid down the return chute. I had to retrieve the books and reshelve them, to be lent out again to the next student who asked. Since there were only a few large courses that had exams on any particular day, it would have been possible to construct several parallel chutes to allow the students to return the books and ease the re-shelving work. But that would have meant some carpentry in the library.

Instead, I came up with a "supply and demand" algorithm. For each big course I could calculate the number of times per hour I would need to put down my own studying to go next door to empty the return bin and reshelve its contents. The data I needed was minimal: the number of students in the course, the total number of copies in the library, the demand rate and the return rate. Even without getting up to check the individual titles being returned, I could get a good estimate for any course just by counting the number of thumps in the return bin—all without having to interrupt my own studying more than once or twice an hour.

It worked! We never ran out of books because they were piled up in the return bin. I got ample time to study. And I was happy to be paid my 55 cents an hour.

At least until the night the head librarian visited the reserve book desk. "Why" he asked, "are you sitting down and reading, while books are piling up in the return bin next door?" Proudly I explained my algorithm, and that we never ran out of books.

I was fired! I spent the rest of the year earning my 55 cents per hour clearing dishes from the dining hall tables. And that was my first innovation. The lesson was clear. Not every invention that works will be appreciated and grabbed up by the market!

Pupil Dilation and Eye Movements

The pupil as a biological servomechanism

Think of the pupil as adjusting the f-stop in our eye. Just as the aperture on our camera adjusts the amount of light that reaches the CCD or the film (remember film?) in the focal plane, so does the pupil regulate the amount of light, called the flux, hitting our retina. When we go outside on a sunny day the pupil constricts. In a dark movie theater it dilates. Along with the slow dark adaptation of the visual purple in the rods and cones of our retina, the variable aperture of the pupil allows us to see in a very wide range of illumination, from starlight to sunlight. The pupil response to light changes is a biological servomechanism that regulates the light reaching the retina. Everyone knows that.

But the first person to cast the phenomenon as a biological servomechanism was a young neurologist, Larry Stark, discharged from the Navy following the Korea conflict and working at Yale-New Haven hospital. Larry had the soul of an engineer trapped in the body of a physician, and sought to describe biological control systems using the new technology of servomechanisms. At Yale he studied with Prof. Schultheiss, the author of a leading control systems textbook. Larry thought of the pupil as part of a feedback system—constricting or dilating to control the light flux hitting the retina. He modelled its stability and its response time to light changes. He even predicted that the pupil reflex could be driven into oscillation if the gain, from pupil diameter to light flux, were to be artificially increased enough.

And he tested this by concentrating the incoming light onto a small disk centered on the edge of the pupil. Even a slight dilation or constriction of the pupil would cause a substantial shift in flux reaching the retina. And, lo and behold, the pupil broke into oscillation—and at just the frequency predicted by his mathematical model! This was a major finding in the 1950s, when cybernetics was attracting increasing attention, especially at MIT and Harvard. It brought Larry to MIT, to the Research Laboratory of Electronics (RLE), successor to the famous "Rad Lab" that developed radar during World War II. And it brought me to sign on as Larry's first graduate student, to do my doctoral thesis on another biological control system—the movement of the human eye. It even convinced Doc Draper, my boss at MIT's Instrumentation Lab, to fund my doctoral research from his own discretionary account.

Developing the Eye-Movement Monitor

Larry's pupillometer was pretty simple. It just reflected incoming infrared light (IR) off the iris and onto a photodetector. The smaller the pupil, the more light was reflected from the iris back to the photodetector. However, I was interested in measuring where the eye was fixating.

I refined the design of a rather simple eye movement monitor, based on a concept Larry Stark came across in Switzerland back in 1959. To extend the pupillometer concept to an eye movement monitor, I used a small infrared illuminator that bathed the eye in invisible low levels of radiation. I placed two small photodiodes, really tiny lightmeters, facing the eye. When the subject looked to one side, the amount of light reflected by the white of the eye, the sclera, would be larger for the photodiode positioned away from the direction of gaze, and the difference between the voltages from the two sides indicated how far the eye had turned.

It required calibration, of course, and only measured horizontal movements initially, but it was simple, cheap to build, and far more convenient than the methods then in use for teaching poor readers how to scan a page. I used the new device for my thesis experiments, and Larry and I included the design in several publications.

Biosystems Inc.

I added vertical eye movement sensing to the eye movement monitors and a method to allow it to be used in any lighting condition, and generated a fair amount of interest in the eye movement community. Those people were interested in clinical applications, from neuro-ophthalmology to balance studies and psychology research, as well as evaluation of advertising, as it could tell if the reader was looking at the product or at the model. It might even help in studies of driving and flying behavior. It was simple, but it worked, and with encouragement from MIT, we got a patent on the device. So, we started a company and incorporated it as Biosystems Inc. in 1962. In addition to our only product, we bid on NASA and Department of Defense (DoD) research announcements in the areas of biological control systems.

At first, in addition to the two Larrys, we had a part-time secretary and a technician, and operated out of a single room in the basement of Technology. Actually, there was a third Larry—the owner of Larry's Barber Shop across the hallway from our office. We would borrow chairs from him to make the office look more occupied when the auditors would visit. We had study contracts from NASA to look into biomedical instruments for space flight as well as the problem of pilot-induced oscillation and manual control of airplane, helicopters and spacecraft. We were able to hire several of our friends on the faculty of MIT and of Harvard to join us as consultants. McGraw Hill signed a contract with us to publish our Biological Control Systems work as a book in a new and rapidly growing field. (Alas, the reports never made it beyond the NASA Contractor Report stage and the book never appeared. My fault. A big mistake!)

When we got a large contract from the Air Force to develop a physical model of the eye that would show exactly what the image on the retina would

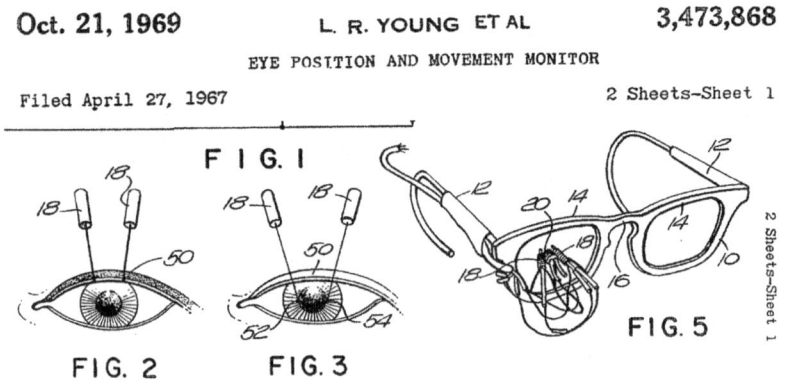

Oct. 21, 1969   L. R. YOUNG ET AL   3,473,868
EYE POSITION AND MOVEMENT MONITOR
Filed April 27, 1967   2 Sheets-Sheet 1

Figures from my patent application for an eye position and movement monitor. A 1967 announcement from Space Sciences Inc. read, "The Eye Movement Monitors (designed by Biosystems Inc., of Cambridge, Mass., which joined SSI in November 1967) are shipped ready for use in a handsome wooden case, complete with spectacle frames and sensor assembly, interconnecting cables, 110 volt recharging cable, batteries and instruction booklet. Prices start at $1550."

be as the eyes scanned a scene, blinked, and dilated the pupils, we were really going strong. (In those days of early interest in applying the principles of biology to the design of machines, it was thought that the model eye could lead to a defensive weapon to incapacitate, or temporarily blind, an enemy anti-aircraft gunner in Vietnam. It never was taken to that next step!) We hired a general manager, Joel Newman, and moved into a whole floor in an old loft building on Ames Street, which is now MIT's Human Resources, but at that time was a warehouse for Brigham chocolates. (I smelled great!) We hired another engineer and wrote more proposals. But management disappointments and difficulties were commonplace—and upsetting. One manager put down more hours than he actually spent on sponsored projects. His justification was that his salary was too low. Another one resented being asked to perform sophomore-level engineering mechanics calculations. He had actually forgotten how to do them, which would have been acceptable if he had owned up to it.

Larry Stark left MIT in 1965 to become Chair of Bioengineeering at the University of Illinois in Chicago. And, most importantly, I was doing well as an assistant professor at MIT, and much preferred it to worrying about the business. It's not that I had any objection to making money, or even to having a lot of it, as long as the accumulation of wealth and the showing off of riches didn't become an end in itself. It's just that, well, it was sort of boring! And I wasn't really good at what is called "compartmentalizing." If something was bothering me with business, say personnel or finance, I couldn't put it aside while I wrote a lecture or a grant proposal or even played squash.

So, with the help of our lawyer, we set about evaluating the company and looking for a partner. We had two offers. The classiest one was from Arthur D Little (ADL), the prestigious engineering consulting company in Cambridge that had deep MIT roots for decades, and was starting up a large biology division. They were cordial, gentlemanly, and experienced in dealing with academics. Everything seemed right—except that their offer was much lower than the other one.

The second offer was from Whitaker Corporation, a growing conglomerate based in LA. They had acquired Space Sciences Inc., a small research group in Waltham, Massachusetts, and were anxious to get into the biomedical engineering field. Whitaker owned Columbia Yachts and spoke of offering a couple of their sailboats to us. They were slick and growing fast in that era of hi-tech conglomerates. Their offer was much higher than that of ADL, and we took it. But the offer was in terms of restricted stock, which we could not sell for a number of years. I consulted for Space Sciences, which took over the eye movement monitor business, and saw it acquired by Gulf + Western and then a private buyer from New Jersey. They were behind on paying me and I began to lose interest. They are still in business, as Applied Sciences Lab in Bedford, Massachusetts, and their engineering director is my friend and former student, Josh Borah.

With time, the Whitaker stock became less valuable. My father bought quite a bit and watched it decline further and further. Larry, who was by that time a professor at U Berkeley, sold his half and used it to buy his house in the Berkeley Hills. I sold my portion, which was quite low by then, to pay the several thousand dollars to carpet the house in Newton.

I learned lessons from that experience. It wasn't that hard to make money in business if you wanted to put that as your top priority. I really hated dealing with personnel issues, especially firing anyone. And finally, I would rather spend my time on science than on business, so I never became rich. But I live as though I were rich and don't lack for money, so I have no complaints.

Consulting

From the very beginning of my career, I was able to find a tie between my scholarly work on human balance and orientation and the interests of "real world" users. It has not only been a useful income source, but it kept me grounded in applications, which made for motivating classroom case studies. Here are some of the ones I recall with pleasure.

My very first consulting job was with Bolt Beranek and Newman, beginning in 1962. I earned only $50/day, but the bagels and coffee were free and Joyce Chen's restaurant was around the corner in Fresh Pond. The big-name project at that time was the design of the acoustics for the new Lincoln Center (Avery Fisher) Hall, but I was off in an area dealing with human response.

My work for Jerry Elkind was on adaptive manual control, which is simply the way people change their manner of control when the vehicle changes its behavior. Think of how you alter your steering and braking when your car hits a patch of ice and you will have the right general idea. Dave Green, who was then still at MIT teaching psychology, worked with me on our experiments, all of which were controlled through an analog computer—a species of electronic computing that was important up until digital computers started getting fast enough and big enough.

Our work on models of eye movements brought Larry Stark and me to the University of Michigan Willow Run Lab, in the old factory where tanks were turned out during World War II. More analog computing. And some work on selecting contractors for the US Army on missile guidance, conducted at the Picatinny Arsenal in New Jersey. For several summers running, my friend and office mate, Walt Hollister, put on a short summer course on inertial navigation at the University of Alabama campus in Huntsville. Von Braun and his colleagues from the German rocket facility were already established there, and I did a little early work for one of them on the Saturn rocket. Our daily tennis game in the park was periodically interrupted by the noise of arriving airplanes at the old in-town airport.

Another exciting branch of consulting involved airplane accidents. Frequently they dealt with my knowledge of spatial disorientation and how a pilot might have lost his sense of position or failed to maintain control. The most complex case was the Northwest Airlines crash on takeoff in Detroit. An early example of the danger of reliance on automatic warnings, this case involved the alleged failure to set the flaps prior to takeoff on a McDonnell Douglas jetliner. All this took place even though an automated voice warning should have announced "FLAPS" when the throttles were advanced for the takeoff roll.

One fascinating case was against a charter operator of a flight, in which a healthy airplane dove into the Red Sea. It involved not only disorientation but the fascinating hierarchy that inhibited a young co-pilot from overriding the control actions of his very senior captain. Still other cases took me to Airbus in Toulouse to look at de-icing systems. Other European visits, as a lecturer for NATO's Advisory Group for Aerospace Research and Development (AGARD), took me all over France and Portugal to look into human factors issues. All of these cases were interesting extensions of the material I taught in class to real world accidents, and brought the real case back to the classroom as case studies the next year.

Pupils and mental workload

The "near triad," consisting of convergence of the eyes, accommodation by altering the power of the lens, and pupil dilation, was of central interest to us. It had already been known that the pupils reacted to certain emotions, such as excitement, fear, or arousal. Artists had known that a model looked more attractive, and even appeared more attracted to the viewer, if her pupils were dilated. The pupils also dilated in response to fear, so pupillometry was added to the battery of lie detector measurements. Larger pupils also correlated with sexual arousal and other emotional drives. Kahneman and Beatty showed that they also opened up depending on how difficult the material was! Even the military intelligence services asked for our help in adapting an instrument for help in the interrogation of Viet Cong prisoners. Would their pupils dilate when they were shown a photograph of a village that contained a Viet Cong hideout?

After Larry and I sold our company to Whitaker Corporation, their Applied Science Laboratory improved and marketed the eye movement devices. They continued to press for applications in the advertising field, but without much success. My remaining research interest in the field was as a means of measuring mental workload with a non-invasive physiological monitor.

The concept of limits to mental workload is based on the idea that, even with full attention, a human will get overloaded when the task demands too much. Many variables go into determining that limit, including training, fatigue, motivation and environment. As one approaches that limit, the ability to also perform secondary side tasks goes down and the number of errors goes up. Subjective workload scales are widely used in aviation to rank the difficulty of a task. We sought to validate some physiological measure, which would objectively signal when a task was too demanding and required more training, better displays or a lower demand. Some of the promising measurements were heart rate and its beat-to-beat variability, respiration, galvanic skin resistance, muscle tension and sweat rate. We concentrated on pupil dilation and eye movements with support from NASA.

We were fortunate to get Danny Kahneman, then a young researcher working for Jerry Brunner at Harvard, to advise us on the pupillometry interpretation. Many years later, Danny went on to win the Nobel Prize in Economics for his work on fast and slow decision making, as described in his best-selling book from 2011, *Thinking Fast and Slow*. It was unrelated to our work on pupillometry. Pupillometry became a commercial emphasis of a few small companies in the US and in Germany, headed by former students or post docs of ours.

Crabs in Puerto Rico

In 1961, Jody and I took advantage of a joint research grant my advisor, Larry Stark, had with José del Castillo. I made a plan to spend the winter in Puerto Rico, working on the eye movements of land crabs in his lab at the School of Medicine. I had been measuring human eye movements in Cambridge and wanted to investigate the way the crab stabilized its eyes when it was rotated or exposed to a moving visual surround. That problem, of visual-vestibular interaction as an example of multi-sensory integration, was a constant during my entire career.

My plan was to measure the lateral eye movements. I would affix a miniature light bulb to each stalk with fast-setting epoxy and track the motions by measuring the current from a pair of photodiodes positioned above the crab. The crabs were about eight inches across. They were reputed to be delicious, and prepared as a Puerto Rican specialty, but there was no way I would eat my test subject or any of his kin. Until the day that one of them clamped down on my finger with its claw and wouldn't let go. It was painful and I had to get the technician in the next room to pry me free with a screw driver. Dinner that night, in a good restaurant, was, of course, land crab. And it was delicious indeed.

Monkeys and cats in Zurich and Paris

Volker Henn was a fantastic colleague in Zurich and later, when we coau-thored the translation of Ernst Mach's *Fundamentals of the Theory of Movement Perception*. He was good friend, who died when he was quite young. Our skills complemented one another's, and we cooperated rather than competed. I did the engineering and modeling and Volker did the surgery and neurophysiology.

Monkeys were our partners in the vestibular research that we did together at the Kantonspitaal in Zurich during my 1972-73 sabbatical. They were ju-venile rhesus monkeys and participated, willingly or not, in our experiments on single unit recordings during visual and vestibular stimulation. Seated in chairs, strapped in with striped seat belts, and eating bananas, they actively made the eye movements we required. Unlike Volker, I had no affection for them, and managed to avoid being bitten. (I was less fortunate in that regard during my astronaut training with rats in Houston years later.)

When the monkey eye movements began showing a slow drift, rather than the snappy saccade we wanted, Volker and I would get strong coffees and the monkey would get a shot of amphetamine—and fifteen minutes later all three of us were ready to get back to science. The only times the monkeys would show us any active fight was when we loosened the straps before taking them out of the experiment chair and back to their cage. Volker said that, just like people, if they are kept in tight restraint they are passive, but give them a little freedom and then the revolution is underway. (I still miss Volker, who died much too young. He was a great friend and my best collaborator.) I continued with some monkey vestibulo-ocular experiments when I returned to MIT in 1974, in conjunction with Emilio Bizzi, but they didn't really go anywhere and I lacked the sense of participation and fun I had in Zurich.

We were performing parallel experiments about eye movements during rotation on rhesus monkeys and on human volunteers. We hit pay dirt on our very first experiments. I had modified a gyroscope rate-testing table I sent over from MIT to spin monkeys while recording activity from their brain cells. The thrill of "listening" to a cell in the brain as its firing rate signaled just what we had hypothesized was amazing—to both of us. For me it remained unmatched until I got my first live results from a space experiment, some ten years later. But I was not about to become a neurophysiologist—too much standing around, and not enough theory. However, the collaboration was terrific. I wore my white coat in the hospital, and at first accompanied Volker and Dr. Baumgartner on rounds to learn about clinical cases, but too many of the patients spoke only "Swiss German" and I could only barely keep up with the "High German" spoken by Volker in the lab.

We came up with a preliminary finding that the adaptation of the monkey's vestibulo-ocular reflex in the horizontal would not transfer to the vertical axis, but it didn't really feel right to me. So, other than mentioning the experiment in a meeting abstract, I did not publish it. I was right. David Robinson and a student of his at Johns Hopkins showed the contrary result a little while later. It is not a bad idea to trust your instincts.

In 1972-73, I divided my time between Zurich, where we were living, and Paris, where I went every other week to do research with my dear friend, Alain Berthoz, at the Laboratorie du Physiologie de Travail, just up the street from the Luxembourg Gardens. We had two projects there. One was on human "linearvection," the self-motion induced by a moving visual field, much like feeling that your train is moving when it is actually the train on the next track that is crawling ahead. The other one, much more interesting, involved drunken cats.

We know that the vestibular system adapts. For example, a patient who loses all function from the labyrinth of one ear, say by an operation to remove a tumor, recovers nearly normal balance and eye movements after some time. Lower animals adapt even more quickly. We were interested in the possibility that we could undo this adaptation and look at the underlying asymmetry of a previously adapted subject. Think about the business of trying to walk a straight line under the influence of alcohol. We all have some underlying asymmetry between the two labyrinths. Is it possible that we learn to compensate for the imbalance, but that one of the effects of alcohol is to undo this compensation and reveal the underlying imbalance? Well, we were about to study this in humans—but decided first to look at cats.

We would create a drastic imbalance in the cat by plugging the semicircular canals on one side (Alain did the surgery). And sure enough, shortly after the operation they were strongly unbalanced, leaning toward one side, and with asymmetric eye movements. But they recovered in a matter of a few weeks. Then came the alcohol, delivered by injection since they would not drink any spiked drink we offered. Measuring their exact blood alcohol level was not so easy, until Alain made contact with colleagues at the Pernod laboratories where they had the facilities and came to our lab in their little truck with the liqueur bottle painted on the side, and picked up our refrigerated tubes of cat blood for analysis. The drunken cats, in addition to their general depression that comes with alcohol, and accounting for the previously established effect of the lighter alcohol on the denser inner ear fluid (endolymph), also showed us what we hoped for. They returned toward their previous, unadapted, post-surgery behavior—at least their eye movements did. In our 1977 paper, Alain and I claimed that the alcohol was selectively inhibiting that part of the vestibulo-ocular system that was changeable, or plastic. Nobody has followed up on this to my knowledge, and anyway the whole business of the pharmacology of alcohol was too complex for me to jump into as an outsider—and an engineer at that. The one thing I did carry forward from that year of experimenting with cats was an allergy to cat dander, which is with me to this day and makes my eyes itch and nose run.

Eye movements to probe the vestibular system

By the 1980s, my interest in eye movements shifted from understanding and modeling the eye movement control mechanisms to using eye movements as a tool. They served as a convenient way to look into the response of the vestibular system. I moved on to research the control of eye movements when the head is turned. We recorded eye movements during extended head rotation as well as during the nauseating experience of turning the head during rotation. We measured torsional movements of the eye during head tilts in the lab, in parabolic flight and especially during space flight.

Prediction and the Internal Model

In looking back over my sixty-year research career, I am struck by several themes that keep reappearing. (*Around and Around*, as the title says.) Is this admirable perseverance or stubborn single-mindedness?

In fact, a look back over my research and even over my daydreams reveals a remarkably consistent, even monotonous, revisiting of some of the same knowledge and reapplication of the same ideas. One such theme, for example, is that of "Prediction and the Internal Model." The concept is hardly original. Versions of it had been discussed by Erich von Holst, Maseo Ito, Hans-Lukas Teuber, Richard Held and others—at least since the 1930s. The idea was that when we absorb sensory inputs we try to fit them into a meaningful context, which allows us to make continual predictions about the state of our bodies and our environment. Later versions fell into "ecological" theories.

But the internal model idea is somewhat different. It maintains that we are never acting on feedback from the current measurements. Feedback loops are far too slow. Instead, we are using measurements to build up a model of ourselves and our surroundings, which in turn is used to predict the forthcoming input. And does so in time for us to act upon it. This model, which we call an "internal model," can learn and can adapt to changing circumstances.

We walk differently on an icy driveway than on a sandy beach. I may hear familiar 19th century classical music differently from modern or oriental music. We like to listen to "standards" because we know what notes or chords are coming next. But we are always looking ahead and making up a consistent scene and dynamic story. When the subsequent sensory inputs disagree with the predictions we have a "conflict." And conflicts are upsetting. Like pressing the up button and having the elevator descend, or awaiting a classical musical progression, only to be jarred by some twelve-tone alternative or even worse. It is disturbing, even sickening at times. (Think of the sea sickness that develops when the pitch of the boat is not in the expected direction.)

The miracle is that we learn. We progress from crawling to walking to running, and we learn to deal with unexpected falls. When we walk down a flight of stairs we anticipate that the rise and run of each step will be the same as the preceding one—and risk a bad tumble when taking the usual step at the wrong place. (The ancients built their castle stairs that way for defense.) So, whether we are learning a new language by speaking freely, rather than working our way through grammatical tables, or perfecting a batter's swing by predicting the trajectory of the ball and then adjusting the stance or the grip on the next swing, we are always using old sensory information, out-of-date results, and the expectations of an existing internal model, to compare with the actual outcome. And finally, but continually, if we see a consistent pattern of disagreements between our predictions and the actual sensory feedback, making adjustments in the model to do it right the next time.

Most of these ideas were incorporated in Rudy Kalman's "Kalman Filter," at the heart of "Modern Control Theory," which swept over the engineering field in the 1960s. They fit right in with my ideas about how the brain exercises adaptive, predictive control over simple "reflexes" like head and eye movements. (Not really simple sensorimotor at all!)

I know the internal model works in science and I try to imagine that it can also be applied to real life too! (Aren't the social dynamics of a family based upon internal models, predictions and adaptation? How about geopolitics too? Or the expectations we place on the performance of our leaders?)

The Birth of Bioengineering

[*These notes were written in 2014. In 2018, the Man-Vehicle Lab was renamed the Human Systems Lab (HSL). —LAY*]

The Man-Vehicle Lab - Fifty-two years and counting

Draper hired me to initiate some bioengineering activity in the department. He put me together with Y.T. Li to provide adult supervision. Y.T. had been on my thesis committee and taught controls and instrumentation, and furthermore was a generous and amazingly innovative man. To describe the beginning of the Man-Vehicle Lab (MVL) I refer to Y.T.'s own description, taken from Y.T.'s autobiography, *Freedom and Enlightenment. My Life as an Engineer in China and the United States* (The Lexington Press, 2003).

> During the late 60s, my closest colleague was Larry Young. He had been a student of mine and had asked me to be the advisor for his doctoral dissertation with Dr. Draper as its Chairman. In fact, his experiment was conducted in the lab of

Professor Stark of Harvard Medical School. It was a study of the movement and response of human eyes. He was the first to discover that human beings go through different stages of sleep, with each stage being marked by different patterns of eye movements. Thereafter, experts studying sleep often used the movements and responses of the eyes as a significant reference in their studies. Larry's discovery constituted an important contribution to the field of physiology. He was engaged as an Assistant Professor in our department soon after the completion of his dissertation.

At that time, I was interested in the relationship between man and the movement of a vehicle in which he is riding. Take for instance the biker. When he is biking, he can choose his direction by turning his front wheel while relying reflexively

[In 2021 and 2022, several offices were converted to a Human Systems Lab (HSL, formally called MVL) student space. Larry's office, in particular, became the HSL reading room. This photo was taken Feb. 15, 2022 by Michael Person of MIT Department of Earth Atmospheric and Planetary Science. —LAY]

on the same front wheel to keep his balance. Indeed, riding a bike gives a sense of freedom. I was experiencing bothersome traffic jams during rush hour, and realized how we Americans had gotten used to driving big and spacious cars everywhere. It occurred to me that the length of the vehicle does not affect traffic jams as much as its width. But if we cut down the width of the vehicle too much, it would cause a series of problems in maintaining the needed stability, both static and dynamic. Finally, I made a donation to support one of my students, Bill Resner, to do a Master's thesis studying a three-wheeled vehicle whose two back wheels were capable of self-tilting and self-balancing, The tricycle should be able to stop without toppling over by adjusting itself automatically to the banking of the road surface and also to tilt automatically when turning the corner, just as the biker does. The principle involved is in fact not at all complicated–the gravitational force simply needs to negate the centrifugal force when the bike is turning a corner.

The first half-century of the MVL is described in the MIT Department of Aeronautics and Astronautics Annual Brochure in 2013, "The Man Vehicle Lab at 50," and in a booklet in 2012 (MVL@50, https://hsl.mit.edu/sites/default/files/Final_MVL50_Book.pdf). This lab has created a warm and collegial atmosphere, as well as an extraordinary publication record and participation in over a dozen space flights. The faculty and students get together at international meetings and form lifetime friendships and two marriages.

The successive Directors, Y.T. Li, myself, Chuck Oman, Dava Newman and Jeff Hoffman (jointly) are all friends and skied, sailed and played tennis together. I have the privilege of a spacious and generously appointed office, in which I am surrounded by my computer, desk, files and my library, and almost every bit of paper I have used in fifty years. My lab space reached pieces of three floors in the 1980s, and included our NE-2 simulator, a Link-1 Flight simulator, Howard's microneurophysiology lab, and our ground version of the Space Sled. With the change in physics emphasis of the Kavli Center, with its lack of interest in human space flight, our lab space was constantly threatened, and reduced to less than just the ground floor of Building 37.

We carry on our thirty-year-old traditions of weekly lab meetings and Journal Club, and the Sherry Award for spirit and service. We no longer go out to lunch together and everyone seems over-committed. I am clearly on the old age side of the demographics these days, and often feel like an "old geezer" with old ideas—but that doesn't stop me from offering them and occasionally having them accepted. After all these years, I still enjoy the feeling of entering my office and the privilege of serving as a professor there, with all of those amazing students.

Bioengineering at MIT–A Long Labor and a Painful Birth

We began bioengineering education at MIT with *nothing*. Going back to the early 1960s, we had no department, no degrees, no curricula, no funding, and no mission statements. We had no student admissions and no dedicated "faculty slots." We offered a large number of courses without any unified goals or coordination of requirements. We had no teaching labs nor means of introducing engineering students to clinical practice.

So what *did* we have that propelled MIT and Harvard into leadership in this evolving field during the 1960s and 1970s?

First of all, we had enthusiastic and optimistic faculty. We organized courses around topics we wanted to teach. We got together across discipline boundaries to offer courses to eager and exceptionally talented students. We formed collaborations, between MIT, Harvard Medical School (HMS), and the local hospitals. We followed the money, from private foundations and the government. Enough money was offered by National Institutes of Heath (NIH) to consider founding a new medical school focused on application of the physical sciences to the life sciences. And we won support for Program Projects in Biomaterials and in Rehabilitation. We were swept up in the post-war optimism that allowed us to believe that we could overcome all obstacles with technology. Finally, we were blessed with academic leaders who saw the boundaries between life science and physical science as opportunities for advancement—in education as well as research—rather than insurmountable barriers.

The evolution of bioengineering is described in Walter Abelmann's 2004 history, *The Harvard-MIT Division of Health Sciences and Technology: The First 25 Years, 1970-1995*. The detailed listing of subjects, instructors and programs is contained in "A Guide to Biomedical Engineering and Physics at MIT and Harvard," prepared by the Harvard-MIT program in Health, Science, and Technology (HST), January 1976. I am grateful to Chuck Oman, then the Helmholtz Associate Professor of HST, for recovering this valuable document.

Each of us has a unique story to tell—of how we grew from a collection of individual labs and lectures to a discipline that is vital and widely recognized. In this book, I look back over sixty years, I trace my own journey through this evolution—from graduate student in Instrumentation in 1960 to Chair of MIT's Committee on Engineering and Living Systems in the 1970s, and I recall the contributions of some of the people along the way.

By the 1960s there were over a hundred "courses" (which we at MIT call "subjects") related to bioengineering, loosely defined. Most of these were devoted to the interests of an individual professor and were given irregularly. They ranged from freshman and sophomore physics, with examples from biology, to groundbreaking subjects in quantitative physiology for seniors. In response to the NIH interests, we had organized the Biomaterials

Science Program, the Rehabilitation Engineering Center, the Biomedical Engineering Center for Clinical Instrumentation and research programs in Nuclear Medicine, Optimization of Radiation Dose, and others. Each of these federally funded centers provided support and training opportunities for graduate students.

My journey overlaps the birth of "bioengineering." Many of us have similar tales to tell, but all share one common thread. From our curiosity about biology or our interest in disease, we stumbled into the possibilities for technology to make a difference. A *big* difference. My own adventure began with the quantitative physical description of the way the vestibular system in the inner ear stabilizes the eyes when the head moves. And how it allows us to sense up and down, and to avoid disorientation, even in flight. I was lucky enough to fall in with an amazing crew of students and faculty at MIT at just the right time. I was lucky enough to be at MIT, first as a student, then as a faculty member, and eventually as one of the pioneers of our graduate program in Biomedical Engineering. I was further lucky in my timing—Sputnik was launched and began the Space Age in 1957—the year I graduated from MIT.

This is my story, but I was only one of over 100 faculty, from MIT and Harvard, who assisted in the birth of the new field we grew to call "bioengineering."

Looking back to the 1950s and on through the 1960s, the growth of this new academic discipline may seem inevitable. Following World War II, with the development of new tools to analyze complex systems and the parallel emergence of technology applicable to studying living systems, the time was right for the birth of a bioengineering curriculum. C. P. Snow's influential lecture, "Two Cultures and the Scientific Revolution," had the impact of awakening us to the sacrifice of breadth that followed from our disciplinary schisms. Humanities disrespected Science and Science rarely took notice of the Humanities. Even within science itself the traditional disciplinary divisions inhibited the interdisciplinary collaborations that were calling out to be recognized. Biology was on the cusp of emergence as a quantitative field. The double helix was only revealed in the 1950s. When I went through the five-year undergraduate joint program between MIT and Amherst College, I successfully petitioned to skip biology in favor of chemistry's quantitative analysis. Whether or not we were in the sciences, the boundaries were hurdles rather than "on ramps." And they were daunting. One of the attractions of MIT for me was the chance to meet, and maybe even study with, Prof. Norbert Wiener, whose book, *The Human Use of Human Beings*, introduced "Cybernetics" and the potential for consideration of the brain as a very special kind of computer. I only got to meet him a few times, introduced by my thesis advisor, Larry Stark.

What exactly was "bioengineering" back in the 1960s? We didn't even have a recognizable name—somewhere in the academic mix between medicine and technology? When Larry and I began a small startup in Cambridge to develop eye movement monitors, we called it "Biosystems Inc.," which seemed sufficiently unrestricted.

With or without a recognizable name, a new industry was emerging and it would need a new breed of engineer. Scanners and lab computers, artificial organs, and prosthetic limbs all were emerging technologies. The new industry called out for education in a field we would come to call "bioengineering" or "biomedical engineering" or even "biotechnology." Medical education had barely changed since the Flexner Report of 1910 identified the challenge of teaching physical science to medical students without watering down the content. Where better to bring together these two branches of physical and biological science than here in Cambridge? East Cambridge, between Kendall Square and Central Square, was smelly and decrepit in the 1960s. It is now home to the Broad and the Whitehead Institutes and is the world's cauldron for biotechnology. So who are we and how did we evolve?

Whatever we called it, one couldn't deny or ignore its existence and its growth. From a handful of individual collaborations and a few isolated subjects, our field evolved explosively. The story is rich and complex, involving two great universities and two previously separate fields: life science and physical science.

In this memoir I will restrict myself to my own journey: from an Aero-Astro graduate student in the early 1960s to a faculty member leading the new Interdepartmental PhD Program in Biomedical Engineering. Along the way, I played a role in the establishment of HST and Bioastronautics, but those are separate tales.

My thesis advisor, Larry Stark, liked to tell the following story to define our field. The brilliant and eccentric psychiatrist and mathematician, Warren McCullough, was asked the following question over his second Manhattan at his own "faculty club"—the F&T Deli in Kendall Square: "Warren, we know what engineering offers to biology: instrumentation, sensors, math models and so forth. But what does biology offer to engineering?" Warren's answer was predictably short and direct. "Problems," he said. And problem-solving is what MIT engineers thrive on!

Even within our emerging field of biomedical engineering we saw our own culture gaps—between life sciences and physical sciences and between engineering practice and engineering science as it had emerged following the successes of World War II. When it came to discussions of clinical exposure for HST Medical Engineering and Medical Physics (MEMP) students, we would argue that an engineer didn't need to repeat a circuit design once it had been mastered and our MD colleagues would vigorously disagree. They would argue that no two cases (or patients) were the same and that professional success depended upon seemingly endless repetition.

And then there were the surface issues—trivial but important. What kind of lab coat and identification would the biomedical engineers wear in the hospital? Where would they eat?

Even up at the level of the HST Executive Committee, these cultural wars were being fought—or suppressed. Pride and prestige were always lurking somewhere. Apparently, a major objection was aimed at Henry Rozovsky, Dean of Harvard's Faculty of Arts and Science. His proposal was that MIT faculty in HST would not only carry Harvard professorships—but would be listed as such under Harvard's Faculty of Arts and Science. "My God," exclaimed one classicist, "The next thing you know, professors in the Business School will want to be listed!" It certainly supported the old saw that faculty meetings are so rancorous because the stakes are so small!

Consider the reasons that Harvard and MIT, two of the world's recognized leaders, in science and technology on the one hand, and in medicine on the other hand, took so long to jointly form the Program in Health Science and Technology. As Derek Bok said, in his forward to Abelmann's book, "Every Harvard President early in his term begins to think that there should be much more collaboration with MIT. It is, after all, a remarkable thing to have two of the world's most renowned research universities only two subway stops apart," or just down the Charles River. Individual collaborative research projects, ranging from sanitary engineering and public health to high energy radiation therapy, had been going on for decades—and blossomed in the post-war atmosphere of peaceful uses of technology. Walter Abelmann's history of HST traces the long background and multiple obstacles involved.

My question is not, "Why did it happen?" but why did it take nearly a half century for Harvard and MIT to join forces in research and education in biomedical engineering? Part of the answer lies in funding. There was a lot on the table—but not enough. According to which account you read, the proposal from NIH's Director, Jim Shannon, was to fund MIT for a new medical school based on science. The clinical training would be conducted at Massachusetts General Hospital (MGH), which would require a substantial additional contribution. That was too much for MIT, led by its new president, Howard Johnson, to swallow, and the proposal was declined. But it got a lot of the faculty thinking, and eventually led to the formation of HST. The academic leadership at MIT (Weisner and Rosenblith) could not ignore the discussions begun at Harvard Medical School (HMS) about establishing a major biomedical engineering program within HMS. Many of us participated in a substantive summer study at MIT's Endicott House in Dedham. Finally, we began to hear from all sides about how to successfully bring about a joint enterprise.

The Interdepartmental Doctoral Program in Biomedical Engineering was proposed by the MIT Committee on Engineering and Living Systems (CELS), established by Dean Gordon Brown. Dean Brown asked me to take over the CELS in 1967 and encouraged us to define a PhD curriculum in Biomedical Engineering within the MIT School of Engineering. I was involved from 1967 through the establishment of its natural successor in HST, the Medical Engineering and Medical Physics PhD program, begun in 1978.

Bioengineering and the Aero-Astro Department

As far as I know, MIT's earliest bioengineering collaboration was with the Harvard School of Public Health—early in the 20th century. But by the 1960s, there was little visible collaboration between MIT engineers and biologists or physicians. Little—but not none.

A human radiation facility on the corner of Mass. Ave. and Vassar Street delivered experimental radiation doses. Prof. Walter Rosenblith edited a volume for the IRE (now the IEEE) on biomedical applications and included Prof. Bill Seibert as a senior faculty member. There were a handful of other brilliant faculty members at MIT who were attempting to apply mathematics to life sciences—but there was no academic or research organization to draw it together. Possibly the most influential group among us were those invited participants at the first Josiah Macy Foundation conference, held in New York in 1948. Warren McCulloch attended, and Norbert Wiener introduced the concept of cybernetics, which laid the groundwork for his influential book. The theory of servomechanisms, developed during World War II to improve the accuracy of gunsights and artillery, suddenly seemed applicable to the regulation of physiological systems as well. Stability and oscillations were observed in the regulation of blood pressure. Homeostasis was identified as a basic principle in physiology.

I became aware of the pioneering work of Larry Stark, a neurologist who had just moved from Yale to MIT to extend his work on the pupil reflex to light as a servomechanism. Larry set up a lab in the Research Laboratory of Electronics (RLE) and the Electronic Systems Lab, guarded carefully at its entrance by an owl that would track all who entered or left. I did my ScD thesis there on human eye movements as a sampled data system. When I joined the MIT Aero-Astro faculty at Doc Draper's invitation in 1962, there was no such thing as "bioengineering." Within the Aero-Astro department we had nothing—no courses, no labs and no faculty research devoted to applications of theory in biology or medicine. However, Doc discussed his own interests in the capabilities of men and machines in performing the kinds of sensory-motor and cognitive tasks inherent with spacecraft guidance and navigation. He reminded me more than once that he had studied psychology at Stanford before moving East.

In my first year on the faculty, Doc assigned Prof. Phil Whitaker and me to work with him on a paper on the relative advantages of human-in-the-loop vs automatic control of aerospace vehicles. We presented it at the 1984 International Astronautical Congress in Warsaw to international acclaim. When I was identified there as Doc's co-author, I was immediately welcomed and feted, especially by the Eastern Bloc delegates—with lots of bear hugs and plenty of vodka! Both the paper and my presence as "Draper's Boy" were important for my early career and gave me recognition on both sides of the Iron Curtain.

Doc encouraged me to continue the PhD work that I did with Larry Stark in RLE on the subject of mathematical models of human eye movements. He gave me space—in fact the entire basement of the empty Building 41—to set up an eye movement lab. He supplied the necessary start-up funds that allowed me to buy used optics from Edmund's Scientific.

When it came to research funding, with my background in eye movement control and my interest in space travel, the obvious sponsor was NASA. Early in the Apollo era, NASA's interest in the protection of astronauts from space motion sickness was significant. Thanks to the support and confidence shown to me by Capt. Ashton Graybiel of the United States Navy, head of the Navy's Aeromedical Lab in Pensacola, Florida, and Dr. Walton Jones, head of Life Sciences for NASA, we were funded to explore human spatial orientation during unusual motion, on Earth and in space.

At that point, my former advisor, mentor, and lifelong friend, Prof. Y.T. Li stepped up to help me and my first PhD student, Jacob Meiry. We designed a horizontal human acceleration device, which we installed in Building 17A, part of the former "blow-down wind tunnel." Together we established the Man Vehicle Control Lab—later shortened to MVL. Meanwhile, I became more and more aware of the developing interest in biomedical engineering at MIT.

Our first Aero-Astro course offering in bioengineering grew out of a summer course I organized on topics in Aerospace Medicine. Sherman Vinograd, MD, had been leading a NASA effort to develop a standard set of lab facilities for use in human space flight. It was called Integrated Medical and Biological Laboratory Measurement System (IMBLMS). We worked with Richard Brubaker, an ophthalmologist at Massachusetts Eye and Ear Infirmary (MEEI), to develop a non-invasive device for measuring venous blood pressure. (Incidentally, several students got up and left my seminar on "central venous pressure" when they learned I was discussing pressure in veins on the human body and not on the planet Venus.) Sherman was preparing to return to Wisconsin after years at NASA HQ and he needed to tune up his clinical skills. A year with us at MIT, combined with hands-on refresher training at Beth Israel, met his needs. In return, he helped me put on our first Aero-Astro bioengineering subject. We covered everything from acceleration tolerance to dealing with thermal stress. Sherman called in his friends and former NASA grantees as guest lecturers. Among other star performers was Raymond Loewy, the famous designer of everything from the post-war Studebaker to the Coke bottle. Loewy taught us about individual space and habitability for long flights.

This summer course evolved into a regular graduate course in Man-Machine Systems, relating to displays, controls and decision aids for the pilot and for air traffic control. I joined forces with my dear friend, Tom Sheridan from Mechanical Engineering (ME), to offer this joint course for grad students in Aero-Astro and in ME. It has continued over the decades. Aero-Astro continued to support the subject with talented faculty, including Ren Curry, who moved on to NASA's Ames Research Center, Rafi Sivan, a leader in "modern control systems" on sabbatical leave from the Technion in Israel, and Missy Cummings, the first female Navy pilot to land on an aircraft carrier. Support from ME was more difficult to obtain. Tom was frustrated by the absence of additional faculty in ME and eventually accepted a joint appointment in Aero-Astro, where he and his work were more appreciated. The basic subject matter was renamed to the more politically correct "Human Engineering Systems" and has continued, to this day. It serves as one of the core subjects for graduate study in Human Vehicle Systems, within HST and Aero-Astro.

Some, if not most, of the early bioengineering subject at MIT grew out of the mutual interests of faculty from different departments or labs. A good example, for me, was the graduate "Seminar in Sensorimotor Processes," which I taught for three hours every Wednesday night. The subject of the seminar was adaptive control—in physiology and in systems. I teamed with Profs. Dick Held and Emilio Bizzi of the Psychology Department. Dick, along with Prof. Alan Hein, had pioneered experiments showing the importance of active rather than passive motion in allowing cats to adapt to movements on a centrifuge. Klaus Hepp, on sabbatical from ETH, Zurich, where he held the theoretical physics chair once occupied by Einstein, was a friend who became increasingly interested in the neural circuitry underlying saccadic eye movements. Bizzi was a leading neurophysiologist, recruited by department head Hans-Luke Teuber, to strengthen that department's basic science core. Emilio went yet deeper and recorded single units in the monkey brain stem during adaptation to head movements while they were wearing image shifting spectacles. And I related it all to "Model Reference Adaptive Control Systems," which had been introduced by Phil Whitaker of the Aero-Astro Department. The students and the faculty debated the fundamental nature of sensor-motor adaptation in animals and machines. It was the most enjoyable teaching activity of my entire career! I hope the students felt the same.

The last graduate course I introduced at MIT was Flight Simulation, begun as a joint effort with my Aero-Astro colleagues, Profs. Bob Simpson and Antonio Elias of the Human Transportation Lab. Their Boeing simulator, contributed to MIT when the US SST program closed down, made for realistic demonstrations. I taught mostly about simulator motion systems and their relation to pilot disorientation.

Within my first year on the faculty, in 1962, I was called in to meet our Dean of Engineering, Gordon Brown. To my surprise, he asked me to take over MIT's Committee on Engineering and Living Systems (CELS). The goal was to establish a doctoral program across departments. MIT already had several senior faculty in the field. I knew only Prof. Murray Eden of Electrical Engineering (EE) and Prof. David Rutstein, the head of Preventive Medicine at the Harvard School of Public Health. They taught a course in Biomathematics, which I inherited and offered in the early 1970s as an alternative to Biostatistics for HMS students who were facing a "math requirement." I emphasized feedback control systems in the context of homeostasis and attracted a small but dedicated following. Murray moved on to NIH where he established and led their Bioinstrumentation activity.

I was only twenty-seven years old, in my first year on the faculty, and by far the least experienced member of our new committee. Absent any senior guidance, I proceeded to organize an Interdepartmental PhD program in Bioengineering, reporting to Irving Sizer, Dean of the Graduate School. I followed the same structure as the Interdepartmental Program in Instrumentation—Draper's structure, under which I earned my doctorate.

We organized the program with few required courses. Over the objection of many students, we required a passing grade in Biochemistry to at least introduce the engineering students to some basic medical science. We also needed enough rigor to assure Prof. Ascher Shapiro that our new program would not be an easy "back door" to an MIT doctorate!

Admission, as I recall, was by oral exam and interview. The PhD program was listed in the MIT Bulletin under several departments. We attracted many outstanding early PhD candidates.

The assignment from Gordon Brown to lead the MIT Committee on Engineering and Living Systems was a pleasure for me. I was met with encouragement everywhere. Everyone I asked agreed to serve in the planning and implementation of the Interdepartmental Doctoral Program in Biomedical Engineering. And what an outstanding group of colleagues and friends they were.

From Nuclear Engineering we recruited Prof. Gordon Brownell, whose lab at MGH pioneered Positron Emission Tomography Scans (PET). Mechanical Engineering was already well represented in Biomedical Engineering, encouraged by its department head, Ascher Shapiro, whose pioneering work in fluid mechanics was applicable to blood flow on the newly developed artificial heart. He was backed up by Prof. Forbes Dewey. But the powerhouse in ME was Prof. Robert Mann, a designer who was attracted to the field by Norbert Wiener to work on the MIT Arm, a motorized above-elbow prosthesis. Chemical Engineering contributed Profs. Earl Merrill and Clark Colton, whose specialty was in the preparation of blood vessel surfaces that would resist the formation of blood clots. Prof. Bob Rose was called in from Materials Science. He, Prof. Igor Paul, and my college buddy, the orthopedist Eric Radin, specialized in joint wear. Profs. William Siebert and Larry

Frishkopf from EE introduced nerve impulse modeling. Harvard's Division of Engineering & Applied Physics was home to Prof Richard Cronower.

We admitted and graduated about one student per year at first. Rena Bizios studied with Prof. Clark Colton in Chemical Engineering and went on to become Biomedical Engineering (BME) Department Head at Rensselaer Polytechnic Institute (RPI). Byron Lichtenberg came to study with me because he was advised by Prof. Bob Mann, his SM advisor, that it would be the most direct path to becoming an astronaut. And he was right, having been selected as America's first Payload Specialist to fly my experiments on the Space Shuttle. Greg Zacharias left the Instrumentation Lab to study with me on human spatial orientation and went on to found Charles River Analytics and later to become Chief Scientist of the United States Air Force (USAF). Chuck Oman joined the MVL and stayed as a faculty member in Aero-Astro, holding HST's Helmholtz Chair and has remained a close friend and associate to this day. Prof. Jacob Meiry served on the Aero-Astro faculty in Instrumentation and made important early contributions to modelling human spatial orientation, but drifted out of the field.

Across the board, our group of faculty interested in bioengineering didn't get much attention at MIT until money became an issue. As I heard it, the Director of NIH, Jim Shannon, was convinced that the basis for medical education in the US was completely misplaced. Instead of building on chemistry, especially biochemistry, we should be building on physics. But there were no existing medical schools that were of top level and willing to build a collaboration with engineering or the hard sciences. He needed to start fresh and introduce a medical education program rooted in the physical sciences. But where? The academic hierarchy was already frozen. Not Johns Hopkins or Yale or the like. Only MIT stood out as a major engineering school, recognized for physical science leadership, without an existing medical school. Shannon reportedly held out a multi-million dollar offer to induce MIT to move ahead. That was a lot of money back in the 1960s! But MIT had just inaugurated a new president, Howard Johnson, who was hesitant. The venture would require a strong clinical partner, including faculty. Harvard already had this loose affiliation with top hospitals, and the idea was to bring MGH in as the medical partner. But there would be an additional cost to MIT of upwards of another $100 million. Too much to swallow, especially for a new leader. And most of all, we were lacking a strong individual who could build the bridges between medicine and engineering, and between MIT and Harvard. Several decades earlier, when MIT was about to merge with (or be acquired by) Harvard, there was an outpouring of protests from MIT alums, which eventually squelched the deal.

And then a miracle happened!

MIT leadership identified a world class physician, highly respected within the Harvard Medical community, distinguished, and well-spoken with administrative experience in medicine. And he was a Harvard alumnus as well.

His name was Irving London, and he was then Chief of Medicine at Albert Einstein Hospital in the Bronx. He was recruited to lead an extended summer study at MIT's Endicott House in Dedham. Almost all of the interested parties at Harvard and MIT were invited to attend. Even me!

Walter Rosenblith, then Associate Provost at MIT, said of his 1970 recruitment of Dr. London, "I was very impressed with his broad knowledge, his research, and his willingness to look at new institutional forms that had to be created at the frontiers where medicine, the physical sciences, and engineering meet. When it was time to find a director for this new enterprise, I was enthusiastic in supporting the selection of Dr. London. His appointment turned out to be most fortunate. He has guided HST into its present fruitful and prospering position." [from Walter Abelmann, The Harvard-MIT Division of Health Science and Technology, 2004.]

We discussed the economics of health care and how it would be altered by new technology. Jerry Weisner provided support from the top and HMS was represented by major players like Henry Rozofsky, Robert Ebert and Eleanor Shore. By the end of the summer a plan emerged and the Harvard-MIT Program in Health Science and Technology was born. I was appointed to the Executive Committee, which met every Wednesday morning in London's office. The tasks of melding two proud and independent universities were not simple, and required endless negotiation. Whose class calendar to use and what to do about tuition? Could faculty be paid by BOTH schools? Who would grant the MD (Harvard) and the PhD (either one)?

To raise the money for the new HST Program, MIT brought in Walter Koltun from the President's Office. Walter would travel to Palm Beach and return with generous donations. Fred Bowman, a young researcher, added administrative support. And over all of these complex bi-university negotiations, sat the calm and effective team of Rosenblith and London.

However, we still had no proof that this kind of engineering/medical training would be useful, and accepted in the hospital environment. Then came another miracle. A charming and well-spoken young man, recently out of the Air Force, appeared on the scene. He had a PhD in EE from MIT and an MD from Harvard. He was an internist at Beth Israel Hospital. And everyone liked Roger Mark. Roger was recruited as co-director.

As time went on through the 1970s and 1980s, HST became the home for graduate education in bioengineering. The PhD track through HST, called Medical Engineering and Medical Physics (MEMP) was formalized and grew its own procedures for admissions and research, with the leadership of Prof. Ernie Cravalho. I continued to administer the interdepartmental PhD program through the 1980s, assisted by Gordon Brownell, who stepped in while I was on sabbatical at Stanford in 1987. But it was by then redundant and its functions were transferred to MEMP. By then, Biomedical Engineering had leapt out of the cradle and was toddling toward recognition as an independent department with world-class faculty and students. Today's version incorporates MIT's Institute for Medical Engineering and Science (IMES) and collaborates with biotechnology in one of MIT's major impacts on modern health and society.

By the 1970s, the bioengineering educational activities began to attract the attention of others in the School of Engineering. We submitted and were awarded an NIH Training Grant. The focus of the training grant was the development of three undergraduate subjects in Quantitative Physiology. Each would assume at least a junior level of engineering ability (electricity and magnetism, fluid physics, feedback control theory, etc.). It would appeal to the growing number of MIT undergrads applying to medical school. Each subject would be accompanied by laboratory sessions.

Over several decades, the courses matured and attracted many of the School of Engineering faculty. In the fall we offered "Cells and Tissues," led by Tom Weiss and Bill Peake of EE (Electrical Engineering Department). Their extensive notes on the Hodgkin Huxley Equations for nerve transmission were later published as a significant textbook. In the spring we offered one course in Organ Transport Systems (heart, lung, etc.), organized and largely taught by Roger Mark and Forbes Dewey, and another in Sensori-Motor systems. This last one, which I directed for many years, covered vision, hearing, balance, proprioception, energetics and locomotion. For each subsystem we recruited an outstanding engineering professor who made appropriate use of mathematical models, as well as active weekly labs. Among the key contributors were Bill Siebert, Larry Frishkopf, Bob Mann, Chuck Oman, Dan Merfeld, Conrad Wall, and Neville Hogan. It was great fun! And over the years, I have run into several of our alums who reported that they learned far more physiology in their undergraduate Quantitative Physiology courses at MIT than they ever did in medical school!

My emphasis on Quantitative Physiology is not meant to imply the absence of other courses developed for MIT undergraduates. The 1976 edition of "A Guide to Biomedical Engineering and Physics at MIT and Harvard," listed over seventy-five "Subjects of Interest to Biomedical Engineering Students" at Harvard and MIT. Of course, most of these subjects were well-established courses and were listed multiple times. But still, it represented the pool of talent and interest even before organized programs and curricula were introduced.

By now, in 2021, there is no doubt as to the effectiveness of Biomedical Engineering and the influence of the HST Program. The establishment of the Biological Engineering Department in 2005 recognizes the importance of research and education in this vital direction.

Air and Space

D-1 MISSION

The D-1 (D for Deutschland) Spacelab Mission was an unexpected bonus for us. Going back to 1976, when we first decided to propose experiments on the Spacelab, the pressurized manned lab to be carried in the cargo bay of the Space Shuttle, our aim was to understand and counteract the motion sickness most astronauts were reporting when they got into orbit. This was a not-very-well-kept secret that only became known after it nearly caused the mission cancellation during Apollo because of severe motion sickness, not quite to the point of vomiting, during a transfer involving the Lunar Excursion Module and the Command and Service Module.

Thanks are due to my friend and old MIT grad student buddy, Rusty Schweikart. The central piece of equipment supporting our proposed experiments for the first Spacelab mission was the "Vestibular Sled," a four-meter-long track on which a chair could be moved back and forth in the Spacelab. The idea was to use the sled acceleration to test the function of the human balance system, essentially the otolith organs in the inner ear, and to see how it adapted to weightlessness, in which there was no longer the constant gravitational pull we experience on Earth. Actually, there is gravity in Low Earth Orbit, but since we are in orbit and "falling" at an acceleration equal to gravity, we "feel" weightless. Together with my colleagues at the Defense and Civil Institute of Environmental Medicine in Toronto and at McGill University in Montreal, we proposed and were selected to do a major in-flight investigation.

But the Shuttle was not yet built or tested, and as time went on and costs mounted while the schedule slipped, the allowable payload mass was reduced, and the NASA team in Huntsville, Alabama, began to rigorously impose their rationing of all critical resources, including experiment power, communication bandwidth, crew time and especially mass. Every gram counted in our experiment. The understanding was that the two partners in Spacelab 1, NASA and the European Space Agency (which built and paid for Spacelab in return for some rights to use it), would evenly share these resources. When it came to weight, ESA was over the limit and was told to significantly slim down.

The only really large ESA facility on board the Spacelab was the Vestibular Sled, some 200 kg, as I recall. The ESA response tactic was to propose removing the sled from the mission, which was clearly not going to happen, they assumed, since the sled was the key facility in major research programs of both NASA (including our MIT-Canadian program and another from NASA's Johnson Space Center) and a huge ESA program lead by Prof. von Bamgarten, with researchers from Germany, France, Belgium, Sweden and elsewhere in Europe. This strategy was referred to as the Washington Monument Strategy. When threatened with a budget cut, the National Park Service would supposedly respond by proposing to close the Washington Monument. Since that was unthinkable, the budget would be restored. As ESA hoped it would be for the sled. But guess what! NASA said go ahead, and the sled disappeared from the mission. We were allowed to keep our other resource allocations and hastily invented a new set of protocols and a small, light hand-rotated chair was provided by our British colleagues. In the end, Spacelab 1 was a success for us, but we still had yet to run our sled experiments in space.

The next Spacelab mission available for us to consider was a German mission, D-1, which flew in the fall of 1985 on STS-61A. (STS stands for Space Transportation System, usually just called the Space Shuttle, or simply Shuttle.) The German teams argued to fly the sled there, and I was able to convince the NASA head of Life Sciences, Gerry Soffen, to bring our team back on board and fund another mission for MIT. Great, I thought. A chance to spend a lot of time in Germany for testing, simulations, and crew training. I would be able to improve my ability to speak German, which had deteriorated in my decade away from Zurich. And there would be lots of opportunities to ski in the Alps or hike in the Black Forest.

By now, I thought, we would have worked out all of the petty jealousies and operational details that plagued us on Spacelab 1. I got along very well with "Von B," my German counterpart, and settled into extended stays in the charming Hotel zum Quelle, in Porz-Wahn, Cologne, Germany. The ESA and German Space Agency (DLR) Life Science activity was located on the edge of the Cologne airport, and the local expression for welcome was "gemütlich." When I returned to the hotel with a nasty cold one rainy day, the manager's wife told me to go to my room and go to bed, and that she would take care of the cold. Her prescription included hot tea with lemon and schnapps. And I guess it worked—I don't remember much.

But dealing with the DLR engineers was something else entirely. They made every exaggerated caricature of German stubbornness seem understated. Schedules were schedules and there was no room for flexibility. When a technical problem arose, of the type that would have brought on a brainstorming session and shared assignments in Houston, we would instead have a formal meeting in which all the managers and engineers brought in their briefcase full of files. Designed, not to find a solution, but to make it clear that the failure was not their fault. My two natural allies, the NASA Mission Specialists, were treated like poorly educated technicians. They weren't. It may not have helped matters that one (Guy Bluford) was black and the other (Bonnie Dunbar) was a woman who weighed less than the minimum for which the sled was designed and couldn't ride it.

Only the presence and good humor of our MIT technician and training supervisor made the whole experience tolerable. In the final analysis, the mission was another success. We got our data, and although the sled never flew again, it was used for pre/post flight testing in Houston for several more years. And as to my proficiency in German, I could understand most of the conversations but wisely chose to keep my mouth shut, or restricted to English and the list of NASA acronyms when in technical meetings. And there was no skiing or hiking. I hurried back to Boston at the end of each session.

Playing Soldier

I was never in the Army—or the Navy or the Air Force, for that matter. But when I did get involved in the military in the 1980s, it was as an Air Force three star general, or rather the civilian equivalent, called a Distinguished Visitor (DV-9). As a freshman in college, with the Korean conflict (not a war, mind you) still going on, most of my Amherst classmates joined the ROTC to avoid the draft. I didn't, but I kept my grades up to maintain a student deferment, and, on graduation from MIT, I took a job as an engineer for the Sperry Gyroscope Company in Great Neck, New York. The work was designing circuits for the advanced bomber, the B-58 "Hustler," using a new component, the transistor. The job carried a defense deferment, so I was again free of the draft for a while. (In those days, if you could make it to age twenty-six you probably would avoid military service in "peacetime.") Then graduate school carried a further deferment, and by then the draft was abolished (before the Vietnam War).

I worked on some DoD research programs, both at MIT and as a consultant during my early professional life. I was not a pacifist, but I was certainly against any actions that would lead to an unwarranted war. What a wimp. Did nothing about it. Never marched in a protest. Never thought about the results of the use any of my contributions to destroy homes or villages—only for "defense." The technical challenges were really interesting, so I gladly went ahead and did my research. But the more appealing problems, for me, lay in the training and utilization of pilots and astronauts in space travel. I began working on manned spacecraft just as soon as I could after Sputnik was launched. When I returned from Paris to MIT in 1958, I was lucky enough to be re-hired by the Instrumentation Lab and resumed working for Jim Nevins.

My early work and my master's thesis were on the propagation of errors in inertial navigation for an orbiting spacecraft. Each afternoon I would submit my punch card Fortran simulation program to be run overnight on the lab's IBM 650 Digital Computer. The next day I would get back my stack of cards and a printout of the simulation of the error propagation. Only after many runs, all of which showed a periodic oscillation in the error, did I realize that the problem could have been solved analytically, with pencil and paper and old-fashioned math, if only I had thought harder about it. An important lesson for me.

Afterwards I was put to work on the DynaSoar, which was a program to place an Air Force pilot in command of a reusable space vehicle that could glide back to a landing on Earth, as sort of a predecessor to the Space Shuttle. When DynaSoar was cancelled, I wanted to do something where I would have more control over my professional future. I was convinced to return to graduate work and pursue a doctorate in the Instrumentation Program, overseen by Doc Draper. That lead to application of control theory to physiology (specifically to human eye movements) and to being hired by Draper to the MIT faculty, and the establishment with Y.T. Li of the Man-Vehicle Lab. Our activity was all non-military, sponsored by NASA, and brought me closer and closer to the issues of man-in-space. I had no relationship to the military until the late 1970s when I was appointed to the Air Force Scientific Advisory Board (SAB).

The SAB was a blast! Started after World War II by Dr. Theodor Von Karman, it was a prestigious and wide-ranging assembly of leading engineers and scientists who were called upon to advise the Air Force on matters of science and technology that could have national defense implications. Of course, it involved clearances to see classified sites and materials. And it opened my eyes to a host of fascinating issues, many of which have come to pass and others of which remain in the realm of science fiction. It brought me the civilian rank of a three-star general, which meant that when I travelled, an Air Force T-38 jet would come to pick me up at Hanscom Field in Bedford, Massachusetts, and bring me back at the end of the trip. No flying experience—but lots of time to look over the shoulders of the pilots. We stayed in the fanciest of the military quarters and were briefed by the top engineers. And best of all, they even seemed to listen to us.

I was put on the Airlift panel, which included flight simulators and the Air Force support of Special Operations. We were shown aerial refueling to a large transport plane off the coast of Nova Scotia and I nearly jumped out of my seat when I heard the sudden, loud, and unanticipated bang as the refueling boom made contact. I flew and evaluated all sorts of simulators (aerial refueling is really stressful—do you truly want to get that close to another airplane? Even in a simulator?) One trip we took was to Eglin Air Force Base in Florida, where we experienced what it was like to fly around the Florida panhandle on a very dark and moonless night, looking out of the helicopter with night-vision goggles. Once I took off the goggles momentarily and realized how blind we (including the pilot) would be. It was terrifying.

On another SAB trip to Oklahoma I was involved in critiquing the very old moving-base flight simulators for the venerable C-130 transports. When I then was asked if I would like to compare the flying qualities to a real flight, I agreed and was put into the co-pilot's seat. The young captain in command asked for some written authorization to allow me to sit there. Within a few minutes, a written message came back to his base commander from MAC

HQ at Scott Air Force Base in Illinois, saying something like, "Prof. Young is approved to do anything he wants!"

And then there were demonstrations of dropping men and vehicles out the back of cargo planes at low altitude, and seeing Army paratroopers relaxing on the tarmac at McGuire Air Force Base in New Jersey (how could they be so cool before jumping?). But the most memorable of the SAB trips were our annual inspections of foreign locations. Air Force Bases in Japan, Korea and Germany were all notable for looking like little bits of the US displaced abroad. Finally, as the Chair of the panel, I was asked where to go for my final such trip. Now I had always wanted to go to Antarctica, ever since I was a kid and read about Admiral Perry at Grandpa Retman's house. My Air Force counterpart, Gen. Don Brown, told me that the request would be denied as frivolous. Instead, he suggested that I ask for the panel to be sent somewhere that would combine being dispatched from a foreign country, and presenting challenging issues of communication, navigation, meteorology, and a long flight with no reasonable alternate landing sites. The response to my request was that the Air Force could only arrange that if we went to Antarctica. And indeed, we had an amazing trip, to Hawaii, Samoa, then Christchurch, New Zealand to await better weather, and finally McMurdo Bay. No penguins there but Antarctica was amazing even for a brief look-see.

Some of the other SAB trips were equally illuminating. On one inspection trip to Korea, which of course included brief overnight stays in Hawaii and then in American Samoa, we spent time at a base that looked just like the M*A*S*H set. The knowledge that the North Korean military was only a few miles away was daunting to me, but part of the challenge to the troops. The highlight to Gen. Brown was taking us shopping on the local economy, having a suit made to measure, and picking up a "Members Only" jacket (then a hot fashion item) for a song since it was made in the factory "after hours" and outside the regular inventory. Other trips, to Tokyo and Frankfurt, were interesting, but the biggest surprise was Berlin. This was during the Cold War, and the listening facilities at the US air base were truly amazing.

PI in a Box

My 1988 Stanford sabbatical research topic suggested itself to me on the basis of my previous Spacelab flight experiments. On our first flight, the principal astronaut operator in space was my own recent PhD, Byron Lichtenberg. He knew both the experiment hardware and the scientific rationale for each calibration and measurement as well as I did. He knew what to do when a piece of hardware failed. In fact, when our fancy new Nikon 3 camera with its thin film 250 frame cassette failed in fight, I radioed up to try substituting a TV camera. But Byron had already started to install it. Our next flight was crewed by highly intelligent Mission Specialist astronauts who had not benefited by training closely with the Principal Investigator (PI). Our experience was altogether different. Like other astronauts, they were trained and motivated to follow the check lists and to refer to the Malfunction Procedures if something went awry—but were understandably reluctant to depart from the written plan the Principal Investigator had submitted and approved. The lesson seemed clear to me. If we couldn't fly the real PI to oversee the flight experiment, then how about flying a computer with AI—a knowledge-based system—that would observe the experiment and its data, and could respond to the complex space flight constraints, like available power or downlink bandwidth.

Gradually, the idea of a science-based AI computer looking over the shoulder of an astronaut began to take shape. I called it "PI in a Box," abbreviated [PI]. I sold the idea to my MIT colleague, Prof. Peter Szolowitz, an acknowledged expert in medical AI. I further sold the idea to Peter Friedland, a Silicon Valley AI leader who was in charge of the AI branch at NASA's Ames Research Center. His enthusiasm and support extended to funding my sabbatical by appointing me as a NASA Visiting Scientist under the Intergovernmental Policy Act (IPA). He further assigned Dr. Silvano Colombano, a highly productive computer scientist familiar with LISP and the other AI languages, to supervise the task of putting all of the PI's reasoning into a rather small IBM Thinkpad. We added Stanford students and an Apple staff person to build up a dynamite team of six.

The PI in a Box concept would allow the on-board astronaut to benefit from the real time advice and trouble shooting from the actual PI. It all worked, without any problems. We flew it on two Spacelab missions. The first one was for my own experiment on Spacelab Life Science 2, for which I was also the Alternate Payload Specialist. It advised the crew on calibration and timelines, and took quick looks at data analysis. The second time it flew was on Neurolab, as a real-time aid to Chuck Czeisler's sleep/activity experiment. John Glenn was one of my subjects, on his return to space at age seventy. He was very complimentary about the balance testing he underwent pre and post flight.

Space Children

Our older children likely caught the space bug from me and made successful careers of their own in planetary astronomy. I include a picture from a feature piece in *Nature* magazine in 2015, prior to the New Horizons Pluto encounter, for which Leslie was Deputy Project Scientist.

Do You Want to Be an Astronaut?

If you ask almost any kid, "Do you want to be an astronaut?" the response is sure to be, "You bet." Well, me too—except that I wasn't a kid anymore. The first time I ever thought about becoming an astronaut was back in the Apollo days. After the "original seven" astronauts had been chosen, all military test pilots, NASA was pressured by the National Research Council to include astronaut scientists in the next selection, in the 1960s. Some of these guys would fly to the moon on Apollo, and naturally MIT was a logical place to recruit. Since the MIT Instrumentation Lab had received the first NASA Apollo contract—for the Guidance and Control System—we were all aware of the opportunity. By 1962 I was a junior faculty member in Aero-Astro at MIT, and never far from the excitement of human space flight. I was a consultant to NASA's Marshall Space Flight Center in Alabama. I had started our MIT Man-Vehicle Lab with Y.T. Li, and we obtained early NASA funding to look at how the motion of the Apollo spacecraft might interfere with the ability of an astronaut to hand-control the launch of the Saturn rocket. Fortunately, a backup system was never needed.

Several of my fellow graduate students, Buzz Aldrin, Ed Mitchell, Dave Scott and Rusty Schweickart, flew on Apollo—and Phil Chapman was se-lected but didn't get to orbit. Charlie Duke, who drove the Apollo rover on the moon with John Young, was my first graduate student. His master's thesis was on the human role in lunar orbit rendezvous. My old Amherst fraternity brother, Bob Parker, who was then teaching astronomy at the U of Wisconsin, was selected as an astronaut scientist.

Leslie and Eliot as "The Pluto Siblings."   Bear Gutierrez

So naturally I was tempted to apply myself. But, with young children at home and a wife, Jody, who wouldn't think of letting me take the risk (or of moving to Houston, for that matter), my fantasy was put on hold. For thirty years.

When the Space Shuttle was introduced in the 1980s, it promised to broaden the base of astronauts to include working scientists. I saw another opening. NASA began recruiting and interviewing for the positions of Pilot, requiring extensive test pilot training, and Mission Specialist (MS), aimed at practicing engineers, scientists or physicians. And they introduced a new category of non-NASA crew called Payload Specialists (PSs). The PSs would apply their specific expertise to performing the scientific payload experiments on a particular mission. PSs would be on loan to the space program. At first, they would come from the European Space Agency (ESA), as well as from American universities and hospitals. They would work on orbit in the pressurized Spacelab (SL), a schoolbus-sized lab carried in the Shuttle's cargo bay. The very first such PS, for Spacelab 1 (SL-1, on STS-9 in 1983), was my own PhD student, Byron Lichtenberg. When the time came in 1990 for crew selection for Spacelab Life Sciences 2 (SLS-2) on STS-58, I saw my own last chance to fly myself. It would be my fourth mission as a Principal Investigator (PI), devising and supervising experiments that would go into space to study human adaptation to weightlessness. So far, I'd done that from the ground.

Jody told me to go for it. And my three grown children, Eliot, Leslie, and Rob, all told me to give it a try. Well, if they weren't worried, why should I be concerned? Except that I was fifty-five by then and twenty years older than the other crew members. As for the PS slot, I was conscious of the advice that the first step to winning is to show up.

Project Scientist Candidate

My application as a PS went in and I was selected as one of about a dozen finalists by the Investigators' Working Group meeting in Cocoa Beach. And for the first time, I thought seriously about a space flight. I was up early the next morning and went out for a walk on the beach—one of my favorite ways to exercise and think. I fell into a long conversation with Rhea Seddon, the SLS-2 Payload Commander. I knew her well from from the 1991 SLS-1 mission and earlier—even back to the time of her selection in 1978 as one of the first female astronauts. A level-headed MD, she had been thoroughly familiar with the stresses that can be caused by PSs marching to a different drummer than the MSs. She was frank about what is needed to be an effective PS, and said nothing to discourage me.

So, I proceeded to start a serious effort to understand both the science and the technology of the other disciplines and experiments to be flown. I also had an opportunity to look into the risks. We had already experienced the tragedy of the *Challenger* accident in 1986, but here we also had the risks associated with human testing. The most obvious was the insertion of a catheter into the great veins leading back to the heart. Gunnar Bolmqvist and his colleagues, from the University of Texas Southwest, were using an invasive (and slightly threatening) technique involving the insertion of a catheter-tipped transducer, which was slid up the inferior vena cava into the entrance to the right atrium of the heart. This was necessary to measure central venous pressure directly to answer the important questions how the cardio-vascular (CV) system responds to weightlessness. The CV guys had indirect measures, and only one direct pressure measurement from SLS-1. The procedure seemed dangerous, and led to a fracas over the continuing presence of one crew on SLS-1 and the reluctant participation and exposure to fluoroscopy several times on SLS-2. I wanted to get some unbiased advice from the medical specialists, so I went to Dr. Eugene Braunwald's Cardiac Catheterization clinic at Beth Israel Hospital [*or maybe Boston Children's Hospital—Larry's notes are ambiguous.—LAY*], where the resident performing the insertions was Terry Sanger, the son of an old Harvard friend of Jody's. I left the observation satisfied that the risk was minimal—but then again, most risks were low compared to sitting on top of a rocket!

There followed a wonderful family trip to Hawaii, where Leslie and Paul informed us that they were getting married, and where Leslie showed me the Green Flash (both outstanding events). I read through all of Guyton's physiology textbook, and certainly expanded my knowledge of human physiology well beyond the vestibular system I had been studying.

The final interviews and selection were held in Houston shortly after Thanksgiving. I was concerned that I didn't know enough biology, that I had so little "wet lab" hands-on experience, and especially that I was so much older than all but one of the other candidates. (I was fifty-seven, and had been a lab director and full professor for nearly thirty years by then.) The medical exams were thorough, but I passed them all. My old friend Jeff Hoffman, by then an experienced astronaut and later a close colleague on the MIT faculty, had told me that the trick was to "pass" the physical exams, like the treadmill stress test, but not to try to show how strong I was by pushing my heart rate beyond the target rate. I complied, and tried not to show discomfort during the famous endoscopic exam. (The endoscopies showed you the view of your intestines, from colon on up, through live TV).

Unfortunately, my endoscopy took place just before my interview, so I didn't really have time to think through what I might discuss there. In fact, at the famous astronaut interview they didn't ask me anything about the science to be done on the mission. We talked about my hobbies, including sailing and ski patrol, and they asked me how I would deal with a reporter who wanted to know about the justification for doing animal experiments in orbit. I later learned, from Rhea, that the committee already knew that I was qualified scientifically, and that I could be trained to do the ultrasound and the animal experiments, but they wanted to know about my ability to work as a member of a team. They knew me as a senior scientist and as a lab director, but they wanted to be sure that I could function as a junior member of a team and follow the direction of a commander. Apparently, they were most impressed by my experience as a ski patrolman. That reflected my ability to respond to a time-critical situation as a member of a team. My sailboat navigation might have helped too. So much for all of my physiology self-study influencing my selection chances. But I did find it of interest and valuable. I was better prepared as I travelled around to the different PI sites and learned about their experiment methods in some detail.

On the last evening of the selection process, the NASA team had us all to dinner and announced that the selections were Jay Buckey and Marty Fettman. Then, in view of the expectation that there would be two PSs flying on the mission, they decided that three PS candidates were to be selected, and I was named the third. (The project scientist, my old friend and colleague, Frank Sulzman, enjoyed pulling my chain a bit by announcing my selection as an apparent afterthought.)

So, I packed up the Texas-size Ford Crown Victoria handed down to me by my thoughtful mother-in-law, Ruth. It was the perfect vehicle for Houston. It was large enough to take up a full lane, and the AC always worked. I moved to Egret Bay, just outside of the NASA Johnson Space Center (JSC), in an apartment I shared with Marty Fettman. My bedroom sliding doors overlooked Egret Bay, where my wind-surfer, Drew Gaffney's day-sailor, and my kayak awaited me after work. I began my two years of training as a PS. Marty and I were separated by twenty years and other interests. We got along well enough but led very independent lives. I don't recall any instances in which competition for the PS slot got between us.

As it turned out, of course, Shannon Lucid, a mission specialist with a background in biochemistry, took one of the PS slots, so we were down to one, which eventually went to my roommate, Marty. He did a great job.

Alternate Payload Specialist

In her marvelous autobiography, *Go for Orbit* (Your Space Press, Murfreesboro, TN, 2015), my friend and Payload Commander, Rhea Seddon, wrote, "The difficulty with having three great candidates train with us was that we knew only one would fly. Some felt it cruel that we make them compete" But my experience was outstanding, and I wouldn't have traded it for anything. Nor was I surprised that my roommate, Marty Fettman, was chosen as the PS and that Jay Buckey and I were designated as APSs (Alternate Payload

Specialists). Marty was a skilled veterinarian at Colorado State. I was a novice at the precise dissection of rats, which would need to be done on board. The rats were comfortable on Marty's arm—but they bit me. Marty fit all of the astronaut criteria.

My own assignment was as a backup astronaut, fully trained and ready to be launched if anything prevented Marty or possibly one of the MSs (Rhea Seddon, Shannon Lucid or Dave Wolf) from flying. Jay and I were also the Payload Communicators. For all of the simulations and for the fourteen-day flight itself, we were the principal interface between the Payload Operations Control Center (POCC) and the fight crew. We were thoroughly familiar with the payload and its constraints, so the crew was at ease discussing payload problems with us over the Air-to Ground radio loops. The POCC was at the Johnson Space Center in Houston for the simulations and in Huntsville, Alabama for the flight.

We were very much part of the crew. We had the same training and were fully capable of following the check lists for all of the nominal (regular) and "off-nominal" experiment procedures and repairs. We went through all of the Shuttle operations and procedures—including all of the safety drills. We were exposed to the g-forces of launch and fitted for our Launch and Entry Suits (LES) for the eight-minute centrifuge exposure at Brooks Air Force Base in San Antonio. Our "Water Survival Week" included parachuting into Pensacola Bay. At the Kennedy Space Center (KSC) in Cape Canaveral, we learned to drive the armored personnel vehicle (APV) to escape from the safety bunker in the event of a shuttle explosion at the launch pad. We put out fires. We participated in press conferences, invited our families and friends to the pre-launch party at KSC, stayed in the Crew Quarters at "the Cape," and dressed in the official crew rugby shirts for the flight, just as the flight crew did.

I never had a dull moment during the two years of training. We began working with the General Electric (GE) mission management team off-campus. I was surrounded by contractor engineers who regularly went home at 4 p.m.. I felt rather removed from the real NASA activity. After a while we were moved into the astronaut offices on the top floor of Building Four at JSC, and only then did I really feel part of the space team. As PSs we were at the bottom of the astronaut pecking order, but on the other hand we were recognized as part of the team and we were assigned to a mission. Some of the older astronauts, with whom I had worked since 1980, were especially helpful. They even encouraged me to sit with them in their undesignated but well-established corner of the JSC cafeteria.

During the two-week flight, Jay and I shared the APS communication duties. I remained in regular communication with the PIs on the mission—off-line—and was pleased to be part of an important scientific campaign. My relations with the Deputy Mission Director had been frosty, since my earliest contretemps over permission to fly back to New England for my childrens' weddings. She ran the mission and the POCC professionally and effectively, with no nonsense. I was relieved that she at least allowed me to position my MIT coffee mug in camera view of NASA TV, which was broadcast around the world. My role as the Payload Communicator, which I shared with Jay, kept me fully involved in the experiments my buddies were doing in orbit. The only times I felt jealous occurred during the quiet pre-dawn hours, before the crew went to work. During training at JSC, I spent many hours looking through the Earth Observation photos and their interpretations, and learning how to use the Hasselblad camera to take my own shots. Now the live TV images of the Earth, taken from the Shuttle, made me wish I could see them from space.

Our Crew

The scheduled fourteen-day flight would be the longest to date and carry a crew of seven. The flying duties were shared between our commander, John Blaha, and our pilot, Rick Searfoss. Rick was a very bright Air Force Academy graduate (first in his class) and test pilot. He was in charge of the "dirt book" of earth observation and took photos for the mission. He later commanded the Neurolab shuttle mission on STS-90 in 1998. He died at the young age of 62 in 2018.

Our Payload Commander, Rhea Seddon, was my "Boss" for the mission—and that's what I called her, except when we were being monitored by NASA. She was a charming and level-headed MD who spanned the gulf between space flight requirements and the needs of the scientists. She was my friend and supporter throughout this adventure. Rhea was married to fellow astronaut Hoot Gibson, later head of the astronaut office. SLS-2 was her third and final mission.

As Rhea repeatedly pointed out, our *real commander* was Air Force Colonel John Blaha, on his third space flight. John was proactive, forming a crew team and maintaining crew spirit. He made sure of the little things that made me and Jay feel part of the crew, like inclusion in crew photos and the printing of our own astronaut pictures. I was tickled to respond to requests for autographed photos. He arranged for Jay and me to use the astronaut gym and to attend the Monday morning astronaut briefings when John Young went over all of the technical issues for each flight. And he made sure we were included in all the crew activities at KSC, including stays at the well-equipped crew quarters, and at the astronaut beach house.

A veteran of 361 combat missions and a research flight to over 120,000 feet, John was the ideal leader of our group. During the simulations, when cascading problems were thrown at the crew, he could calmly prioritize them and assign responsibilities. He assured me that in-flight, things never got that bad—and they didn't. He respected all our interests. He told us, no matter how much the crew enjoyed the flight, it would be a failure if we didn't accomplish the scientific goals.

The Payload Specialist, Marty Fettman, was excellent at animal procedures and almost everything else. He and I shared an apartment overlooking Egret Bay, off Clear Lake, for two years and remained friends. At a press conference shortly before launch, when asked how I felt about my roommate being Prime, I said that he didn't like my cooking now. Marty blurted out that he *never* liked my cooking

In addition to Rhea, we had three other MSs on board. Dave Wolf, on his first Shuttle flight, was an engineer and physician from NASA who had been involved in the development of the bioreactor for simulating zero-g with cells and tissues on the ground, and the flight echocardiogram equipment we used in Spacelab. An outgoing and fun-loving astronaut, twenty years my junior, he took me on as a surrogate for his uncle who had so influenced his career. Bill McArthur was a brilliant engineer, a career army officer, and a lovely person, with a very broad background, also on his first flight. Shannon Lucid was harder for me to get to know. Shannon went on to fly on Mir for 188 days, setting the record at that time as the longest-flying US astronaut. She still holds the record for the longest-flying US astronaut on Mir.

The SLS-2 Crew, Front Row, L-R: Dave Wolf, Mission Specialist,. Shannon Lucid, Mission Specialist. Rhea Seddon, Payload Commander and Mission Specialist. Marty Fettman, Payload Specialist. Top row: Jay Buckey, Alternate Payload Specialist. Rick Searfoss, Pilot. Bill McArthur, Mission Specialist. Larry Young, Alternate Payload Specialist. John Blaha, Commander.

Jay Buckey, an Alternate Payload Specialist like me, became a Professor of Medicine at Dartmouth and worked with us on the Harvard-MIT Bioastronautics PhD Program. He went back to fly as a PS on Neurolab. As Alternate Payload Specialists, Jay and I handled Air-to-Ground communication with the Crew during the fourteen-day mission. It was a privilege to be part of this team.

Payload Training

Most evenings in Houston were spent studying. The training material wasn't hard—but there was a lot of it. By living apart from my wife and by dropping the multitude of academic activities like advising and serving on committees, I found enough time for the training. I learned a lot and enjoyed the process. We each had an assigned "Scheduler" who would fill out our hour-by-hour program for each week and manage to somehow fit in all of the training requirements and, where possible, to comply with our requests, including a few hours each week in the gym.

The payload training was intense, fascinating, and right up my alley. The first year or so involved familiarization with the scientific rationale and especially the operation of all the life science experiments. Even though I had taught the subject, I learned much regarding the effects of weightlessness on human physiology.

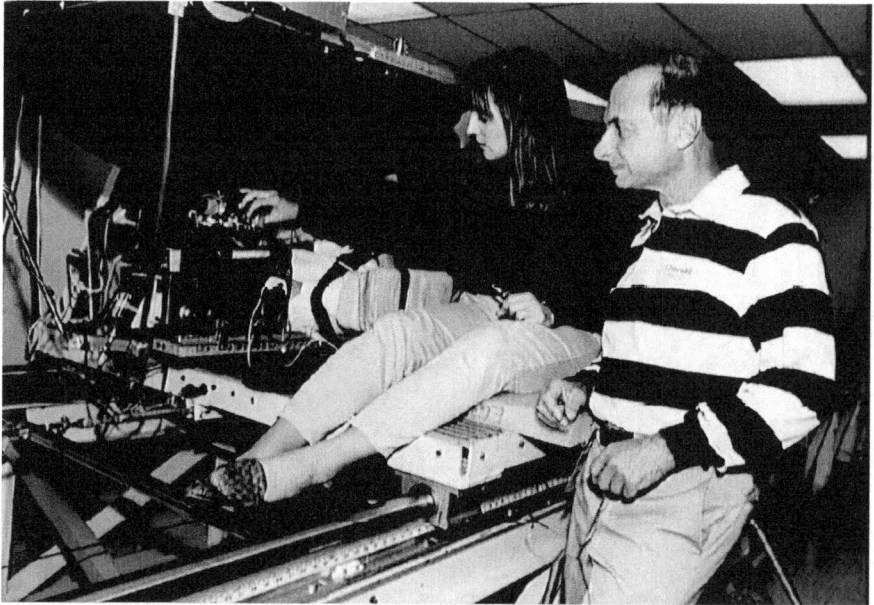

Fettman (face obscured), in an oscillating sled device, participates in data collection for neurovestibular functions. Assisting the test are Dr. Laurence Young, alternate payload specialist, and an unidentified MIT student. Image and caption from NASA: https://science.ksc.nasa.gov/mirrors/images/html/STS58.htm

The Spacelab research covered all the gravity-sensitive systems of the human body, as well as the corresponding organs in our rats. The absence of gravity weakened bones and muscles. It affected respiration and blood cell formation, and influenced the immune system and metabolism as well as the vestibular system, my own special interest.

We spent several days with each of the two dozen PIs in their home laboratories or in Houston and received hands-on instruction from world-class scientists. This included my own lab, MIT's Man Vehicle Laboratory. My long-term friend, former student and colleague, Chuck Oman, took over as Director of our Man Vehicle Lab and led it following my return.

I remained the PI on the extensive set of human vestibular experiments, including the "rotating dome" vestibulo-ocular reflexes and otolith-spinal reflexes. But I left all of the baseline pre- and post-flight testing to my Deputy PI and former student, Dan Merfeld, who performed faultlessly. Dan was a recent PhD of mine, who went on to be a professor at Harvard and then at Ohio State, specializing in the vestibular system.

The flight equipment was all specially designed to work in microgravity. The mass spectrometer analyzed gas exchange in the lung while an astronaut exercised on a bicycle ergometer. My own "rotating dome" device induced the sensation of tilt by rotation of the visual surround. Almost everything else was new for me, and we all had the privilege of being mentored by some of the world's leading experts—the PIs and their assistants.

Beyond the payload science was the technical operation training. We

Astronaut Rhea Seddon, payload commander, spins the Spacelab LIfe Sciences (SLS-2) rotating chair as payload specialist Martin J. Fettman serves as test subject.

Image and caption from NASA: https://science.ksc.nasa.gov/mirrors/images/html/STS58.htm

learned how to identify malfunctions in the equipment and, where possible, how to fix them, following the detailed malfunction procedures. After the introductory tutorials we were individually coached by the very capable and always supportive GE payload training team. We practiced on the wide range of human and rat studies to answer questions like bone loss, muscle deconditioning and cardiovascular or respiratory regulation in weightlessness. I was especially pleased to observe the crew's acceptance of our on-board computer assistant, "PI in a Box," which I had invented to assist the astronauts on board.

Some of the training was hard for me, and I don't mean physically demanding. For me, the most difficult procedure involved inserting a catheter into a tiny blood vessel in the tail of a rat. It was used to draw blood and insert a radioactive tracer for calcium turnover studies. Since this was done with our hands in surgical gloves, inserted into an isolated reduced pressure "glove box," it took all my care to avoid puncturing the vessel wall. It was much easier to insert a catheter into a vein of one of GEs patient volunteer trainers.

First of all, the rats and I didn't get along. They seemed to sense that I was nervous around them and I had trouble grabbing one, first to inject a small catheter into the tail vein and then to sacrifice it in the guillotine. (No wonder they were nervous.) One time I was bitten and was sent to see Dr. Richard Jennings, our flight surgeon at JSC. He had not dealt with rat bites before and together we looked up the treatment. It was nothing special, but from then on I wore reinforced leather gloves. Once the animal was decapitated we had only a few minutes to compete the dissection before the samples would begin to deteriorate. Starting with the identification and removal of the vestibular organs in the inner ear, we proceeded to dissect all the organs for study by the PI teams. My inability to do that rapidly and precisely may have been my major shortcoming in the final PS selection process. I couldn't disagree with the PI's and Mission Director's decision to select Marty for the job in space.

I also needed a lot of guided practice to manipulate the probe of our ultrasound imager to be able to get good echocardiogram images of the beating heart—all four chambers and the valves. It was always a thrill to "look around" with the probe and suddenly see the beating heart–either my own or one of the trainers.

Shuttle Training

Beyond our training on the experiment facilities and operation lay the required familiarization with the Space Shuttle systems. These were similar to the training given the astronaut candidates but much less intense. We learned how to deal with cabin depressurization and other emergencies. Life on the Shuttle entailed preparation of meals, and of course the use of the vacuum systems for disposal of liquid and solid human waste. For voice communication we carried our radios and learned how to safely recharge their lithium batteries. We were shown how to set up and operate the Shuttle TV cameras. We were even given a lesson on the Shuttle Guidance and Navigation computers, although it was highly unlikely that a PS would ever be called upon to touch, let alone to operate, any such critical device.

And then there were many adventuresome days of the kind my fellow Payload Specialist Candidate, Jay Buckey, called "FGE" (Fun at Government Expense). These included learning to parachute and to crawl into a one-man raft, with a flight suit full of water, in Pensacola Bay in late winter. (It's harder than you might think it is). Or driving a tracked armored vehicle to escape from a simulated shuttle fuel tank in danger of exploding. Or putting out fires.

After a year or so of Space Shuttle training, Jay and I were interviewed by the JSC newspaper about our backgrounds and experiences in training. I compared myself to Indiana Jones, a movie hero who was also a college professor and pursued adventure in the name of science. His passion was archeology, mine was space physiology. I knew that life as an astronaut would entail more risks than did teaching in Cambridge, but I was more than ready to jump in—even at my advanced age, twenty years older than my crewmates.

In the Shuttle mock-up at JSC, we practiced bailing out of the Shuttle by dropping onto a slide. That was much like the commercial airplane evacuation slide we all had seen demonstrated—with one exception. We dropped

Astronaut Training. With my payload commander, Rhea Seddon, and with Mission Specialist Dave Wolf on the shuttle scaffold at Kennedy Space Center, reviewing the evacuation procedures.

onto the slide still wearing our parachutes and stepping free of cables, which tended to roll us over sideways. In fact, Rhea broke her leg during one of the sessions and bravely limped around in her cast for a while, but managed to keep on as a key crew member.

During our water survival training we practiced handling our parachute and raft for recovery, both in the JSC pool and in the chilly Gulf water in Pensacola. Dressed in a LES, you were supposed to climb into your inflated one-man life raft. Most of the times I tried, it flipped over on me.

Some of our training was conducted at KSC. One day we took the launch gantry elevator up to the level of the Space Shuttle entry hatch and we proceeded to familiarize ourselves with "Our Space Vehicle." There was a special thrill in sitting in the crew seats some of us would occupy during the real mission.

We learned how to get out of the Shuttle, in the event of a pre-launch fire. We learned how to control the temperature and breathing supply on our pressurized orange Launch and Entry Suits. We practiced an emergency

Wearing a launch and entry suit and navigating a one person life raft, Astronaut Jay C. Buckey, M.D., participates in emergency bailout training in the JSC Weightless Environment Training Facility (WETF). Dr. Buckey is an alternate paylaod specialist for the Spacelab Life Sciences-2 (SLS-2) mission. Nearby is a SCUBA-equipped diver who assisted in the training exercises.   Image and caption from NASA: https://science.ksc.nasa.gov/mirrors/images/html/STS58.htm

egress from the cockpit of the Shuttle mock-up if the main hatch could not be opened from inside. (Shades of the Apollo 1 fire.) In your LES you were supposed to climb up on a seat back and chin up to the overhead window to escape. That was hard, but I managed it. .

Before starting training, I was afraid I would be too old, at fifty-five, to accomplish all that would be required. The rest of the crew were all in their thirties. In fact, there were only two exercises in crew training that required my maximum physical effort: the emergency egress from the cockpit and the climb into the one-man life raft.

Although most of the Shuttle training was intense, it wasn't really difficult. The Shuttle classes were adequate yet perfunctory. The practice sessions in the simulators were effective. And yet we knew we were being observed and "scored" at almost every one. The mental demands were far less than graduate school and the physical demands were mostly trivial. I found that, despite my age, I could absorb all of the procedures of both the Shuttle and Spacelab operations.

Most of the Shuttle training involved study of a manual and then demonstration of mastery of the procedure in a simulator in the training facility at JSC—always under the watchful eye of a trainer who would notice, and report, any mistakes. I typically spent the night before each run-though visualizing the procedure. With my eyes closed I would imagine the scene and then visualize each action I would take, from flipping a switch to pulling the cord to inflate my parachute. It worked pretty well.

Houston—"No Problem"

The mission itself was a great success. The scientific return was enormous and the contributions of Payload Specialists were highly regarded.

All in all, the two years in Payload Specialist training were highlights of my life. I am grateful to everyone who made them possible, from my NASA crew mates to MIT for giving me the time away, and to my supportive and loving family.

No regrets

Usually, when new people learn that I trained for a space flight but never went into orbit, I am asked if I wasn't disappointed. Of course, I was disappointed, though the result of the final selection was fully predictable. The hardest part of the on-board science was the animal dissection, and Marty (and Jay for that matter) was far more skilled at that than I was. Furthermore, Marty was well-qualified in all other aspects of the job. The night following the selection disclosure I felt blue, but it passed quickly.

But I still had an important job on the successful flight. During the actual mission, I was the Payload Communicator, meaning that I was the guy in Huntsville, along with Jay on the other shift, who spoke with the crew. I was accepted as a knowledgeable and collegial member of a very successful crew, and I am proud of my contributions. I took very seriously my ground job and, in fact, the air-to-ground communication and the discussion of technical issues went extremely smoothly during the fourteen-day mission of STS-58. I was too busy and involved in my job to be jealous.

Furthermore, the two years of training were fascinating and mostly good fun. Everything from learning the science and operation of all of the experiments to water survival and parachute training was like a continual summer camp experience. Not only did I learn a lot about space flight–I learned a lot about myself and my ability to keep learning new things at my advanced age. I am grateful for the opportunity to be a "half-ass-tronaut." I wouldn't have traded it for the world. So, no regrets.

Space Grant

I first heard of the idea of Space Grant in about 1988. My student, Peter Diamandis, introduced it to me by telling me I was invited to meet with a small group at MIT, including President Chuck Vest. Peter is the phenomenon who initiated the X-Prize (the first private near-space voyages with a repeat within a week), Students for the Exploration and Development of Space, International Space University, Singularity University, and a private venture to mine asteroids. He is a space nut who also earned an MD from the Harvard-MIT HST Program and was my advisee from his undergrad and master's degree days. He built our MVL centrifuge that has spun people and enabled graduate theses for over two decades. I once introduced Peter at a dinner, where he was getting a major award, by announcing that he owed his success at least partially to the fact that I was his advisor and that he almost *never* followed my advice!

The subject for this high-level meeting was proposed legislation to establish "Space Grant Consortia," one per state, much in the manner of Land Grant and, more recently, "Sea Grant" consortia. The idea was to spread public awareness and support for space activities broadly. Chuck was opposed to the idea since MIT had been on record as strongly opposing designated federal research awards. However, he eased up and MIT won the competition to become the lead of the Massachusetts Space Grant, with my Aero-Astro colleague Dan Hastings as its head. After a while, Jack Kerrebrock, later department head and Dean of Engineering, took over. While I was at the end of my stint in Houston, Jack asked if I would be willing to take over Space Grant when I returned to MIT. It wasn't much work, he assured me.

Well—he was wrong. My feeling, supported by my recent space experience at the Johnson Space Center, was that space research was a demanding field and not for everyone. In fact, it was only for the best and the brightest. Others would fail or be discouraged. Space Grant, I thought, was a way to attract outstanding young engineers and scientists and to ease their entry into space activities through mentoring and financial support.

Shortly after returning to MIT in 1993 and taking over the program, ably assisted by Helen Halaris, I paid a visit to Julius Dasch, who directed the overall NASA Space Grant program in Washington. He was very gracious. When he asked about the composition of our consortium, I proudly replied that we were broader than just MIT. I explained that we also included Wellesley, Tufts and Harvard. Well, he explained, that's not what they were looking for in terms of diversity: geographical, ethnic or otherwise. Working with my assistant director, I proceeded to recruit some Western Massachusetts schools, including the Five Colleges (Amherst, Williams, Hampshire, Smith and Mt. Holyoke), as well as U Mass Amherst. Still not good enough. Then I added Worcester Polytechnic Institute and Boston University, both of which had active space research activities. And Holy Cross. Still not diverse enough! Then Roxbury Community College. By this time, I had the benefit of having Jeff Hoffman on our faculty, as our Associate Director, and he was more effective in spreading the word—to NASA and to our sister institutions, about space and diversity.

We had something in excess of $100K per year for direct fellowship support and I used a peer review of all the applicants by the representatives of the member colleges in our consortium. Well, that had a good and bad aspect. We only had enough money to support one, or possibly two, Space Grant Fellows each year, depending upon where they were studying. The top applicants each year were, not surprisingly, from MIT, and that burned up the bulk of our annual fellowship fund. We got strong support from the science director at Goddard, my old friend Gerry Soffen, who had been NASA's Director of Life Science. But, after Julius' retirement, the Space Grant staff at HQ began criticizing us for lack of diversity and for concentrating on the high achievers at MIT.

Finally, after one of our five-year reviews, we were told, to retain our high funding status, I would have to be replaced and the program altered and broadened. I was dissatisfied, since we had amply fulfilled our mission of recruiting and supporting future leaders in space activities. Jeff took over and did what was required, in his usual diplomatic and capable manner. The full fellowships, intended to recruit leading students, were eliminated and replaced by a large number of small grants, largely for summer internships, spread broadly across the consortium. The overall Space Grant program has had its ups and downs in terms of funding, but continues to this day.

And Still a Space Cadet

After a career of contributing to human space exploration, I still remain enthusiastic. Here I am, standing in front of a student prank mockup of the Lunar Excursion Module, trying to hitch a ride to space with Neil Armstrong and Buzz Aldrin—from MIT's Kresge Lawn.

And how about the future?

I believe we will see people explore Mars in the next couple of decades. My New Hampshire license plate expresses my commitment to going "2-Mars." On the other hand, this is now my third car to carry the plate. Yet I remain hopeful.

Here I am with Neil Armstrong and Buzz Aldrin in 2010 on MIT's Kresge Lawn, still trying to get a ride to space.

My career has changed over the years, but my faith in human exploration of space remains evident on my license plate.

Teaching

Becoming a Professor

Nobody ever taught me how to teach. Nor did anyone observe my teaching and critique my approach or style. Nobody ever exposed me to books about good pedagogy. Nobody spoke to me about student counseling or office hours or use of any AV beyond viewgraphs. The little bit I picked up from my wife, while Jody was studying for a PhD combining education and psychology at Harvard, was of little practical value. The introduction of technology in the classroom, like clicks to let the students register their understanding during a lecture or the use of extensive computer-based assignments and grading, all came about long after I had established my own way of doing things.

Doc Draper offered me an entry-level position as an Assistant Professor in the Aero Department at MIT as I was nearing completion of my thesis, and Frank Reintjes, head of MIT's Electrical Engineering Department (EE), offered me a two-year appointment to teach in EE. I never applied for either position—or for any other, for that matter. There were no meetings with search committees or faculty interview seminars. There was no question but that I would accept one of the MIT offers. After all, I was going to teach engineering and MIT was the top choice. The EE offer was for a Ford Professorship, one of many funded by the Ford Foundation, and it had a limited duration. Even though my undergraduate and master's degrees were from EE at MIT, and I knew next to nothing about airplanes, or even spacecraft, other than what concerned my background in guidance and navigation, I was persuaded by the smaller size and collegiality in Aero.

In 1962, Draper was Director of the MIT Instrumentation Lab, which was gearing up to provide the guidance system for the newly announced Apollo program to send an astronaut to the moon, and also Head of the MIT Aero Department. He used the former to support activities in the latter when it suited him. He liked to refer to the Department as an Athenian Democracy, in which each faculty member was a citizen who could voice his opinion. I don't know of anyone who ever actually spoke openly in opposition to Doc. Anyone who opposed his views on the superiority of spinning wheel gyroscopes (as opposed to laser gyros, for example) was subject to his blistering put-down.

Very fortunately, I was on his favored list. He personally supported my doctoral research on human eye movements, after letting me know he had a degree in psychology from Stanford and would be looking over my shoulder. Also, that there was an outspoken psychologist in the region who also worked on eye movements, and if she ever showed her face in my lab that would be the end of my funding. Period. No explanations. And no, she never did show up, although she knew about my work and would call me at home to ask for some detail about a citation, often in the wee hours of the morning.

Courses I Taught

During my half-century as a full-time professor at MIT, I only taught five different full semester subjects: Comparative Instrumentation, Aerospace Human Factors, Quantitative Physiology (Sensori-Motor), Flight Simulation, and Engineering Apollo. Of course, there were also the shorter, one- to four-week offerings, which gave me a chance develop some area of interest to me. These included: Engineering and Skiing, an undergraduate seminar combined with on-slope testing of ski bindings; biomathematics for Harvard medical students; and summer courses in Flight Simulation and in Inertial Guidance, taught at the University of Alabama in Huntsville. Aerospace Human Factors remains a popular senior "capstone" subject and Engineering Apollo, offered biannually, has become the largest graduate course offered in the department. For each one of these subjects we emphasized the principle of "learn by doing," including laboratory sessions and individual projects and reports. There were no existing textbooks to use for these topics, although some books were available for reference. As an overall guideline we rejected the classic lecture and recitation mode of teaching in favor of one that involved the students in "active learning." And, the faculty learned from our students every time we offered the subject.

Comparative Instrumentation

As my first course I was assigned to teach Comparative Instrumentation with Y.T. Li. This was a grad course with a rich heritage, starting with Draper, and later taught by Sid Lees, who went on to teach at Dartmouth, and then to Tufts Dental School. Draper's book, *Instrument Engineering*, published by Mc-Graw Hill, treated the emerging field of feedback control systems. It adhered to Doc's insistence on using his elegant but hopelessly cumbersome "Draperian notation," and was eventually dropped. Y.T.'s idea was that instrumentation, like anatomy, could be shown to have certain fundamental concepts that transcended the applications and that could be taught. He had successfully introduced some of these concepts in the outside company Dynisco, which he founded with his younger brother, MIT Mechanical Engineering Professor Shih-Ying (S.Y.) Lee. I was more familiar with accelerometers and gyroscopes, the instruments for inertial guidance, than with pressure transducers, which had been the chief product of the Li-Lee brothers. I relied upon my colleagues in the I-Lab to help me develop examples of Y.T.'s basic principles.

Y.T. Li arranged for a book contract with McGraw Hill, for us to write a volume on Comparative Instrumentation. I only wrote one chapter. The project never got off the ground, I regret to say. Forgive me please, Y.T. and S.Y.—you were the most innovative colleagues I ever encountered. What a mistake I made, not to have pursued this book with these extraordinary engineers. And, to further compound the error, I never followed through on another agreement with McGraw-Hill to produce a book on Biological Control Systems, using largely the NASA reports that Larry Stark and I had already prepared. No excuses.

In hindsight, these projects should have been kept at a higher priority. In my entire career I only wrote two books, and edited a third, and probably should have followed the advice of my old friend, Alain Berthoz, Professor at the Collège de France, who regularly encouraged me to write all of my ideas on models and space in one book. Both books I co-authored with Volker Henn. The first was *Visual Vestibular Interactions*, one of the series brought out by the Neuroscience Research Program, and co-authored with Bernie Cohen of Mt. Sinai School of Medicine in New York, Volker and myself. The other, published by Kluwer Academic/Plenum Publishers, was the annotated translation of Ernst Mach's classic, *Fundamentals of the Theory of Movement Perception*. Hans Scherberger picked up the translating burden following Volker's early death, and was the third author. Later in my career, I edited the *Handbook of Bioastronautics*, a major reference co-edited with Dr. Jeffrey Sutton of Baylor College of Medicine and published by Springer. [*He can add this volume as a third book. —LAY*]

Aerospace Human Factors

Since my own interest was in aviation human factors and in aerospace medicine, I decided to introduce a graduate course on the subject. This all seemed pretty remote from the hard, quantitative engineering subjects offered by my colleagues, but there was a fair bit of student interest, so I plunged ahead. I was encouraged by the year-long visit of Sherman Vinograd, an MD from NASA Headquarters, who had sponsored one of the projects we did as consultants at Biosystems, in preparation for the Skylab and later Life Science Space Shuttle missions. The concept was to provide a "tool box" of standard space-worthy instruments for the use of any researchers doing space life sciences. It was called Integrated Medical and Behavioral Laboratory Measurement System (IMBLMS).

Our chief contribution, through our little company (Biosystems), was a non-invasive instrument to measure central venous pressure. We extended a technique used for measuring intraocular pressure by seeing how much pressure was required to inflate a small balloon until it just flattened the jugular vein. It worked, but was never picked up by NASA nor did we patent it. Ironically, thirty years later when I was a Payload Specialist training to go up on the Space Shuttle, central venous pressure was still a measurement of great interest.

Taking advantage of Dr. Vinograd's presence at MIT, we put on a short summer program emphasizing those aspects of aerospace medicine and space human factors that would be critical to a successful manned mission. Sherman knew everybody and invited them to MIT to lecture, including the avant-garde designer, Raymond Loewy.

The series of lectures grew into a course on Human Factors that I offered jointly with Tom Sheridan of the ME Department. Tom became a friend and close colleague. A few years older than me, Tom had studied psychology at Harvard and had a more classical view of human-machine interaction than I did. His classification of the different levels of human vs. machine control became a classic—and is every bit as valuable in the world of self-driving autos at it was in our earlier consideration of autopilots. He is a gentle and amusing colleague. However, his home department was never as supportive of human factors as was my Aero department. Whereas I was able to support the appointment of a series of assistant professors in these "softer" disciplines like human environmental physiology or cognitive processes, Tom had difficulty hiring and retaining junior colleagues. Eventually Tom threw his lot in with our spacey and more collegial faculty and joined us for the remainder of his active teaching years.

Meanwhile, the course in human factors grew in popularity as a joint Aero/ME offering and was included as a senior elective in our department. After Tom retired. I was able to get the help of a number of talented younger colleagues to share the load with me, including Jim Kuchar and my close friend and colleague, Chuck Oman. Visiting faculty were also brought in to introduce their own perspectives. Rafi Sivan, Dean of the EE faculty of the Technion in Israel, contributed his approach of optimal estimation to our treatment of Manual Control. Prof. Mica Endsley, during her year with us at MIT, discussed her concepts of Situation Awareness.

I began introducing real-life case studies, and eventually had the students read and present the human factors aspects of some actual aircraft accidents, as analyzed by the National Transportation Safety Board (NTSB). Those case studies, presented by students, did a lot to bring home the lessons that "pilot error," as frequently listed as the cause of the accident, was a gross over-simplification. Most of the accidents could be attributed to the failure of the designers, of the cockpit or of the air traffic control system, for example. Or they could be attributed to failure of airline management in specifying training or work/sleep schedules. Gradually the case studies became integrated with the lectures and brought reality to the academic reading. They also made some of the students a bit leery of flying. I had more difficulty finding illustrative space human-factors cases at first, but eventually added some instructive cases—like the *Mir-Progress* collision or the *Challenger* accident. The introduction of the case studies presented by the students was an important factor in bringing home the relevance of the more academic models, such as Signal Detection Theory or Manual Control.

When Missy Cummings, an ex-Navy F-18 pilot with a degree in Industrial Psychology, joined the Department, she was given control of the class, which was later passed on to Prof. Leia Stirling when Missy moved to Duke University. Leia later moved on to teach at the University of Michigan. It became obvious that our attempt to teach even a survey course on the role of the human in aerospace systems would take more than a single course. I couldn't squeeze in subjects as diverse as atmospheric requirements and g-tolerance with concepts like workload assessment and ergonomics. Eventually, thanks to the presence and enthusiasm of Dava Newman on the faculty, we introduced a Space Life Sciences subject she taught, and which became an important requirement for our NSBRI-sponsored Bioastronautics PhD program.

Quantitative Physiology—Sensori-Motor Systems

Although some introduction to human physiology is now a core element of the biomedical engineering curriculum in almost every university, that was not the case in the 1960s. Our engineering students, including those who were pre-med, found no instruction tailored to their needs and interests. The Harvard Med courses were generally not a good match, and often were closed to non-medical students. What was really needed was teaching of physiology that fit with the interests and background of our MIT engineering students.

As it happened, the NIH was interested in the same thing in the early 1970s. A stellar group of engineering faculty was assembled to develop an undergraduate set of subjects along these lines. Some of the key players were Ascher Shapiro, MIT's leading fluid mechanics professor and head of ME, Bill Siebert, an electrical engineer with research interests in the auditory system, Roger Mark, an MD-PhD with clinical and research experience in cardiovascular function, and Tom Weiss and Bill Peake, who concentrated on bioelectric transduction and nerve impulses. The effort resulted in a three-term sequence in Quantitative Physiology: neural signals, mass transit systems (chiefly cardiopulmonary) and sensori-motor systems.

When I returned to MIT from my sabbatical in Zurich in 1973, I was drafted into leading the sensori-motor offering, along with Larry Frischkopf, Chuck Oman and Bob Mann. We introduced a heavy dose of linear control systems into our teaching about the vestibular systems. I put together a series of hands-on labs concentrating on human eye tracking movements. The students seemed to appreciate the exercises. For example, they would observe the predicted "square wave" oscillations of their eyes as they tried to follow a dot on the screen when the target, in turn, was being driven by those same eye movements.

I was delighted, years later, to hear from a former student that he learned more physiology from these three quantitative physiology subjects than he did in medical school. And I learned to appreciate the power of fundamental engineering concepts in teaching biology. On the other hand, many of the first year HST medical students felt I missed the mark. Most of the students wanted to know the clinical relevance and not the beautiful mathematical theory, even though it explained how we, as unstable inverted pendulums, could stand and walk without falling. A second, half-term course that I introduced was called "Biomathematics," and was aimed at Harvard Medical School students who needed to fulfil a math requirement but had already taken biostatistics. It was fun to teach and continued for several years until the early 1970s.

Flight Simulation

The field of flight simulation became of interest to me as a result of a long series of basic psychology experiments I had been doing on visual-vestibular interaction. My desire was to understand and model the way a human develops a sensation of self-motion, based on both the acceleration detected by the inner ear and the moving scene shown on a screen or seen out the window. The latter phenomenon, called "vection," is the illusory motion we feel when the train next to ours begins to move out of the station, or when we are looking over the bridge railing at the river flowing below us. Of course, it is just such a feeling of self-motion that one tries to induce in a pilot of a flight simulator, which both moves around (although not as much as the real airplane or space vehicle) and presents the pilot with an "out the window" view on one or more screens.

Our work came to the attention of the Air Force simulator specialists at the Wright Aeronautical Laboratory in Dayton, Ohio. They in turn persuaded the Link (Trainer) Division of Singer in Binghamton, New York to hire me as a consultant to work on advanced simulators. I did some work with the Air Force large multi-screen flight simulator at Williams Air Force Base in Mesa, Arizona. The motion illusions were so strong that operational Tactical Air Command pilots were not permitted to fly the same day as their simulator exposure. A general was once given a demo ride and said the motion in the simulator was just great, only to be told that the motion system was turned off for his demo. That just about killed the advances in Air Force motion drive algorithms, which was my particular interest!

With Gerry Kron and Frank Cardulo of Singer-Link, we worked on the problem of inducing a sense of pulling "Gs" in a fixed base simulator. The G Seat was one candidate we pursued. It would change its shape so that, when the plane was supposed to be accelerating in a tight turn, the pilot's seat pan would change shape, giving him a real "pain in the butt." Later I borrowed a G Seat from NASA Langley Research Center and used it to determine the influence of tactile forces on illusions of movement in our "Space Sled" at MIT. We were called in to support the suit against Disney for their use of the G Seat software in their Mission to Mars ride. We failed!

Flight Simulation was of increasing use for pilot training as well as for development of airplane control and display systems. It further came into great significance in space travel, where simulation was an absolute necessity. There was no way to train an astronaut by practicing landing on the real Moon. The first landing was "for real," whether on the Moon or back on Earth. Sophisticated simulators of various kinds, both flying and fixed, with moving TV cameras and later with computer graphics, became essential in the Apollo program. Astronauts commented that landing on the Moon was "just like the simulation."

I began to appreciate the rapid growth of the field of flight simulation, for vehicle development as well as for training, and for space as well as for aviation. The MIT-MVL bought a Link Trainer—one of the famous "Blue Boxes" used to pitch, roll and yaw a cockpit while simulating some of the elementary aspects of flying a small plane. We installed it in the basement of the MIT Center for Space Research and used it for over a decade, mostly for basic studies of visual-vestibular interaction. Test subjects indicated their perceived orientations while we spun them and projected simple patterns of stripes on the windows. I admit that, as a non-pilot, just for fun I practiced plenty of simulated takeoffs and landings in that box. We used it to assess the effects of space flight on a subject's ability to "fly right" following a week or two in space, and the trainer was moved to Houston in 1991 for pre-post flight testing of astronauts on the 1993 SLS-2. We loaned it to Dan Merfeld at Massachusetts Eye and Ear for related vestibular experiments later. I was disappointed that nobody at MIT wanted it back, not even the Flying Club.

With all of that interest in Flight Simulation as a rapidly growing industry, it seemed like the right time to introduce a graduate course on the subject. I divided it into three parts: motions systems, visual systems, and computer modeling of the vehicle dynamics. I covered motion systems. Of course, simulators could not really reproduce all of the aircraft motion. Their travel was limited by mechanical support. Hydraulic or electric motors moved the cockpit commanded by a computer that supplied "motion washout." That was supposed to take care of the compromise between the real motion of the airplane and the necessarily limited motion of the simulator. The goal, of course, was always to make the motion illusion in the simulator agree with the sensation that the pilot would feel in real flight, using visual as well as motion cues.

I prevailed on my old friend and colleague, Prof. Walter Hollister, to teach the "math model" part of the course. Walt was an ex-Navy pilot who had been a doctoral graduate student with me. Computer models of the actual airplane orientation drove the simulator motion and the out-the-window scene. Finally, we went outside the department for help with the computer graphics. The new and rapidly developing field of computer image generation was not limited to video games. It allowed one to generate a realistic-looking visual scene, with sufficient resolution and speed, to make it look as though you were actually flying above real terrain, with real houses, trees and even other airplanes. We began working with Mark Connolly, of the Electronic Systems Lab. Mark and Bob Simpson, of our department, had a Boeing commercial aircraft fixed-base simulator that was available for student demos and projects. As time passed, other talented faculty, from the Media Lab as well as Aero-Astro, came in to help me teach the increasingly popular course.

When I moved onto space studies, nobody jumped up to take over the flight simulator course. For several years we offered a one-week summer program covering the highlights of the graduate course. It attracted a number of experts from the airlines and from the military, both American and foreign. The summer program was continued while I was away in Houston for two years. I was grateful that my colleague, Frank Cardullo from SUNY Binghamton, with whom I had worked at Link, came over to teach it, but nobody was around to teach the graduate course during my second year at JSC, and it ended.

That would have been the end of my involvement with flight simulation, were it not for the appearance of a stimulating and unusual man in our midst. John Tylko, a space buff like none other, who went from being a student in our Engineering Apollo course to taking over the lead in teaching it with me. John was also the Chief Innovation Officer at Aurora Flight Systems (Boeing). They were located in Kendall Square and hired many of our students as well as their professors. John's knowledge and recall of space and aviation facts were matched only by his enthusiasm. His PhD thesis, under David Mindell's supervision, was to be on the history of modern flight simulation, from the early "blue box" through its vital role in the moon landings. I was pleased to serve on his doctoral committee and we became friends. John promoted the award to me of the AIAA's Louis de Florez Award for contributions to flight simulation.

Engineering Apollo

The last MIT subject I introduced was the brainchild of David Mindell, who organized and led it through its early years. David's faculty appointments were in Aero-Astro and Science Technology and Society. In addition to his engineering background, he was a respected historian of technology. Our offering spanned history, politics and engineering as related to the conception and implementation of the Apollo program.

When we first offered the course, many of the pioneers of human space flight were still alive and graciously accepted our invitation to speak at MIT. We listened to Bob Seamans, Joe Gavin, key members of the MIT Instrumentation Lab who designed the guidance system, and countless others—astronauts, managers and engineers. They gave students the true story of Apollo. It was a history of the first-ever large-scale Systems Engineering effort and arguably the pinnacle of technology reached in the 20th century. One of the students, a middle-aged engineering manager, came up to me after one of the classes and said, "Now that's why I came to MIT." This course became the most popular graduate subject in the department, most recently lead by John Tylko of Aurora Flight Sciences.

Engineering and Skiing

Back in the early 1970s, the aerospace industry was caught in the midst of a real downturn. Newspapers showed photos of Aero PhDs pumping gas in California and parents warned their children not to go into the field. Sophomore registration in our department got smaller and smaller. We were threatened with being forced to join with Ocean Engineering—or worse yet, to be gobbled up by Mechanical Engineering, from which we were spawned nearly a hundred years earlier. (Years later, with Ocean Engineering undergraduate interest withering, they were indeed forced to merge with ME.) Our department head, Rene Miller, requested that we teach anything that would bring students in. I asked about a freshman seminar course on Engineering in Skiing, and it was quickly approved.

I put together a course covering everything from the design and manufacture of skis and bindings to the biomechanics of making a carved turn. I had some backing from Salomon, for whom I was consulting, and brought in guests from the industry. It was quite popular—especially when I combined it with the opportunity to spend a week or two at the rented house in Campton, New Hampshire. Those students did the on-slope binding evaluations and participated in the papers and presentations we gave at the International Society for Skiing Safety every two years. It was a blast to teach. Our studies of binding function also advanced safety in alpine skiing. For example, we provided data to support the inclusion of machine testing of binding release torques in rental operations, and we demonstrated the limitations of the "voluntary twist" technique for checking the binding.

Good Enough

I just recently heard some discussion of a book on the subject of teaching young people to settle for "good enough" rather than to suffer the stress of going for excellence. The example was to encourage the student to take time off from studies and get a lower grade in geometry while allowing for more social time with his friends. I could not disagree more! For me, the drive, and the satisfaction, comes from working hard to achieve—not the best in the class or the fastest in the race—but to know that I have reached the best I could possibly do. I wasn't the top student at Science or Amherst or at MIT, but I really studied hard to get the best results I could. When I would finish third in a Masters' ski race, if I had two good clean slalom runs, I was really pleased—far more than if I had finished first and beat my competition who missed gates. (That happened to me in the Nationals at Sugarbush one year and, although I keep the 2000 Combined 2nd Place trophy stowed on top of my bookshelf, it didn't bring anything like the pleasure of skiing really well and, as Eliot has put it "barking with the big dogs.")

So, it gets down to setting challenging yet achievable personal goals and working toward them, rather than trying to beat everyone else. When I concluded my psychiatric evaluations during the astronaut payload specialist evaluations, the shrink asked me if I had any questions for him.

"Yeah," I offered, "what did you find out about me after a day of testing and interviews?"

"Well," he summarized, "you are a bit of a perfectionist and rather hard on yourself."

I guess he had that right. I am frustrated when I don't do as well as I think I could, whether professionally or athletically. All too often, that frustration spills out onto the tennis court in childish and inappropriate behavior. But hey, maybe next year when I am eighty, I will have learned to control my outbursts and get down to serious play—and isn't all play serious? So, anyway, I do not endorse "good enough"—not when there is still room for personal improvement. Maybe that is why I always enjoyed ski training more than the actual racing.

Epilogue

Dealing with Aging

[*These remarks were written in 2015, five years before Larry was diagnosed with cancer.—LAY*]

When your last name is "Young," you get used to a lot of pithy comments like "forever young," or "you'll always be young." But it's not true. I recall vividly trying to convince my father that his symptoms, especially his "senior moments," were just part of the natural aging process. Needless to say, I didn't succeed. But now that I am almost eighty and seeing my own aging process—well, things seem different. I'll try to explain:

My father used to joke that the way to make an old Jew happy was to have him find something that he thought he lost. It's true. When I find my missing checkbook, or keys, or sun glasses—or even when I finally come up with the name of an old friend after running through the alphabet unsuccessfully for days, I am pleased. But there are certain things I notice that I have lost—not serious, mind you, but disturbing nonetheless.

For example, my height. Ever since my teens I had been six feet tall. And very proud of it—six feet was a tall guy. When I was a student in Paris in 1957, I was always the tallest person in the metro car, and the garlic and wine odors wafted up to my level. Then, recently I was standing next to Leslie, at the New Horizons Pluto Flyby reception, when I noticed that I was no longer looking down at her to see her eyes.

"Are you wearing high heels, Leslie?"

"No, why do you ask?"

Well, it was simply that I had not noticed how much my spine had compressed and I had gotten shorter in my late seventies. My medical record shows that I have lost three inches. And the sense of my own height.

And I've lost a lot of hair and have a very definite male pattern bald spot. I only became aware of it when a friend took a picture of our Bermuda race crew on Eric's sailboat, looking down from the mast head. *Hey! Who is that bald guy at the wheel? Could that be me?* Yeah, it was. I can't see my bald spot myself—it is hidden from my own view. It reminds me of that old story of the guy who says to the shaving mirror, "I don't know who you are, but as long as you are here I might as well shave you!"

And teeth. I have been losing teeth for a few years now and need dentures to chew. What a pain—in all senses. *That* really makes me feel old. My several ventures with implants have failed and molars have been removed. I tend to order fish rather than beef at restaurants. And I eat really slowly. But I still enjoy food.

And mobility. I had three concussions in one year when I was seventy-five (one from falling off the hood of our car while trying to trim a branch on the apple tree in front of our Waterville Valley condo—and the other two during ski race training). I had my head examined and they found nothing wrong! But I have become convinced of the real danger of falls and repeat concussions. So, I stopped ski racing, though I miss it to this day, especially when I pass up a Masters' training course here at home. And I try to be super careful about avoiding falls. I was told that when two-time Nobelist Linus Pauling was asked what he thought was the single biggest factor in longevity, the great scientist and promoter of Vitamin C said, "Hold onto the hand rail."

This year, my arthritis in my knees got so painful that I had a total knee replacement in April 2015 and have restricted my athletics to golf, using a cart, and gentle bike riding. Aside from the post-op pain and loss of sleep, it seems to be working out well and I have yet to decide about the other knee. It's kind of funny to observe that, with one knee straightened, I am decidedly half-bow-legged. I hope to ski this winter, when my eighty-year status will finally qualify me for free skiing, and I may no longer need to cant my ski boot—at least the left one.

Of course, the loss we all worry about is cognitive ability. For a professor, the ability to think clearly and communicate is life itself. No problem with "senior moments" in which I forget names or why I went into the other room for something or other. But when I start a sentence and then don't quite know how to end it—or what the point was—that is scary.

I am sure there are some other things I have lost, but I don't remember. So far, I have been spared serious illness, for myself and my loved ones. And I really am grateful!

Passing Remarks

I've had a wonderful life. Glitches? Of course. But taken all in all, it's been a very merry go-round.

About the Authors

Laurence "Larry" Young was the Apollo professor in MIT's Aeronautics and Astronautics department, the founding director of the National Space Biomedical Research Institute, and was a backup astronaut for the Spacelab Life Sciences 2 mission on the Space Shuttle. He was born in the Bronx, and divided his time between Cambridge, Massachusetts, and the White Mountains of New Hampshire. He began writing *Around and Around* when he said his knee hurt too much to ski a lot, and completed it while battling cancer in 2021. He passed in August, 2021.

Leslie Young, Larry's daughter and editor for his memoir, caught the space bug from her father—and the secret tip to try to get paid to have fun. She was the Deputy Project Scientist for NASA's New Horizons mission to Pluto, and an editor for *The Trans-Neptunian Solar System* and *The Pluto System after New Horizons*. She lives in the Rocky Mountains of Colorado, where she is a planetary scientist at Southwest Research Institute in Boulder and a member of the Allenspark Fire Department.

Larry and Leslie in Cambridge, working on the memoir in the spring of 2021.

Made in the USA
Middletown, DE
28 September 2022

11414828R00109